MAKING GERMAN JEWISH
LITERATURE ANEW

GERMAN JEWISH CULTURES

Editorial Board:

Matthew Handelman, Michigan State University
Iris Idelson-Shein, Ben-Gurion University of the Negev
Samuel Spinner, Johns Hopkins University
Joshua Teplitsky, Stony Brook University
Kerry Wallach, Gettysburg College

Sponsored by the Leo Baeck Institute London

MAKING GERMAN JEWISH LITERATURE ANEW

Authorship, Memory, and Place

Katja Garloff

INDIANA UNIVERSITY PRESS

This book is a publication of

Indiana University Press
Office of Scholarly Publishing
Herman B Wells Library 350
1320 East 10th Street
Bloomington, Indiana 47405 USA

iupress.org

© 2022 by Katja Garloff
Cover image: Lynne Avadenka, *Sudden Heart* from *Dan Pagis: Six Poems* (2007)
Photo credit: R. H. Hensleigh

All rights reserved
No part of this book may be reproduced or utilized in any form or by any means, electronic or mechanical, including photocopying and recording, or by any information storage and retrieval system, without permission in writing from the publisher. The paper used in this publication meets the minimum requirements of the American National Standard for Information Sciences—Permanence of Paper for Printed Library Materials, ANSI Z39.48-1992.

Manufactured in the United States of America

First printing 2022

Cataloging information is available from the Library of Congress.

ISBN 978-0-253-06371-7 (hardcover)
ISBN 978-0-253-06372-4 (paperback)
ISBN 978-0-253-06373-1 (e-book)

CONTENTS

Acknowledgments vii

Introduction 1

Part I Performing Authorship

  1 Authorial Self-Fashioning in Second-Generation Writers: Maxim Biller, Esther Dischereit, and Barbara Honigmann 25

  2 Playing with Paratext: Benjamin Stein's *Die Leinwand* 43

Part II Remaking Memory

  3 Memory and Mobility: The Novels of Doron Rabinovici 59

  4 Memory and Similarity: Katja Petrowskaja's *Vielleicht Esther* 78

Part III Claiming Places

  5 Returning: Diasporic Place-Making in Barbara Honigmann 101

  6 Transitioning: Migration Narratives in Vladimir Vertlib and Julya Rabinowich 117

7 Arriving: Arrival Stories in Lena Gorelik,
  Dmitrij Kapitelman, and Jan Himmelfarb 137

Conclusion 153

Notes 161

Works Cited 181

Index 193

ACKNOWLEDGMENTS

This book was born out of the spirit of collaboration. It began with a seminar, titled "German Jewish Literature after 1945: Working through and beyond the Holocaust," that Helen Finch, Erin McGlothlin, Agnes Mueller, and myself organized at the 2014 German Studies Association Conference in Kansas City, Missouri. After three days of spirited discussions, we were still debating whether and how the years 1989–91 marked a caesura in the development of German Jewish literature after the Holocaust. There was no doubt that postreunification Germany was seeing a wave—in fact, several waves—of literary publications by self-identified Jewish authors, and that there was much that was novel and exciting about their writing. The time seemed to have arrived for taking stock and reflecting more deeply on this new German Jewish literature.

In the years after that first seminar, the discussion continued in panels and seminars at the GSA and the Association for Jewish Studies Conferences and the biennial Workshop in German Jewish Studies at Duke University and Notre Dame University. A volume of essays I coedited—*German Jewish Literature after 1990* (Rochester, NY: Camden House, 2018)—was one of the tangible results of this ongoing conversation. My deepest thanks are due to all who participated in it: to the coeditor of the book, Agnes Mueller; to its contributors, Luisa Banki, Caspar Bettegay, Helen Finch, Elizabeth Loentz, Andree Michaelis-König, Jessica Ortner, Jonathan Skolnik, and Stuart Taberner; to the editors of the series in which it appeared, Erin McGlothlin and Brad Prager; and to other panelists and respondents who added valuable insights, including Sarah Horowitz, Michael Levine, Leslie Morris, Anna Parkinson, Leo Riegert, Rebekah Slodounik, Corey Twitchell, and Sebastian Wogenstein. Without the inspiration of this network of scholars who simultaneously and enthusiastically turned their attention to contemporary German Jewish literature, I would never have attempted to write this book. The project also benefitted from the ideas and comments of other colleagues and interlocutors in German Jewish studies and related fields, including Leslie Adelson, William Donahue, Helga Druxes, Stefani Engelstein, Abigail Gillman, Sander Gilman, Jeffrey Grossman, Martha Helfer, Paul Reitter, Maria Roca Lizarazu, Sven-Erik Rose, and Scott Spector. Sadly, my longtime friend and mentor Jonathan Hess, a towering presence in German Jewish studies, passed away much too early in 2018. We are still mourning the loss of this brilliant scholar, beloved colleague, and genuine Mensch.

At a crucial juncture of this project, I became the lucky recipient of a fellowship from the American Council of Learned Societies and a research grant from the German Academic Exchange Service (DAAD), which allowed me to spend the year of 2018–19 in Germany. I would like to thank all the people who made that stay possible, productive, and thoroughly enjoyable: Doerte Bischoff (University of Hamburg) and Kerstin Schoor (European University Viadrina Frankfurt, Oder) sponsored my DAAD application, invited me to lectures, and gave me access to the resources of their institutions. During the year, I also received speaking invitations from Irmela Marei Krüger-Fürhoff (Free University of Berlin), Robert Gillett and Godela Weiss-Sussex (University of London), and Ruth von Bernuth and Eric Downing (University of North Carolina, Chapel Hill). I fondly remember the Selma Stern Center for Jewish Studies Berlin-Brandenburg, where I gave a talk and attended several others, as a site of lively debate about German Jewish culture and history. It was there, as well as at a few other Berlin institutions, that I first met several contemporary scholars who gave fresh impulses to this project, including Yael Almog, Micha Brumlik, Max Czollek, and Yael Kupferberg. Throughout my time in Berlin, I cherished the intellectual conversations with my dear friends Eva Lezzi, Dagmar Deuring, Cornelia Manikowsky, Andree Michaelis-König, and Christoph Schulte.

Back in Portland, Reed College provided the stimulating and supportive environment I needed to finish this book. My departmental colleagues past and present—Jake Fraser, Ülker Gökberk, and Jan Mieszkowski—have long modeled exciting interdisciplinary approaches to German studies. I take much inspiration from other Reed friends and (current and former) colleagues—including Diego Alonso, Michael Breen, Ann Delehanty, Jacqueline Dirks, Elizabeth Duquettte, Ariadna García-Bryce, Marat Grinberg, Jing Jiang, Dana Katz, Laura Arnold Leibman, Mary Ashburn Miller, Geraldine Ondrizek, Paul Silverstein, Steven Wasserstrom, and Catherine Witt—who manage to combine original scholarly or artistic work with an unwavering commitment to teaching. I would also like to thank my students at Reed, who continue to inspire me with their curiosity, hard work, and intellectual courage. One of these students, Nathan Modlin, assisted me in the final phase of manuscript preparation by drafting translations and checking the bibliography.

The Dean's Office of Reed College generously funded his work as well as several research trips I undertook to Germany.

I would like to express my appreciation to everyone who helped turn the manuscript into an actual book: to Kerry Wallach, who invited me to submit the manuscript for consideration in the German Jewish Cultures series, to the staff at Indiana University Press, including Gary Dunham, Carol McGillivray, and Laura Larsen, who made editing and publication a smooth, efficient, and enjoyable process. I am especially grateful to Lynne Avadenka, who gave me permission to use her lithograph *Sudden Heart* as the cover image for this book. *Sudden Heart* is part of a series of collages which the artist created from maps included in a 1910 Baedeker Guide to Southern Germany, in response to the poetry of Dan Pagis.

Finally, heartfelt thanks to my family, both in Germany and the United States. My parents, my siblings, and their partners and children are a constant reminder of how family ties and love can flourish over geographical distance. My greatest debts are to my husband, Asher Klatchko, and our son, Yona. Having lived through a family tragedy, they know more than most people about the importance of new beginnings. I marvel every day at their resilience, their spiritedness, and their creativity. This book is for them.

Earlier versions of the following chapters of this book have been previously published: Chapter 1 in *German Jewish Literature after 1990*, ed. Katja Garloff and Agnes Mueller (Rochester, NY: Camden House, 2018); Chapter 2 in *Persistent Legacy: The Holocaust and German Studies*, ed. Erin McGlothlin and Jennifer M. Kapczinski (Rochester, NY: Camden House, 2016); Chapter 5 in *Rebuilding Jewish Life in Germany*, ed. Jay Howard Geller and Michael Meng (New Brunswick, NJ: Rutgers University Press, 2020). I would like to thank the publishers for permission to reprint this material.

Throughout this book, I use published English translations whenever possible. All other translations are mine.

MAKING GERMAN JEWISH
LITERATURE ANEW

INTRODUCTION

> There are a number of drawers I can be put in and taken out of at will. For example, in one review I was referred to as a "Russian living in Austria," which is valid, even if it is not the entire truth. Additionally, I was a "Russian writer," an "Israeli living in Germany," a "Jewish-German writer of Russian descent," an "Austrian Russian," a "German Jew," and even a "Hebrew author," although I can just barely formulate a couple of pleasantries in that language."[1]
>
> Vladimir Vertlib

Thus, in a public lecture, Vladimir Vertlib, who was born in Russia to Jewish parents, resides in Austria, and writes in German, characterizes the reception of his literary work. The lengthy list of descriptors in this passage reminds us that in their efforts to label the author, critics easily confuse aspects of national, cultural, linguistic, and religious belonging. Above all, the list draws attention to the very act of labeling and the fact that minority authors are frequently reduced to their biographies. Moving back and forth between quotations from his literature and remarks on its reception, Vertlib goes on to create a loop in which his public lecture, his literary writing, and his critics' responses all seem to inform each other. At one point he cites a scene from his novel *Letzter Wunsch* (Last wish) that raises the question of what it means to speak publicly as a Jew to a non-Jewish audience. The novel's protagonist, Gabriel Salzinger, is a German Jew who wants to fulfill his deceased father's wish to be buried in the local Jewish cemetery next to his late wife. When the Jewish community turns down his request after a staff member discovers the father was not Jewish by halachic criteria (since his maternal grandmother had converted to Judaism in a non-Orthodox ceremony), Gabriel decides to discuss his case on a live radio show. However, instead of engaging with the questions at hand—who is a Jew and who gets to define who is a Jew?—the callers inundate Gabriel with their opinions about Israeli politics, Jewish community leaders, the causes of antisemitism, and so on. By citing this scene in which the protagonist is treated as a representative of all Jews, Vertlib suggests that the novel itself reflects on its own future reception as well as the public identity of its author.

The self-reflexivity displayed in Vertlib's novel and multiplied in his lecture is a hallmark of the new German Jewish literature that began to develop in the mid-1980s. Around this time, and especially in the decade after the 1990 reunification of Germany, a new generation of German-speaking authors emerged who self-identified as Jewish in interviews and other public forums; they included Katja Behrens, Maxim Biller, Esther Dischereit, and Rafael Seligmann in Germany; Ruth Beckermann, Doron Rabinovici, Robert Menasse, and Robert Schindel in Austria; Chaim Noll in Israel; and Barbara Honigmann in France. Their writing quickly drew critical attention, especially in the English-speaking world, where scholars identified a "reemergence," "rebirth," or "renaissance" of German Jewish literature.[2] These terms signal both the novelty of the literature and its connectedness with an earlier period of cultural vibrancy and artistic innovation, presumably German Jewish culture before the Holocaust. The writers themselves emphasized the novel, collective, and precarious character of their literature and often reflected on their Jewish identities and position vis-à-vis German-language culture and society in nonfictional forms such as essays. In 1995 Maxim Biller went so far to claim that there is only one country in the world apart from Israel "in which an original, autonomous Jewish literature will be produced for a long time to come," and that is Germany.[3] He explained that the proximity to the perpetrators of the Holocaust and their offspring will not allow German Jews to either forget its horrors or assimilate to mainstream German culture. Instead, it compels them to think more deeply through their identity and articulate it more clearly: "That one should not live and write as a Jew in Germany is naturally the first and most compelling reason why, precisely as a Jew in Germany, one lives and writes particularly Jewishly."[4]

Both Biller and Vertlib perceive the German-language environment as conducive to Jewish creativity and self-reflection, even if these are initially foisted upon writers by a history of genocide and a literary public inclined to pigeonhole Jewish authors. In *Making German Jewish Literature Anew*, I take my cue from this perception to trace the development of German Jewish literature from 1989 to the present. Whereas earlier comprehensive volumes have focused on the second generation of German Jewish writers after the Holocaust, my analysis extends to third-generation writers, many of whom come from Eastern European and/or mixed-religion backgrounds.[5] The writers who have begun to publish more recently, including Katja Petrowskaja, Julya Rabinowich, and Benjamin Stein, bear out one of Biller's claims: that the reinvention of German Jewish literature is an ongoing project that involves repeated acts of creation. This insight into the reiterative nature of innovation is the starting point and the organizing principle of this book, which highlights the foundational moments of a new diaspora literature. *Making German Jewish Literature Anew* is structured around a series of "founding gestures"—that is, literary strategies by means of which authors self-consciously posit a new beginning. I focus on three such founding gestures: *performing authorship, remaking memory*, and *claiming places*.

The verb *to found*, as I use it in this book, has a range of meanings that I can only begin to sketch here. It can mean to posit a beginning, such as happens in the origin stories analyzed in part 1 of this book, in which second-generation writers dramatize the moment they became self-conscious German Jewish authors. *To found* furthermore hints at the metadiscursive dimension that characterizes many literary texts published in the last few decades, especially those engaged in the remaking of Holocaust memory discussed in part 2 of this book. At the moment when the remaining eyewitnesses are passing and the Holocaust is turning from memory into history, we see a proliferation of what I call fictions of metamemory—that is, literary texts that explore the medial, institutional, and neurological foundations of memory. Indeed, I argue that the new German Jewish literature as a whole is metaliterary in that it reflects on its own conditions, possibilities, and limitations—and therefore invites us to rethink the very concept of Jewish literature. Finally, the verb *to found* has a distinct spatial dimension—the Latin verb *fundare* means, among other things, "to lay the bottom" and "to lay a foundation"—and often denotes the marking of a place, the drawing of a boundary, or the enclosing of a site. In part 3 of this book, I discuss acts of diasporic place-making—of returning, transitioning, and arriving—that can be understood as founding gestures in that sense.

After the Holocaust

The founding gestures have been necessary because the Holocaust had all but eradicated German Jewish culture. For decades after the end of the war, Jewish writing in the German language meant searching for ways to speak about the unspeakable—the systematic mass murder of the European Jews—to an overwhelmingly non-Jewish audience that was reluctant to listen. German Jewish literature became a literature of exiles and survivors.

Many of its exponents returned belatedly to their German-speaking home countries, did not return at all, or left again after a period of time. Those who were writing from within East and West Germany often either suppressed their Jewish identities or felt like they were "sitting on packed suitcases" in the land of the perpetrators. Dan Diner has aptly called the postwar relationship between Germans and Jews a "negative symbiosis" that is based on a shared reference to the Holocaust from radically different perspectives: "After Auschwitz it is actually possible—what a sad irony—to speak of a 'German-Jewish symbiosis,' albeit a negative one. For both Jews and Germans, the aftermath of mass murder has been the starting point for self-understanding—a kind of communality of opposites."[6] Diner's term captures the abyss that separated the former victims and perpetrators and made an in-between position almost impossible. The existential crises suffered, for example, by Peter Weiss, Nelly Sachs, and Paul Celan in response to their increased reception in 1960s West Germany testify to the difficulty, even impossibility, of sustaining relations between the small group of Jewish survivors who continued to write in German and the German language, literary heritage, and public sphere.[7]

Yet by the time of Diner's writing in 1986, changes were underway that would ultimately challenge his dichotomous notion of a "negative symbiosis" centered on the memory of the Holocaust. The sense of a clear separateness of Germans and Jews began to wane as second-generation intellectuals such as Cilly Kugelmann and Micha Brumlik self-consciously identified as "Jews in Germany"[8] and intervened, for example, in the public debates surrounding the planned staging of Rainer Werner Fassbinder's antisemitic play *Der Müll, die Stadt und der Tod* (Garbage, the city, and death) and Ronald Reagan's 1985 visit to the Bitburg military cemetery, which houses some graves of SS troops. These debates, in turn, revealed the inner heterogeneity of the postwar German Jewish community, whose members came from diverse geographical and cultural backgrounds and espoused a range of religious and political views. Thus, the public statements of Diner, Kugelmann, and Brumlik constituted a left-wing dissent from the declarations of the official German Jewish community. One symptom of these two ongoing trends—toward a more tangible *presence* and an increased *diversity* of Jewish life and culture in Germany—has been the founding of new journals meant to promote inner-Jewish debates, including *Babylon: Beiträge zur jüdischen Gegenwart* (1986–2010) and, most recently, *Jalta: Positionen zur jüdischen Gegenwart* (since 2017). These same two trends can also be observed in literature. If the number of German-language works published by self-identified Jewish authors has grown dramatically over the past three decades, so has the diversity of this literature—and what critics have variously called its transnational, transcultural, translingual, exterritorial, and cosmopolitan character.⁹

An important vehicle of diversification has been Jewish migrants who came to Germany with different historical experiences and memories and whose works, among other things, call into question the centrality of the Holocaust for the construction of Jewish identity today. Nothing has accelerated the shift toward a greater Jewish presence *and* diversity in contemporary Germany more than the influx of Russian Jewish *Kontingentflüchtlinge* (quota refugees) in the wake of German reunification. The migration began with the disintegration of the Soviet Union in the late 1980s and became regulated in 1991, when a new law allowed Jewish citizens from the former Soviet Union to enter Germany and become naturalized within six to eight years. The law became inoperative when Germany's new immigration act took effect in 2005, and additional stipulations introduced shortly later—which require applicants to pass a German-language test and receive approval by a Jewish community—reduced the influx of Jewish immigrants from the former Soviet Union to a trickle. Over this relatively short span of time, about two hundred thousand quota refugees entered Germany (this number includes the non-Jewish relatives many brought along), roughly half of whom registered with the state-recognized Jewish community. This immigration dramatically changed the demographic composition of that community. It is estimated that between 80 and 90 percent of the about one hundred thousand current members of the Jewish community trace their origins back to the former Soviet Union. Among those who are not officially affiliated with Judaism but still identify as Jewish in one way or another, the percentage of people with Soviet background is similarly high.¹⁰

The migration of Russian Jews to Germany ushered in a process of transformation and reinvention that continues to this day. At the outset their Jewish identity was often tenuous. Leaving at the tail end of a longer exodus of Jews from the Soviet Union, the migrants who ended up in Germany tended to be both less Zionist and less religious than those who had already left for Israel or the US. Although they had carried the ethnicity stamp "Jewish" in their Soviet passports and frequently suffered the antisemitic discrimination that went along with it, many did not fulfill the halachic, matrilineal criteria for membership in German Jewish communities.

And yet they arrived in Germany as part of a state-sponsored project of revival that placed on them a certain expectation to perform their Jewishness. The German government had admitted them in an effort to revitalize the Jewish community and to that end was making significant investments in infrastructure such as synagogues and community centers. In a recent anthropological study, Sveta Roberman points to the difficulties the new immigrants faced in inhabiting the Jewish identity assigned to them. Due to the Soviet campaigns of Russification and Sovietization, they had comparatively little knowledge of Jewish traditions, especially Jewish religious traditions. While the collapse of the Soviet system led to a renewed interest in religious and cultural traditions that had been suppressed, including Jewish ones, the outcome of this reinvention was neither predictable nor controllable. For many post-Soviet Jews, "Jewishness had become an "'empty' or 'floating' signifier," which needed to be filled with new meaning.[11] Aware of the long history of antisemitism, they were often either hesitant to embrace their Judaism or inclined to fill the empty signifier of Jewishness with stereotypical images of intelligence or musical giftedness.

Other scholars claim that beyond such stereotypes, true affinities between Jewish cultures past and present are emerging in contemporary Germany. Many post-Soviet migrants carried in their suitcases the great classics of prewar German literature and espoused an ideal of high culture reminiscent of pre-Holocaust German Jewry. Indeed, Dmitrij Belkin predicts that the encounter in Germany between the quota refugees and Jews from other backgrounds will give rise to a "German Jewry 2.0."[12] Recent German Jewish literature provides an archive of this ongoing process of transformation among the quota refugees and their offspring who adopted new Jewish identities. Their literary work is the latest chapter of the story explored in this book: the rise of a new diaspora literature that is uniquely suited to probe recent theories of Jewish literature.

Theorizing Jewish Literature

The concept of "Jewish literature" often seems to raise more questions than it answers. Is a literary text "Jewish" because of the author's identity, intended audience, thematic concerns, and/or stylistic choices? Does such a text have to be written in a Jewish language, such as Yiddish or Hebrew? What kind of unity does Jewish literature form, where are its boundaries, and how are its elements connected? Anthologies of Jewish literature tend to answer these questions both implicitly—by selecting texts and arranging them into rubrics—and explicitly—by justifying their selections and arrangements. Literary criticism in Jewish studies often begins by defining its object—or, alternatively, by tracing the history of such definitions—while easily losing sight of the fact that critical practices also help constitute the object of their critique. Indeed, any critical project involving Jewish literature must consider the warning Benjamin Schreier issues in his book *The Impossible Jew*: that in analyzing Jewish literature, we may too quickly assume that such a literature exists and reproduce this assumption in a circular manner. "Once the decision is made to treat a text as Jewish, the Jewish signified overdetermines the textual signifier, making the text representative of 'its' Jewish identity."[13] Schreier's critique is aimed at the purported self-evidence of Jewish identity as well as the idea of literary representation. In his mind, "Jewish literature" does indeed exist, namely as a heuristic category that can be brought to bear on a body of texts. However, these texts should be read as a site of identity *construction* rather than identity *representation*. Instead of assuming the existence of a Jewish author who precedes the text and uses the text to express a Jewish identity or describe a Jewish experience, we should pay close attention to acts of identity ascription and ways of marking an experience as "Jewish." As Schreier summarizes the critical approach he envisions (and intriguingly calls "semitic"): "A 'semitic' literary criticism would privilege in its readings analysis of the way texts render Jewishness as an attractor or focus, of how texts deconstruct the givenness of Jewish identity. Thus in figuring Jewish identity as an object at once of theorization, historicization, desire, and practice, 'Jewish' literary texts destabilize and displace what 'Jewish' might possibly refer to."[14]

In *Making German Jewish Literature Anew*, I argue that contemporary German Jewish writers can help us develop such a metacritical mindset because they highlight the very act of creating a new Jewish literature. Their writing brings to mind an earlier historical moment, which has been anatomized in one of the most ambitious attempts in recent years to advance an overarching theory of Jewish literature. In *From Continuity to Contiguity: Toward a New Jewish Literary Thinking* (2010), Dan Miron argues that modern Jewish literature began with an *awareness* that something new was beginning.[15] This was the new task given to literature by the circle of Jewish intellectuals around the Enlightenment philosopher Moses Mendelssohn: the task of promulgating humanist thought throughout European Jewry and helping Jews adapt in an age of secularization, rationalism, and nationalism. This sense of newness explains why the emergence of "the modern Jewish literary complex," as Miron calls it, was from the beginning accompanied by intense theorizing about the shape, nature, and function of Jewish literature—and why Miron's own book is, to a large extent, a critical history of these theoretical debates. The rise of a new German Jewish literature, I argue, allows us to probe Miron's ideas about the importance of metaliterary thinking for a literature that falls outside his main area of concern—that is, modernist authors writing in Yiddish or Hebrew. By highlighting the founding gestures of a new Jewish literature in contemporary Germany and Austria, I carry Miron's ideas forward into the contemporary moment and into a different kind of diaspora. Whereas Miron writes about a first founding, I claim that at least in this time and place, but maybe overall as a diaspora literature, Jewish literature is always made anew—and is thereby recreating Jewishness.

Miron's most important contribution to the scholarly debates is his conception of Jewish literature as a multifarious complex lacking unity and cohesion. He argues that modern Jewish literature does indeed constitute an entity but that the connections between its elements are more intangible and equivocal than literary historians tend to assume. To grasp this nonunified whole, we have to turn away from the concepts associated with *continuity*—such as influence, tradition, intertextuality, and generation—toward the more diffuse forms of connectedness associated with *contiguity*. According to Miron, modern Jewish literature has developed and continues to develop through forms of cultural contact that can vary greatly in intensity and can be random, unfocused, and fleeting. Such contact can even consist of the rejection of a cultural trend, such as Franz Kafka's deliberate silence about the Hebrew renaissance—and, we may add, Maxim Biller's polemics against the sanctities of Holocaust remembrance or Barbara Honigmann's self-distancing from her German Jewish forebears. Miron's work allows us to think of contemporary German Jewish literature as an entity composed of disparate elements that, moreover, centrifugally move away from each other. The notion of contiguity has guided the construction of some of the chapters of *Making German Jewish Literature Anew*, chapters that describe parallelisms, intersections, and similarities between different authors without claiming a direct influence or other form of continuity between them. Thus, chapter 1 explores the simultaneous appearance, at the turn of the millennium, of the prose collections of several second-generation German Jewish writers who, in reflecting upon their own positions in German culture, touch upon similar concerns from different angles. Chapter 7 examines another contiguous cluster of narratives that emerged in the following two decades—namely, the arrival stories of post-Soviet Jewish writers who had come to Germany as quota refugees when they were children.

At times, however, Miron's conception narrows to a protonationalist view that diverts attention from the diasporic origins of Jewish literature. In practical terms, Miron is primarily concerned with literature written in Jewish languages, at the expense of important literary traditions in German, English, and other languages. Accordingly, he locates the beginnings of modern Jewish literature in the Hebrew-oriented Haskalah of the late eighteenth century and traces its development through the Hebrew and Yiddish revival movements of the late nineteenth and early twentieth centuries. In contrast, scholars who emphasize the diasporic character of Jewish literature above all tend to go back to a different moment in history—namely, the establishment of the secular *Wissenschaft des Judentums* (science of Judaism) in the early nineteenth century. Thus, Andreas Kilcher shows how Leopold Zunz, the founder of the *Wissenschaft des Judentums*, first coined the concept of "Jewish literature" by distinguishing it from an older Hebrew-language tradition and defining it as an intrinsically hybrid, diasporic, and multilingual medium. In Leopold Zunz's view, the inextricable linkage of particularity and universality in Jewish literature makes it stand out in the world literature to which it nonetheless clearly belongs.[16] Nineteenth-century scholars Moritz Steinschneider and Gustav Karpeles similarly maintained that Jewish literature, in all its particularity, developed in dialog with non-Jewish cultures all over the world. According to Kilcher, these conceptions of Jewish literature put a twist on the nineteenth-century concept of world literature and its Enlightenment-inspired universalism, conjuring up the idea of a radically decentered textual network: "The diaspora transforms the library of Judaism from the closed, Hebrew book to the open, multilingual, and connected intertext of 'Jewish literature.'"[17] More recently, Lital Levy and Allison Schachter (who also cite Leopold Zunz) have further distinguished the diasporic network of Jewish literature from the idea of world literature, which they view as too closely tied to the concept of the nation-state and too much construed from an imagined European center. Drawing attention to the production, distribution, and reception of literary texts, they conceive of Jewish literature as a multilingual web of literary relations that has developed, and continues to develop, through acts of migration, adaptation, and translation.[18]

I fundamentally agree with these theorists that we must presume the hybrid, plural, and dynamic character of Jewish literature and attend to the ways in which literary texts deconstruct any stable meaning of "Jewishness." Yet I also take my lead from Sheila Jelen, Michael Kramer, and Scott Lerner, who enjoin scholars of Jewish literature to take note of boundaries as well as of intersections—they point out that Leopold Zunz himself set a boundary around Jewish culture in order to preserve this culture in changed form.[19] Using this conceptual language, we may say that the founding gestures of contemporary German Jewish literature are acts of boundary setting that give way to new intersections. In part 1 of this book ("Performing Authorship"), I examine how writers who self-consciously perform Jewish authorship imaginatively set themselves apart from their non-Jewish readers yet in that process also challenge and mobilize the meaning of the label of "Jewish author." Part 2 ("Remaking Memory") shows that the metamemorial shift in Holocaust remembrance entails a delineation of boundaries between different memory practices, perspectives, and communities while enabling new comparisons between diverse historical traumas. Finally, part 3 ("Claiming Places") explores how the narratives of flight and migration in contemporary German Jewish writers go hand in hand with place-making strategies by which displaced subjects anchor themselves in new places. The rise of a new German Jewish literature, I argue, helps us recognize the dynamic between the drawing and blurring of boundaries, between the construction and deconstruction of identities, and between the closing and opening of a literary field.

Performing Authorship

The sine qua non for most definitions of Jewish literature is the author's Jewish identity, however broadly conceived or variably expressed. Thus the editors of the 2001 *Jewish American Literature: A Norton Anthology* write that Jewish fiction is "created by authors who admit, address, embrace, and contest their Jewish identity, whether religious, historical, ethnic, psychological, political, cultural, textual, or linguistic."[20] Writing in the same year, literary critic Michael Kramer justifies such an emphasis on Jewish authorship in terms of scholarly developments over the last two hundred years. He argues that a racially inflected notion of Jewish authorship has informed nearly every definition of Jewish literature since its conception by Leopold Zunz and the *Wissenschaft des Judentums*, and he recommends holding on to that definition even today. Perhaps unsurprisingly, Kramer faced an immediate backlash by scholars who objected to his use of the term *Jewish race* and to what they variously called his biologist, essentialist, or maximalist understanding of Jewish writing.[21] Kramer, in turn, defended his terminological choice by pointing to the importance of descent-based models for most definitions of Jewishness and to the overall understanding of human groups and cultures in our time. Importantly, he claims that the focus on Jewish authorship has generated more capacious definitions of Jewish literature, as it expanded the body of works considered under this rubric while bracketing other criteria such as a shared religion, language, or territory. Historically, this approach has allowed the entirety of Jewish writers to come into view, whether they are religious or secular, nationalist or diasporic, self-conscious or indifferent about their Jewishness. According to Kramer, a focus on Jewish authorial identity helps keep the field of scholarly inquiry open and flexible even today: "For me, Jewish literature begins with the Jews—all Jews, regardless of what they do or do not believe or practice."[22]

Kramer's point that the criterion of authorial identity undergirds virtually every approach to Jewish literature is well taken. Even Miron, with his radically decentered model and attention to hybrid formations, posits that works of Jewish literature are produced by authors who self-identify as Jewish, whether in terms religious or secular, cultural or historical. However, there is an interesting tension in Miron's argument that is never fully resolved. On the one hand, he emphasizes the importance of intrinsic definitions: it is the writers' existential (rather than essential) Jewishness, which they define themselves and express in their literature, that sets the boundary around the entity that is the modern Jewish literary complex. On the other hand, Miron cannot do entirely without an extrinsic component, which can be seen in his definition of a Jewish writer as someone "whose work evinces an interest in or is in whatever way and to whatever extent conditioned by a sense of *Judesein*, being Jewish, *or is being read by readers who experience it as if it showed interest and were conditioned by the writer's being Jewish.*"[23] The italicized sentence hints at something crucial for the writers discussed in this book: the fact that their identity often hinges upon the public reception of their literary work. Contemporary German Jewish writers, I argue, help us explore the tension between intrinsic definition and external ascription of identity precisely because these writers are so aware—and often highly critical—of the marketing and reception mechanisms that classify them as Jewish.

In a recent study of contemporary German Jewish culture titled *The Translated Jew*, Leslie Morris seeks to dismantle the connection between Jewish literature and Jewish authorial identity on which Miron and most others still insist. One of Morris's chief accomplishments is the reassessment of W. G. Sebald, the German-born writer who in his adopted British home wrote a number of hybrid memorial works that have become classics. By connecting him to other writers and artists who have dispersed and circulated German Jewish culture across spaces, times, and media, Morris recasts the non-Jewish Sebald as a producer of "Jewish text." In so doing, she relinquishes an author's identity as the main criterion of Jewish literature and instead focuses on the complex transmission of Jewish memory and experience.[24] While I applaud Morris's radical questioning of the idea of Jewish authorship, I pursue this questioning in a different way. Rather than bracket the authors' identity, I draw attention to the self-conscious performance of Jewish authorship in contemporary writers who publicly claim, assert, question, or contest the Jewish identities that are inevitably attributed to them. These writers tend to be keenly aware of their identities in part because they are writing for largely non-Jewish audiences that often display an intense—some would say voyeuristic—interest in things Jewish.

Witness, for example, the literary fallout of the arrival of the Russian Jewish *Kontingentflüchtlinge*. As noted earlier, the German state had promulgated the new legislation regarding quota refugees in hopes that post-Soviet Jewish migrants would help revitalize the Jewish communities in Germany. Aware of these expectations, many migrants found it difficult to embody Jewishness and perform the roles assigned to them. If they turned to literary writing, they often published a first book that explicitly reflected on their Jewishness and/or migration experience before they moved on to other literary themes. Thus, Wladimir Kaminer and Olga Grjasnowa both depict the lives of Russian Jewish immigrants in Germany in their first books—*Russendisko* (2000; *Russian Disco*) and *Der Russe ist einer, der Birken liebt* (2012; *All Russians Love Birch Trees*)—but rarely touch upon the subject in their later work.

One inspiration for my approach in this book is the contemporary poet, essayist, and performer Max Czollek, who envisions new strategies to engage critically with the identity labels affixed to Jewish artists. A co-organizer of the Desintegrationskongress (De-integration Congress, in 2016) and cofounder of the Radikale Jüdische Kulturtage (Radical Jewish Days of Culture, starting in 2017), Czollek sums up his ideas in several interviews and a book with the catchy title *Desintegriert euch!* (2018; De-integrate!). He argues that Y. Michal Bodemann's notion of the German "theater of memory," according to which Jews have been fulfilling a distinct public function in postwar Germany—namely, as living proof that Germany has successfully worked through its Nazi past and once again has become a hospitable place for minorities—still applies to contemporary Germany.[25] The fact that Jewish (and other minority) artists in public discussions are either rendered invisible or reduced to their biography has to be seen in this context: artistic expressions that are labeled "Jewish" can easily serve as evidence that Jews are once again thriving in Germany. Czollek calls for a "de-integration," which works against the instrumentalization of Jewish artists by creating new roles, affects, and forms of agency for them. For example, instead of contemplating the figure of the Jewish survivor who extends forgiveness to German perpetrators, the audience may be confronted with artistic expressions of rage and symbolic acts of revenge. Czollek proposes expanding the positions available to Jewish artists in the German public sphere by working with and upon the adjectives bestowed upon them. De-integration in that sense demands an infusion of the word *Jewish* with new meanings, as happens when someone deliberately appears in front of an audience *as a Jew* and at the same time rejects, sarcastically affirms, or otherwise calls into question the definitions of "Jewishness" held by this audience. As Czollek explains the desired effect of the Radical Jewish Days of Culture: "We want to expand the positions Jews can hold in public space. To do this, we choose a strategy described by a sentence by Hannah Arendt: when one is attacked as a Jew, one must defend oneself as a Jew. That is absolutely central.... The other literature is migrant literature, Jewish literature or women's literature. This is how supremacy works in the literary world: some get an adjective, others don't. Biographies, then, are the capital of the continuously-pigeonholed artists. We are now trying, within the framework of the festival, to work with and on these adjectives."[26]

Thus far, the concept of de-integration has been mostly discussed in the context of theater—which makes sense, given that the primary locus of activity of Max Czollek and his main collaborator, Sasha Marianna Salzmann, is the Maxim Gorki Theater in Berlin. The vocabulary of stages, roles, and actors deployed in the theoretical debates around de-integration also suggests a direct interaction with an audience that is present during the performance. Yet can Jewish writers also de-integrate by means of novels and other prose texts? Can they lay claim to a Jewish identity or authorial position while refusing to play along with dominant German notions of Jewishness? Some critics have argued that writers may achieve this effect through narrative strategies of fragmentation and disidentification, which thwart readers' expectations for readily legible Jewish characters and coherent Jewish family histories.[27] In part 1 of *Making German Jewish Literature Anew*, I gauge the de-integrative potential of literary prose in a related yet different way—namely, by drawing attention to acts of authorial self-fashioning and self-positioning within the literary text and its margins. I explore how the second-generation German Jewish writers Maxim Biller, Esther Dischereit, and Barbara Honigmann each create a recognizably Jewish author persona in prose collections that appeared around the turn of the millennium. I also show that Benjamin Stein makes creative use of paratext to stake out a new authorial position—that of the observant Jew who writes German literature—in his 2010 novel *Die Leinwand* (*The Canvas*). The performance of Jewish authorship in these texts effects a de-integration in Czollek's sense: the authors challenge and expand mainstream conceptions of Jewishness as they become visible *as Jewish artists*—and for that reason, their performance is a founding gesture, the creation of a new possibility.

Remaking Memory

There can be no doubt that the Holocaust was a defining experience for many twentieth-century Jews and its commemoration a central aspiration of postwar Jewish literature. This is true for both first-generation writers, who personally experienced exile, internment, and/or loss of relatives, and second-generation writers, who confronted the long silence surrounding the Holocaust, especially in perpetrator countries. But is it still true for German Jewish literature today now that the Second World War has moved into greater historical distance, most of the eyewitnesses have passed away, and the demographic changes in the Jewish community have brought other past experiences into view? For many contemporary authors from the former Soviet Union, more immediate historical reference points are the terror under Stalin, the antisemitic campaigns of the Communist regimes, and the interethnic conflicts following the collapse of those regimes. If they do write about the Second World War, they often do so from the perspective of the Soviet victors rather than the Jewish victims and/or draw attention to episodes less frequently discussed in Germany, such as the blockade of Leningrad. However, these shifts only mean that Holocaust remembrance has undergone significant changes, not that it has disappeared from contemporary German Jewish literature altogether. Even Benjamin Stein, in his attempt to define a Jewish identity based on religious observance rather than memories of the Holocaust, does so by revisiting a notorious moment in the history of Holocaust remembrance. Throughout *Die Leinwand*, Stein alludes to the scandal surrounding Binjamin Wilkomirski's fake Holocaust memoir, *Bruchstücke* (1995; *Fragments*), to ask probing questions about the nature of Holocaust testimony and its transmission to future generations.

"The year 2000 marks the starting point of a new era . . . the Holocaust went global," Aleida Assmann concludes about the state of Holocaust remembrance at the threshold to the new millennium.[28] The worldwide dissemination of Holocaust films, new scholarly debates about the universal significance of the Holocaust, and political initiatives such as the founding of the Task Force for International Cooperation on Holocaust Education, Remembrance and Research (ITF; currently the International Holocaust Remembrance Alliance, or IHRA) all worked to expand the scope and reach of Holocaust memory. As a result, the Holocaust became a "global icon," "a free-floating signifier that is readily associated with all kinds of manifestations of moral evil, and which today can invariably be applied to any pain, destruction, trauma or disaster."[29] Among other things, the new scholarly focus on the mobility of Holocaust memory—whether achieved through the transnational movement of people, the media circulation of images, or the metaphorical transfer of meaning—challenges the uniqueness paradigm that has long dominated Holocaust studies. A growing number of scholars nowadays argue that the Nazi genocide can and should be compared to other episodes of historical trauma and violence and that such comparisons can create new forms of transcultural connectedness, empathy, and solidarity.

The first to argue for such a political efficacy of Holocaust memory were Daniel Levy and Nathan Sznaider in their book *The Holocaust and Memory in a Global Age*. Levy and Sznaider claim that the global or "cosmopolitan" memory of the Holocaust that emerged during the 1990s helped establish new moral and political norms after the end of the Cold War. At a time of political turmoil and ideological uncertainty, the Holocaust became an important moral touchstone in public debates, a "measure for humanist and universal identifications."[30] In his widely acclaimed book *Multidirectional Memory*, Michael Rothberg takes this idea a step further, arguing that the memory of the Holocaust has facilitated the recognition and articulation of other histories of mass violence and genocide.[31] Rothberg proposes an alternative to an understanding of public memory as competitive and privative, or the notion that any particular event can only be remembered at the expense of others. Rather than competing for limited space and attention, representations of diverse historical atrocities can cross-reference, borrow from, and ultimately enable each other, and they can do so across significant lapses of time.

More recently, Rothberg has supplemented his concept of multidirectional memory by a theory of political affect meant to distinguish even more clearly "politically productive forms of memory from those that lead to competition, appropriation, or trivialization."[32] According to this new theory, the comparison of different traumatic histories can generate relations ranging from equation to differentiation and affects ranging from competition to solidarity, with "differentiated solidarity" occupying the endpoint of the politically desirable spectrum of political affects. Lucy Bond, Stef Craps, and Pieter Vermeulen have summarized the impact of these and other theorists who are currently working on "memory on the move": "Collectively, these critics construe a model of memory as a fluid, inclusive, and open-ended process, rather than a fixed and exclusionary narrative, embracing the possibility that the intersection of disparate commemorative discourses might offer an opportunity to forge empathic communities of remembrance across national, cultural, or ethnic boundaries."[33]

One problem with this scholarly focus on transcultural empathy (i.e., feeling with the other) and solidarity (i.e., acting with the other) is that it tends to privilege connection over contestation and positive over negative affects. However, negative affects such as rage, hatred, and resentment have long abounded in post-Holocaust German Jewish writers, and their expression has its own uses and functions. For example, whereas Rothberg explicitly disqualifies *resentment* as a politically productive affect, Jean Améry, an Austrian Jewish survivor of the Holocaust, defends resentment as a source of moral knowledge in the post-Holocaust world and an effective form of communication between former victims and perpetrators. Other German-speaking Jewish writers who survived the Holocaust, including Edgar Hilsenrath and Ruth Klüger, also self-consciously deploy negative affects in their writing.[34] And as noted earlier, Max Czollek enjoins contemporary German Jewish artists to "de-integrate" by assuming a confrontational stance vis-à-vis the non-Jewish audiences they inevitably address—for example, by giving expression to revenge fantasies. These writers and thinkers are not primarily focused on solidarity with other victimized groups but on a different political affect that is associated with memory competition but nevertheless productive. They suggest that the *contestation* of public memory is a political exigency in a postwar Austria that has long denied its complicity in Nazism and in a postreunification Germany that has been all too ready to "normalize" German-Jewish relations—and to use the work of Jewish artists to that end.

In part 2 of this book, I explore the remaking of Holocaust memory in the wake of its globalization, remediation, and politicization around the turn of the millennium. I argue that the new German Jewish literature reflects the changes in Holocaust remembrance while offering deep insights into the structure of memory itself. In a situation in which the tensions between different commemorative discourses are palpable, writers are prone to reflect on the sources, representations, and transmission of memory. As others have argued, contemporary German Jewish authors have brought about a "metamemorial shift" in Holocaust literature.[35] In *Renegotiating Postmemory*, Maria Roca Lizarazu observes that for many of these writers, the Holocaust is not primarily a personal or inherited trauma but a historical memory shaped by specific political conditions, cultural conventions, and medial frames. Authors such as Benjamin Stein, Maxim Biller, Vladimir Vertlib, and Eva Menasse are conscious of their historical distance from the Holocaust and the existing representations—the stories, images, and symbols—that have molded their understanding of it. As a whole, their literature is characterized by a high degree of metamemorial reflexivity, or an awareness that every instance of literary Holocaust remembrance is also a comment on the memory cultures of the present. *Making German Jewish Literature Anew* brings into focus two authors—Doron Rabinovici and Katja Petrowskaja—who exemplify this metamemorial turn as they probe the remaking of Holocaust memory in an age of globalization, digitization, and transculturation.

Claiming Places

The category of *place* matters in contemporary German Jewish literature precisely because this is a literature of displacement. Many of the writers discussed in this book moved to Germany or Austria from other countries, often when they were children: Maxim Biller came from Czechoslovakia; Doron Rabinovici from Israel; Vladimir Vertlib, Julya Rabinowich, and

Lena Gorelik from Russia; and Jan Himmelfarb, Dmitrij Kapitelman, and Katja Petrowskaja from Ukraine. The balance of this list is tilted toward Eastern Europe, and especially to the countries of the former Soviet Union, not only due to the *Kontingentflüchtlingsgesetz* (Quota Refugee Act) of postreunification Germany but also because of earlier waves of migration that brought, for example, Jews from the Soviet Union to Austria during the 1970s. Other authors have moved away from German-speaking countries while continuing to write and publish in German; these include Barbara Honigmann, who in 1984 left the GDR to resettle in the French city of Strasbourg. The mobility that characterizes the lives of many contemporary German Jewish writers also informs their literary work, which often exhibits a tension between displacement and emplacement. Whereas migration and exile are recurrent and central literary themes, the authors depict scenes of arrival, dwell on locations, and turn spaces into places by investing them with personal meaning and emotional significance.

Inspired by the recent "spatial turn" in Jewish studies, *Making German Jewish Literature Anew* explores new literary strategies of place-making and place-claiming. In particular, Barbara Mann's 2012 *Place and Space in Jewish Studies* allows us to formulate a concept of *diasporic place-making*—which in Mann is not so much an explicit concept as the result of two theoretical currents that intersect in her book.[36] On the one hand, Mann joins the ranks of a number of theorists who in the last few decades have reinterpreted and revalorized life in the diaspora. Paradigmatic for this trend are Daniel Boyarin und Jonathan Boyarin, who have held up the Jewish diaspora as a model of how a minority group can preserve a distinct communal identity while being able to share space with others, who are recognized and respected as others. Because diaspora Judaism grounds its collective identity in a shared genealogy rather than a shared territory, it presents a viable alternative to the modern nation-state, with its tendency toward social homogeneity and exclusion of cultural "others."[37] Mann develops this idea in a new direction as she relinquishes the Boyarins' clear-cut distinction between the space of the nation and the time of the diaspora. For Mann, the diaspora first and foremost requires and encourages acts of place-making. If uprootedness is the precondition of diasporic existence, actual life in the diaspora enables people to put down new roots, make new homes, and create new places.

Mann also draws on a second theoretical current—namely, the dynamic understanding of place in contemporary anthropology and human geography as expressed, for example, in James Clifford's dictum that human places are the result of *routes* as much as of *roots*.³⁸ A route is a path that is tied to a specific human activity—as in travel routes, trade routes, mountain climbing routes, and so on—and on which stops develop wherever human needs meet with the terrain humans traverse to fulfill these needs. Human geographers such as Yi-Fu Tuan (who defines "place" as a pause in the movement enabled by "space") and Doreen Massey (who describes the social construction of places through human activity and interactivity) converge on a similar idea: that all places emerge out of movements that have come to a temporary standstill and are still reverberating in these places.³⁹ On her part, Mann presupposes this never-ending movement and asks how Jewish practice, both traditional and contemporary, creates new places. She develops a vocabulary to describe acts of place-making in religious ritual as well as literature and the arts. For example, travel narratives that attend closely to the physical details of the sites visited and remembered imaginatively inhabit these sites and in that process constitute them as places. Furthermore, a number of contemporary American Jewish artists reference the *eruv*—a religious-spatial practice of enclosure that enables observant Jews to carry objects outside the domain of their homes on the Shabbat—in their works to envision a pervious Jewish space.⁴⁰

As I bring these ideas to bear on contemporary German Jewish literature, I often speak of "place-claiming" in addition to "place-making." Whereas *place-making* tends to connote a *creatio ex nihilo*, *place-claiming* points to an engagement with existing places that can be repossessed, repurposed, and resignified. The term *place-claiming* is capacious enough to describe the many ways places accrue new meanings in contemporary German Jewish writing, from descriptions of a Jewish cemetery that reconnects its visitors to Judaism and of a hidden street that welcomes its immigrant residents all the way to a narrator's attempt to occupy openly hostile places—in one case even a deportation holding cell. The verb *to claim* also reminds us that place-making often depends on language, especially political speech acts such as asserting, demanding, or protesting. This political dimension transpires most clearly in the characters' encounters with bureaucratic apparatuses—for example, in an attempt to obtain an immigrant visa or a special permit to celebrate a Jewish holiday. Beyond the narrated actions of literary characters, the term *place-claiming* conceptualizes the overall effect of the new Jewish writing—that is, the ways these authors lay claim to a place in German literature. Their narrative and writerly claiming of places, I argue, is a founding gesture on par with the performance of Jewish authorship and the remaking of Holocaust memory. Taken together, these three gestures reinstate the possibility of a vibrant German Jewish literature several decades after the Holocaust.

Book Outline

Part 1 of *Making German Jewish Literature Anew* focuses on authorship and how authors publicly claim, assert, or question their Jewish identities. I begin by examining a genre that around 2000 became a key vehicle of authorial self-fashioning for second-generation German Jewish writers: the "prose collection," which combines stories and essays, autobiographical reflection, and sociopolitical commentary. In chapter 1, I identify several key strategies by which Maxim Biller, Esther Dischereit, and Barbara Honigmann define, perform, and ultimately produce Jewish authorship in their prose collections. These strategies include references to other, recognizably Jewish authors; vivid depictions of the author as set apart from non-Jewish audiences; and strategically positioned stories about his or her development into a self-conscious Jewish author. I also suggest that the prose collections can be considered "post-Jewish" in that they self-reflexively engage with the conditions that govern the production and reception of Jewish literature in Germany. Chapter 2 argues that Benjamin Stein's 2010 novel *Die Leinwand*, although formally different from the prose collections, further develops their innate possibilities by staking out yet another authorial position: namely, that of an Orthodox Jew who writes German literature. Drawing particular attention to Stein's creative use of paratexts such as the book title, jacket copy, and glossary, I maintain that Stein, like the second-generation German Jewish writers before him, exposes, questions, and strategically deploys the literary conventions that identify an author as Jewish.

Part 2 of this book is concerned with memory, particularly the remaking of Holocaust memory. Chapter 3 analyzes three metamemorial novels by Doron Rabinovici that explore the foundations of human memory, from neuronal processes and media representations to discursive networks and memory communities. A trained historian and public intellectual who frequently indicts the repression of the Nazi past in postwar Austria, Rabinovici—intriguingly and at times perplexingly—uses his novels to focus on memorial practices that reshape rather than preserve the memory of the past. Even flagrant disruptions of memory can be seen as productive. Thus, in *Ohnehin* (2004; Anyway), the story of a former SS officer suffering from a memory disorder, a mistranslation during a symposium on antisemitism, and a revisionist call for an end to Holocaust remembrance are all shown to forestall the ritualization and routinization of Holocaust memory. In *Suche nach M.* (1997; *The Search for M.*) and *Andernorts* (2010; *Elsewhere*), the interpersonal transfer and international travel of memories similarly spark new discourses and connections, including transcultural ones. Chapter 4 turns to Katja Petrowskaja, one of a number of post-Soviet German Jewish writers who have begun to transform German memory culture by bearing witness to multiple historical traumas. In her widely acclaimed literary debut, *Vielleicht Esther* (2014; *Maybe Esther*), Petrowskaja establishes tenuous connections between the Holocaust and other atrocities before, during, and after the Second World War. Yet, like Rabinovici, she stops short of depicting the actual emergence of a transcultural memory community. Instead, through their metamemorial works, these authors contemplate the principles that would make such communities possible—in Petrowskaja's case, the principle of *similarity* that undergirds the possibility of transcultural witnessing and the connectivity of memory media.

Part 3 examines the tension between displacement and emplacement in contemporary German Jewish literature. This part is organized around three different types or phases of movement from which places may emerge: returning, transitioning, and arriving. Chapter 5 explores how Barbara Honigmann, in several of her autofictional works, critiques the postwar return of Jewish exiles to East Germany while casting her own resettlement in France as an alternative—yet also as a form of *return*. Honigmann's 2015 *Chronik meiner Straße* (Chronicle of my street), which relates how a rundown street in Strasbourg becomes the narrator's permanent home as she retells the stories of the street's residents, is a powerful example of diasporic place-making. Chapter 6 probes the concept of place-making for a very different form of migration, one that leaves its subjects in a state of permanent *transition*. Both Vladimir Vertlib and Julya Rabinowich depict the flight of their families from Leningrad to Vienna in the early 1970s as a traumatic rupture and a cause of lasting displacement. And yet the narrators of their early writings manage to inhabit new places—and, in particular, places of transit—in a way that may explain the interest in ever-new forms of migration in Vertlib's and Rabinowich's subsequent works. Finally, chapter 7 turns to representations of *arrival*. I show how the literary debuts of post-Soviet authors Lena Gorelik, Dmitrij Kapitelman, and Jan Himmelfarb are all structured around emphatic scenes of arrival—namely, of quota refugees in Germany. At the same time, these authors rethink and redefine what it means to arrive in a place, thereby wresting the idea of arrival away from the political call for an "integration" of migrants and infusing it with a new sense of unpredictability and open-endedness.

PART I

PERFORMING AUTHORSHIP

1

AUTHORIAL SELF-FASHIONING IN SECOND-GENERATION WRITERS

Maxim Biller, Esther Dischereit, and Barbara Honigmann

IT HAS OFTEN BEEN NOTED THAT THERE IS something qualitatively new about the literature of the second generation of German and Austrian Jewish writers after the Holocaust. Since the late 1980s, and especially in the decade after the 1990 reunification of Germany, writers such as Maxim Biller, Esther Dischereit, Barbara Honigmann, Rafael Seligmann, Ruth Beckermann, Doron Rabinovici, and Robert Menasse have created a new German Jewish literature reflecting a new set of conditions. Born after the war, these second-generation writers were profoundly shaped by their parents' experiences of exile, internment, and genocidal terror. In their writings they often confront this traumatic legacy by registering the conspicuous silences, ruptured genealogies, and loss of cultural traditions in their Jewish families. At the same time, they also challenge taboos of Holocaust representation and, on occasion, even question the centrality of the Holocaust for contemporary German Jewish identity altogether. Another prominent feature of their literature is its international character; the narratives are often set in different places in Eastern Europe, North America, or Israel. This geographical range reflects the diasporic existence of the authors, many of whom were either not born in Germany or Austria or at some point moved away from these countries. Most importantly, these second-generation writers identify both as self-conscious Jews and as German-language writers who are committed to both these self-identifications, an attitude that differs markedly from the first generation's sense of "sitting on packed suitcases." While they are far from resurrecting the myth of the "German-Jewish symbiosis"—in fact, they rather highlight the tensions between the German and the Jewish—their public presence and self-declared Jewish identity have led scholars to speak of the "reemergence," "rebirth," or "renaissance" of German Jewish literature. Early on in the process, Thomas Nolden used the phrase "young Jewish literature" to characterize this new literary movement.[1]

One way of explaining the rise of a new German Jewish literature is that it served the changing needs of the literary market. Thus, Sander Gilman has read these works in terms of the contemporary interest in ethnic literatures. Although he concedes that the category "ethnic" is rarely used in the German Jewish context, Gilman suggests that the market value of ethnic literature is one of the reasons authors in Germany are labeled Jewish.[2] There is indeed evidence to support this view. For example, Rafael Seligmann initially had great trouble finding a publisher for his first novel, *Rubinsteins Versteigerung* (Auctioning off Rubinstein), and initially published it in 1988 with a small private press. Only a year later, however, the book was republished by the prestigious Eichborn press and received remarkably positive reviews in numerous German newspapers and magazines, not so much because of its aesthetic merits but as a "documentation of a young Jewish life world that has thus far remained largely invisible."[3] And according to Esther Dischereit, it was her publisher who insisted on the adjective *Jewish* in the subtitle of her 1988 novel *Joëmis Tisch: Eine jüdische Geschichte* (Joëmi's table: A Jewish story), apparently because the company had discovered the attractiveness of Jewish literature for German readers.[4]

This chapter explores how second-generation German Jewish writers engage with these market conditions and pressures. One inspiration for my analysis involves the theoretical insights and critical language developed by scholars of postethnic literature. The term *postethnic* was originally coined by the intellectual historian David Hollinger to capture the fluid, multifaceted, and voluntary character of ethnic affiliations in contemporary North America.[5] As a sociological concept, the term does not travel well from North America to the German-speaking countries, where groupings have proceeded along different lines and the term *ethnisch* (ethnic) has exceptionally problematic racial-biological connotations. However, literary scholars have developed the term *postethnic* in ways that are indeed relevant to the analysis of contemporary German Jewish literature. Florian Sedlmeier, for example, analyzes the professional promotion and marketing of ethnic literature to contemporary reading audiences in the United States. Sedlmeier shows that the notion of ethnic literature is based on three assumptions, which together make up what he calls the "paradigm of communal and cultural representativeness."[6] These assumptions are as follows: (1) ethnic authors write about their ethnic identities, (2) they are capable of speaking representatively for their ethnic group, and (3) they describe the group's experience with greater authenticity, or at least greater legitimacy, than authors who are not considered part of the group. With *postethnic* Sedlmeier designates a more recent tendency among authors who are perceived or self-identified as "ethnic" to critically reflect upon these assumptions. Postethnic authors self-reflexively engage with the conditions that govern the production and reception of ethnic literature. In this chapter I argue that second-generation writers similarly reflect on the production and reception of the new Jewish literature in Germany.

This chapter focuses on the period in which the new German Jewish literature clearly emerged as a sizable and recognizable entity—that is, the decade after the reunification of Germany in 1990. I examine a genre that enjoyed particular popularity at that time—namely, collections of essays, stories, and other brief prose texts that were often first published independently and then assembled into a peculiar mix of sociopolitical commentary and autobiographical reflection. Around 2000, several second-generation German Jewish authors published such prose collections, including Esther Dischereit's *Übungen jüdisch zu sein* (1998; Exercises in being Jewish) and *Mit Eichmann an der Börse* (2001; With Eichmann on the stock market); Barbara Honigmann's *Damals, dann und danach* (1999; Back then, then and after) and *Das Gesicht wiederfinden* (2006; Rediscovering the face); and Maxim Biller's *Deutschbuch* (2001; German book). To be sure, these three authors differ in terms of geographical origin—Dischereit grew up in West Germany, Honigmann was raised in East Germany, and Biller spent the first ten years of his life in Prague—and Jewish identity—Honigmann is the only one among the three who clearly identifies with Judaism as a religion. But there can be no doubt that all three were both self-identified and publicly perceived as German Jewish authors, a perception to which their prose collections contributed significantly. Interest in the genre was not limited to Germany. Austrian Jewish writers also contributed to its development: for example, Doron Rabinovici with *Credo und Credit* (2001; Creed and credit) and Robert Schindel with *Mein liebster Feind* (2004; My dearest enemy).[7] The cumulated appearance of these prose collections shows that the turn of the millennium was indeed a moment of stocktaking and self-reflection.

I propose to read the prose collections of Biller, Dischereit, and Honigmann as sites of authorial self-staging and self-fashioning. The titles of these collections all evoke a process of becoming: learning to speak German, practicing to be Jewish, moving from the past to the present. To be sure, the writers did not necessarily author every aspect of the collections. The book titles and the selection and arrangement of the texts, for example, may very well have been the work of an editor rather than the author. Yet the cumulative effect of these prose collections is nonetheless one of authorial self-construction, since they were published under the names of Biller, Dischereit, and Honigmann. In what follows, I identify three key strategies by which these collections define, perform, and ultimately produce Jewish authorship: (1) They create webs of references to well-known and recognizably Jewish authors, including contemporary American Jewish authors and pre-Holocaust German Jewish writers. In so doing, they conjure an idea of "Jewish literature" as an entity based on contiguity. (2) They describe the author, often vividly, as set apart from his or her main audience, whether as a perpetual immigrant, a speaker on a theater stage, or a German-language writer in France. (3) They feature one or more strategically placed stories about the author's coming of age as a Jewish author. These stories are marked by a tension between a narrative of self-discovery or self-actualization on the one hand and an awareness of processes of labeling and classification on the other.

To emphasize this again, I do not make an argument about actual people writing about their actual selves. Rather, I suggest that the texts assembled in each of these prose collections work together to create a distinct author persona. If I use expressions such as "Biller writes," "Dischereit depicts," or "Honigmann claims," it should be remembered that I understand "Biller," "Dischereit," and "Honigmann" to be simultaneously the producers and the products of the collections. Because I conceive of the author as both the agent and the effect of writing and publishing, I forego the conventional distinction between author and narrator, even in my analyses of fictional stories. The point of this chapter is to identify three distinct strategies by which these prose collections produce—and simultaneously interrogate—notions of Jewish authorship and Jewish literature.

Creating Webs of References

One cumulative effect of the prose collections is that they create networks of references to other Jewish writers that together conjure a broader idea of Jewish literature. References to other Jewish writers are especially numerous in Maxim Biller's *Deutschbuch*, which is based on columns and reportages he previously published in various German newspapers and magazines. *Deutschbuch* contains reflections on North American Jewish authors, including Saul Bellow, Mordecai Richler, and Philip Roth; an essay on Robert Schindel and other contemporary German-language Jewish writers; and portraits of Aleksandar Tisma (a Serbian Jewish author who wrote about the Holocaust), David Vogel (a Russian-born Hebrew modernist), and Henryk Broder (a contemporary German Jewish journalist and author). Explicit comparisons between himself and these writers and descriptions of moments of contact with them—such as his meeting with Broder in the writer's Berlin apartment and his telephone conversation with Tisma—create a sense of personal connection between Biller and the Jewish writers he references. Esther Dischereit's *Übungen jüdisch zu sein* includes a recollection of the awarding of Germany's most important literary prize to Nelly Sachs, which the young Dischereit watched on TV, and an essay on the American-born German Jewish writer Jeannette Lander, which first appeared as the afterword to one of Lander's novels. There are not many references to Jewish writers in Barbara Honigmann's *Damals, dann und danach*, which consists mostly of autobiographical stories and reflections. However, Honigmann's subsequent prose collection, *Das Gesicht wiederfinden*, features essays on Albert Cohen and Thomas Brasch, as well as a lecture on the tradition of German Jewish female writing exemplified by Glückel von Hameln, Rahel Varnhagen, and Anne Frank.

Among the three authors, Maxim Biller most emphatically posits the existence of a cohesive body of Jewish writing in contemporary Austria and Germany. In "Goodbye, Columbus," he argues that these are among the few countries that are still home to a vibrant and autonomous Jewish literature. According to Biller, the contemporary literature of Honigmann, Schindel, Menasse, and Rabinovici is the product of a long process of dissimilation— the "Absonderung der Juden von der deutschen Gesellschaft" (segregation of the Jews from German society)—that began in the early twentieth century and only intensified after the Holocaust.[8] It is precisely because the life of Jewish writers in contemporary Germany and Austria is so anomalous that they depict Jews and Judaism with such focus and urgency and that they live and write "besonders bewußt jüdisch" (90; particularly deliberately Jewish). Biller insists on the truthfulness and authenticity of their writing despite his critique of the trite rituals of the literary establishment. Another one of his essays in *Deutschbuch* begins with a description of an invitation the New York Goethe Institute issued to five German-language Jewish authors, including Biller and Robert Schindel, who went on to perform their rather stereotypical Jewish parts in front of reading audiences. However, the essay ends with a scene in which Biller, after leaving the reopening of Suhrkamp's Jüdischer Verlag (Jewish Publishing House) in Frankfurt full of anger at the host's hypocritical philosemitism, resumes his reading of Schindel's novel *Gebürtig* (*Born-Where*), reveling in the book's strengths: "Es warten noch fünfzig Seiten Schindel auf dich, ruhig Blut also, fünfzig Seiten Wahrheit und Güte und sehr viel Erinnerung" (101; You still have fifty pages of Schindel waiting for you, so keep calm, fifty pages of truth and goodness and lots of remembrance). In Biller's eyes, the public instrumentalization of German Jewish authors takes nothing away from the truth and power of their writing.

If Biller posits the existence of a Jewish literature, however, the concept remains remarkably fluid and nonessentialist. The idea of such a literature arises from references to various Jewish writers who do not have much in common other than that they enter Biller's sphere of consciousness and become the subject of one of his essays. And in "Goodbye, Columbus," Biller actually distances himself from the Jewish writers who initially had the greatest influence on him—namely North American Jewish writers such as Saul Bellow, Mordecai Richler, and especially Philip Roth. He concludes that these authors paid for their sense of relative normalcy with assimilation and that this normalcy is neither possible nor desirable for German Jewish writers. American Jewish literature and German Jewish literature developed under fundamentally different conditions and in opposite directions. What marks both of them as "Jewish," then? It seems that Biller bases his idea of Jewish literature, to use Dan Miron's fruitful theoretical concept, on *contiguity* rather than continuity.[9] According to Miron, modern Jewish literature has developed and continues to develop through forms of cultural contact, spatial proximity, or intellectual affinity that can vary greatly in intensity; they can be random, unintended, or fleeting. Such contact can even consist in rejection or self-distancing—such as, we may add, Maxim Biller's deliberate dissociation from American Jewish literature. Like Miron, Biller invites us to think of Jewish literature as a multifarious entity in which elements are drawn together and pulled apart by centripetal and centrifugal forces.

The same is true for Esther Dischereit, who repeatedly references other Jewish writers in *Übungen jüdisch zu sein*, most prominently in an essay that probes the conditions of her own writing in postwar Germany titled "Vom Verschwinden der Worte" (On the disappearance of words).[10] The title of the essay refers to the difficulty of writing about the Holocaust, which defies linguistic representation, as well as to the silence and loneliness it inflicted on postwar German-speaking Jews such as Dischereit herself. How can she write about the loss of her Jewish family, traditions, and identity in a language in which words such as *Rampe* (40; ramp) have become permanently fraught with connotations of danger and menace? The references to other Jewish writers in this essay, then, do not provide an answer to this question but rather rearticulate the impasse in different ways. By invoking the names of these authors, Dischereit creates a network of associations around a fundamental negativity.

Dischereit cites two well-known Holocaust writers to capture the double bind in which German Jewish writers find themselves. She transfers the cynical title of *Bei uns in Auschwitz* (*Here in Our Auschwitz*) by Tadeusz Borowski (a non-Jewish survivor of Auschwitz) to Germany, which suggests that extreme cruelty has become a social norm there: "In Deutschland ist es unser liebes Dachau" (38; In Germany, it's our dear Dachau). She also recalls Jean Améry's statement that after the Holocaust one has to accept one's Jewishness even if it has no concrete meaning for oneself. Dischereit then evokes the writings of the pre-Holocaust German Jewish writers Heinrich Heine, Else Lasker-Schüler, and Franz Kafka, which give expression to ineffable suffering, and the language struggles of the female protagonist in Jeannette Lander's 1972 novel *Auf dem Boden der Fremde* (On the soil of a foreign country). Finally, she identifies a common trait in her own writing and that of contemporary German Jewish writers Barbara Honigmann, Matthias Herrmann, and Chaim Noll, all of whom have embarked on a literary search for a Jewish identity that has no roots in their own childhood experiences. As is the case with Biller, Dischereit's references to other Jewish writers are not always affirmative. Thus, she finds the use of physiognomy in Alfred Döblin's early twentieth-century writings on eastern European Jews disturbing because, as a post-Holocaust Jew, she cannot isolate it from the Third Reich's use of racial ideology. Overall, the names of Jewish writers function as signposts that guide Dischereit's search for a language and aesthetics for the post-Holocaust German Jewish writer. The names help create a web of similarities and differences, of affiliative and conflictual relations, that never coalesce into a homogenous whole but rather conjure an idea of Jewish literature as an entity based on contiguity.

More so than Biller and Dischereit, Barbara Honigmann describes a *continuum* of Jewish literature that spans several generations—namely, German Jewish literature before the Holocaust—to which she haltingly links her own writing. *Damals, dann und danach* features a story (which I analyze in more detail later in the chapter) about three of her paternal ancestors who were authors of literary texts and eager participants in the project of Jewish acculturation. In a lecture delivered a couple of years later, Honigmann discusses three famous female writers who belong to a different, yet similarly continuous, tradition of German Jewish writing: Glückel von Hameln, Rahel Varnhagen, and Anne Frank. Honigmann reads their works as elements of a "truly minor literature," using a variant of the phrase coined by Franz Kafka—and made famous by Gilles Deleuze and Félix Guattari—for a literature that is composed at the margins of a dominant culture and used as a medium of self-understanding for a minority group.[11] Although von Hameln, Varnhagen, and Frank write at different historical moments—before, during, and after the period of Jewish emancipation and assimilation—their works have several things in common. They use preliterary forms such as the letter and the diary, they take their subjects from everyday life, and their language is not quite German. According to Honigmann, they constitute a German Jewish literary tradition characterized by a high degree of authenticity, immediacy, and intensity:

> Es sind Werke, in denen uns Frauen Geschichten, Begebenheiten, Gedanken und Träume erzählen, die von ihrem Leben als Angehörige einer kleinen Minderheit in einer großen Kultur handeln, unter starker innerer und äußerer Anspannung geschrieben und deshalb von so unvergleichbarer Intimität und Intensität. Eine "ganz kleine" Literatur des Anvertrauens, in der uns die Autorinnen durch die Geschichte hindurch anzublicken scheinen.[12]
>
> They are works in which women tell us of incidents, thoughts, dreams and stories about their lives as members of a small minority in a large culture, written under intense inner and outer pressure, which explains their incomparable intimacy and intensity. A "truly minor" literature of confiding, in which the authors seem to glance at us through the story.

Toward the end of her lecture, Honigmann intimates that her own writing still belongs to the "truly minor literature" and that this literary tradition has inspired and empowered her. It is interesting, then, that the few evocations of these authors in *Damals, dann und danach* are interspersed with criticism of the clichéd use made of them and of the public representation of Jews in general. Their names appear only in scenes in which Honigmann protests against the social roles she is made to play. When she compares herself to Rahel Varnhagen, for instance, she is well aware that she thereby echoes a construction of German artist friends who cast her in the role of a *salonnière*:

> Sie nannten mich manchmal im Scherz die Gertrude Stein vom Prenzlauer Berg, und sie meinten damit, daß ich sozusagen einen Salon hielt, eine Vermittlerin also war. . . . Daß ich jüdisch war, paßte natürlich noch besonders gut zu dieser Salonrolle, sie hätten auch "Rahel" vom Prenzlauer Berg sagen können.[13]
>
> They sometimes referred to me in jest as the Gertrude Stein of Prenzlauer Berg, with which they meant that I held a sort of salon, that I was a facilitator. . . . The fact that I was Jewish fit particularly well into this salon role, of course; they could also have said "Rahel" of Prenzlauer Berg.

Honigmann adds that she could not have become a writer in Germany in part because the role into which her friends pushed her stifled her own creativity.

Playing the part of Anne Frank is even more problematic. In *Damals, dann und danach*, Honigmann recalls how non-Jewish Germans often commented on her supposed similarity to Anne Frank, drawing an attention to her physical difference that she did not welcome (75). And the book begins with a text entitled "Ich bin nicht Anne!" (I am not Anne!) in which Honigmann recounts an episode from her time as a student in East Germany when an alcoholic neighbor repeatedly mistook her for a Jewish girl named Anne, whom she had apparently protected during the Third Reich. Honigmann senses that she is being forced into a "role" in the neighbor's own "drama" (9)—a drama of guilt feelings and longing for catharsis—and that the ostentatious philosemitism of her other neighbors is not much better. With the exclamation in the title—"Ich bin nicht Anne!"—she objects to her own (mis)representation as the iconic Jewish child in hiding. Like Biller and Dischereit, Honigmann undermines any sense of continuity through the depiction of contiguity; her invocations of other Jewish writers highlight the role of external ascription, random association, and misidentification in the definition of Jewishness.

Inscribing Authorial Positions

A second cumulative effect of the prose collections is that they stake out an authorial position that sets the author at a distance from, even in direct opposition to, his or her main audience. They use spatial images that visualize the author's position: the immigrant who is perpetually on the move (Biller), the author who writes across the French-German border (Honigmann), and the Jewish writer who speaks as if from a podium (Dischereit). The repeated depictions, whether literal or figural, of the authors' spatial relations to their German readers translate into rhetorical stances that are marked by some degree of alienation, such as that of the observer, the skeptic, or the polemic.

The last of these is the case with Maxim Biller, whose diatribes against German mentality, German culture, and especially German contemporary literature make up a substantial part of his *Deutschbuch*. The collection contains the famous Tutzing speech, delivered in 2000 to prominent German writers of his generation, in which Biller denounces contemporary German literature as a vapid, colorless, impotent "Schlappschwanz-Literatur" (325; limp-dick literature). Some of the essays draw attention to the presence of a speaker and his identity as an outsider: as an Oriental ethnologist studying Germany (173) or, less clearly embodied, as someone who is able to apostrophize Germany as if from afar: "So wird das nichts, Deutschland" (257; It won't work like that, Germany). Other essays explicitly connect Biller's oppositional stance to his position as an immigrant to Germany. *Deutschbuch* includes stories and portrayals of immigrants—some of whom, especially the Polish-born journalist and satirist Gabriel Laub, serve as figures of identification for Biller—and several essays hint at, refer to, or retell in more detail the story of his own immigration to Germany.

The essay "Deutscher wider Willen" (German against my will) is exemplary of Biller's self-identification as an immigrant who never truly arrives or even wants to arrive. The essay, which largely consists of a polemical reckoning with German history, society, and culture, repeatedly mentions that Biller immigrated to the country at the age of ten and calls him a "Emigrantenkind" (120; emigrant child) and "Edelausländer" (121; noble foreigner). Toward the end, Biller briefly entertains the possibility of identifying as German—provided that the Germans could overcome their tendency toward self-pity, xenophobia, and calculated egotism—before he recalls, once again, his Armenian grandfather. The figure of this grandfather, whom Biller never saw again after his family's emigration, is central to the essay. As an Armenian, the grandfather is the representative of a "gehetzten Minderheit" (115; hounded minority) and the opposite of everything German; it was in his company that Biller first saw intimidating Germans on Soviet TV. By conjuring the image of the grandfather in its very last sentence, the essay firmly establishes Biller's position as an immigrant: "Manchmal, Großvater, denke ich an dich, und ich denke auch, wir hätten niemals in die Fremde ziehen sollen" (133; Sometimes, grandfather, I think of you, and I also think that we never should have moved to a foreign place). It is telling that Germany is still called a "Fremde" (foreign place) and that the last image is one of Biller on the move toward this "Fremde." Biller's spatial distance from Germany—the memory of which he preserves long after his arrival in the country—is both a condition and an expression of his polemical stance. His self-stylization as a perpetual immigrant buttresses his oppositional attitude toward his German readers. It helps him stake out an authorial position from which he can critique, provoke, and chastise his audience.

Biller immigrated to Germany, but Honigmann made the opposite move. In 1984 she left what was then the GDR for the city of Strasbourg, which is close to the German border and home to a sizable and vibrant Jewish community.[14] It is there that she wrote her first collection of short stories, which in 1986 became an instant success on the German book market. Honigmann would stage and restage this central fact of her life—that she became a German-language writer at the very moment she left Germany—in several auto-fictional novels. In her prose collection *Damals, dann und danach*, she repeatedly extols the benefits of writing at some distance from Germany. Going to France enabled her to escape the daily reminders of just how fraught with tension the relationship between Jews and Germans is and how the awareness of the violent history shapes and strains so many everyday conversations. The move to Strasbourg positioned her as "ein Zuschauer, ein Gast, eine Fremde" (17; a spectator, a guest, a foreigner) who observes Germany from a certain distance. This separation from her home country, the adoption of a position "am Rande" (45; on the margins), made it possible for her to begin writing in earnest.[15] In a next step, Honigmann universalizes this position and claims that all writing means to be speaking from a distance to an "Other" who may or may not understand:

> Ich begriff, daß Schreiben Getrenntsein heißt und dem Exil sehr ähnlich ist, und daß es in diesem Sinne vielleicht wahr ist, daß Schriftsteller sein und Jude sein sich ähnlich sind, wie sie nämlich vom Anderen abhängen, wenn sie auf ihn einreden, mehr oder weniger verzweifelt. Es gilt ja auch für beide, daß eine zu große Annäherung an den Anderen für sie gefährlich ist, und eine völlige Übereinstimmung mit ihm ihren Untergang befördert. (47)
>
> I understood that writing means being separated and is very similar to exile, and that it is in this sense perhaps true that being a writer and being a Jew are similar as well, in the way they are dependent upon the Other when they speak to him, more or less despairingly. It is true of both that approaching the Other too closely is dangerous for them and that agreeing with him too completely will bring about their downfall.[16]

In contrast to Biller and Honigmann, Dischereit locates herself exclusively within Germany, a position she describes as lonely and problematic in *Übungen jüdisch zu sein*. When Dischereit was growing up, her mother, who had survived the Third Reich in hiding in Berlin, felt isolated not only in her non-Jewish environment but also within the Jewish community, as everybody else seemed to have immigrated from somewhere. The public for which Dischereit then began to write—in German, the only language at her disposal—reinforced this sense of segregation and parcellation. Unable to grasp how deeply embedded in German life Jews once were and still are, literary agents and editors insisted that she document Jewishness as a "pures Stück" (17; pure piece) instead of presenting Jewish topics in fictional form or linking them to questions of gender and sexuality. Like Biller and Honigmann, Dischereit translates her own position as a writer into spatial images that assert a certain distance from her audience. The dominant spatial figure in her texts is that of the stage, the podium, or the TV screen, from which the Jewish author addresses an overwhelmingly non-Jewish German audience. This position on a platform may expose and objectify the Jewish author, but it can also afford her protection or surround her with an aura of authority.

In *Übungen jüdisch zu sein*, Dischereit conveys the risk of objectification in metaphors culled from the imagery of the exhibit, the display, and the show. She likens the treatment of Jewish individuals to that of an endangered species (214); the literary work of Jewish writers to a "Demonstration der Jüdischkeit" (49; demonstration of Jewishness); and herself during public readings to a "Jüdin zum Anfassen" (205; Jewish woman you can touch). In several essays, she uses the metaphor of prostitution to express a sense of indecent exposure: "*Vor* dem deutsch-deutschen Publikum jüdisch zu schreiben hat einen lästerlichen, einen prostituierenden Zug—wie das Ausziehen einer Frau vor den Augen der Männer. Ich weiß es. Aber ich sehe keine Alternative." (34, my emphasis; To write in Jewish *in front of* a non-Jewish German audience has a profane, prostitution-like element—like a woman getting undressed before the eyes of men. I know this. But I don't see any alternative.) Dischereit's formulation that she is writing "in Jewish" *vor* (in front of) rather than *für* (for) a non-Jewish German audience is intriguing. She not only posits that she writes "in Jewish"—probably referring to the linguistic constraints experienced by post-Holocaust German Jewish writers—but also spatializes the relationship between the Jewish writer and her audience. The author who writes *in front of* an audience seems to be simultaneously distanced from and overly close to her readers, which leads—as the prostitution metaphor suggests—to objectification and exploitation.[17] At other times, the image of the stage implies a protective effect of distance. In an essay published in a subsequent prose collection, Dischereit compares her writing to an actor's speech on a theater stage: "Mit dem Schreiben tritt eine Ich-Erzählerin zutage, die vor der Distanzlosigkeit des unmittelbaren Sprechens geschützt ist. Ich spreche gleichsam in einen dunklen Raum hinein, wie auf der Bühne."[18] (In writing, a first-person narrator comes to light who is protected from the lack of distance that characterizes direct speech. I speak as if into a dark room, as though I were on the stage.) As we will see, Dischereit sees this protective distance as first realized in the TV appearance of Nelly Sachs to accept a literary prize.

Narrating Origins, Establishing Genealogies

A third shared feature of the prose collections of Biller, Dischereit, and Honigmann is that they explore the origins of contemporary German Jewish literature by narrating, in one or more strategically placed stories, the authors' development toward being consciously Jewish writers. These stories exhibit a tension between a desire for an authentic Jewish literature and a critique of the classification mechanisms of the literary market and the literary public.

In the first three texts of *Übingen jüdisch zu sein*, Esther Dischereit moves between two very different conceptions of the public role of the German Jewish writer. On the one hand, she recalls how she glimpsed the transformative power of Jewish authorship while watching a telecast of a literary award presentation to Nelly Sachs (the famous German Jewish author and Nobel Prize winner who continued to reside in Sweden after the war). On the other hand, Dischereit compares her own writing for a largely non-Jewish audience to prostitution. While several critics have commented on the prostitution metaphor, what has gone unnoticed is its proximity, in the prose collection, to the scene that depicts the public celebration of Nelly Sachs as empowering. *Übungen jüdisch zu sein* never resolves the tension between empowerment and debasement in the act of public recognition. Yet the story of Sachs's TV appearance, which is set in Dischereit's adolescence and opens the prose collection, posits a new beginning and a new possibility—a German Jewish literature that is not a form of prostitution.

The telecast of the 1965 ceremony in which Sachs was awarded a prestigious literary prize, the Friedenspreis des deutschen Buchhandels (Peace Prize of the German Book Trade), strongly affected Dischereit and her mother for two reasons. On the one hand, they saw a Jewish writer who was able to fully and authentically express herself in Germany—"so vollständig Jüdin, wie es uns an keinem Tag gegeben" (15; as fully Jewish as we have never been)—and who, in return, was treated with dignity and respect, honored by the ovations of the political elite. The loftiness of the occasion, which was mediated through television, seemed to forestall the sense of exposure Dischereit elsewhere captures in the prostitution metaphor. Sachs's appearance on TV was marked by auratic distance rather than the unwanted closeness Dischereit would later experience in her own encounters with audiences. On the other hand, the event had such a powerful impact on the young Dischereit and her mother precisely because the TV temporarily disappeared as a medium, creating a sense of immediacy and the possibility of identification for the Jewish spectator. The vocabulary of encounter and intimacy that informs the text—which is entitled "Ein sehr junges Mädchen *trifft* Nelly Sachs" (9, my emphasis; A very young girl *meets* Nelly Sachs)—is one indicator of such immediacy. The immediacy of the experience enabled Dischereit's mother, who used to write poems during her years of hiding, to identify with Nelly Sachs. Watching the well-known German Jewish author and her enthusiastic reception by the German public also left a deep impression on the young Dischereit: "Diese Begegnung mit Nelly Sachs hat mir einen tiefen Eindruck gemacht, weil sie für einen Moment die Einsamkeit auflöste; sie saßen da in diesem Wohnzimmer, zwei, meine Mutter und Nelly Sachs. Bis der Moment verlosch." (15; This encounter with Nelly Sachs left a deep impression on me because it dissipated the loneliness for a moment; they sat there in that living room, the two of them, my mother and Nelly Sachs. Until the moment expired.) Even if this experience dissipated the loneliness that otherwise suffused their family life only for a moment, it was a significant originary moment for Dischereit.

With this story about herself, her mother, and Nelly Sachs, Dischereit establishes a genealogy of female German Jewish authors and a possible point of origin for her own writing. As noted previously, the figure of genealogy plays an even more important role in the work of Barbara Honigmann, who at one point relates her own work to the "truly minor literature" of Glückel von Hameln, Rahel Varnhagen, and Anne Frank. Honigmann's prose collection *Damals, dann und danach* features a story, entitled "Von meinem Urgroßvater, meinem Großvater, meinem Vater und mir" ("On My Great-Grandfather, My Grandfather, My Father and Me"), that posits a different kind of literary genealogy—one that is constituted by three of her paternal ancestors, all of whom wrote literary texts. In the story she describes how she herself became a German Jewish writer through two forms of distancing: spatial (she moved from Germany to France) and temporal (she broke with the tradition of German Jewish writing embodied by her father, grandfather, and great-grandfather). These ruptures are, in fact, related, since it was her move to Strasbourg, where none of her paternal ancestors had lived, that allowed her to avoid the assimilatory pressures to which they had succumbed. However, what first looks like a radical break and a new beginning is still based on a sense of genealogical continuity. This is so because the very act of writing in German is a form of return:

> Vielleicht war das Schreiben aber auch so etwas wie Heimweh und eine Versicherung, daß wir doch zusammengehörten, Deutschland und ich, daß wir, wie man so sagt, nicht auseinanderkommen können, gerade jetzt nicht, nach allem, was geschehen war. . . . Ich hatte mich doch ganz anders aufführen wollen als mein Urgroßvater, mein Großvater und mein Vater, und nun sah ich mich, genau wie sie, wieder auf den Anderen einreden, hoffend, gehört zu werden, vielleicht sogar verstanden, ihn anrufend: Sieh mich an! Hör mir zu, wenigstens fünf Minuten! (46–47)

> But perhaps writing was also something like homesickness and an assurance that we really did belong together, Germany and I, that we, as they say, could not get away from each other, especially not now, after everything that had happened. . . . I wanted to present myself completely differently than my great-grandfather, my grandfather, and my father, and now I saw myself, just like them, speaking again to the Other, hoping to be heard, perhaps even to be understood, calling to him, "Look at me! Listen to me, at least for five minutes!"[19]

Honigmann situates her own literary project in the space between the recovery and the rejection of the German Jewish literature her paternal ancestors helped create. In other words, she relates her project to existing categories of German Jewish writing, just as she does a couple of years later in her conception of the "truly minor literature" of German Jewish women.

Biller also invokes Franz Kafka's concept of a "minor literature" in a text that narrates his own development into a Jewish writer: from a child in Prague who is unaware of his difference from others to an adolescent in Germany who gradually becomes aware of that difference to a writer who consciously relates to Jewish history and culture. The title of the text, which is strategically positioned at the very end of Biller's *Deutschbuch*, is "Kleine Autobiographie" (Small/minor autobiography). One may, in fact, trace a line between Kafka's conception of a "minor literature" as a self-contained, quasi-organic entity with limited contact to other literatures to Biller's understanding of German Jewish literature as the communication medium of a minority group and the promotion of ethnic literatures by contemporary literary publishers and institutions.[20] As Sedlmeyer and others have argued, the concept of ethnic authorship assumes that literature gives expression to real-life experience and that individuals speak representatively for their ethnic group. Biller often advocates similar ideas in his programmatic writings, although he does not use the term *ethnic literature*. In a 2014 article in *Die Zeit*, for example, he calls on German-language authors with a migration background to use their experience as the starting point and thematic center of their literary writing. However, like Honigmann—who objects to facile public comparisons between herself and the German Jewish females who in the past composed a "truly minor literature"—Biller establishes a genealogy of Jewish writing without ever losing sight of the social mechanisms that produce the very idea of Jewish writing. He, too, exhibits the self-reflexivity that is the hallmark of the postethnic literary.

In "Kleine Autobiographie," Biller plots the birth of the Jewish writer as a bildungsroman of sorts, in which an individual realizes his or her inner potential in the encounter with new environments. Biller describes his childhood in Prague, his arrival in Germany, and the realization of his outer (*äußerlich*) differences from his environment—by which he means that he does not speak the language and grew up with different "Geschichten, Mythen und Spiele" (331; stories, myths, and games"). Once these outer differences erode in a process of acculturation, he discovers what he calls his *inner difference*—namely, his Jewishness—which is said to inform all his writing.

He claims that the experience of the Holocaust, in particular, gives his own literary characters the seriousness, wisdom, and depth that he demands as a critic. However, at the very end of his text, he suddenly contemplates the possibility that his writing lacks all truth and profundity and that he may just as well accept the derogatory label he first received as a child in Prague, when his Czech playmates branded him a gypsy, giving him a first taste of what it means to be labeled "other": "Vielleicht hatten sie damals eben doch recht, die blassen tschechischen Kinder, und ich bin nichts weiter als ein kleines, dreckiges Zigeunerlein" (333; Maybe the pale, Czech children were right back then after all, and I'm nothing but a small, dirty gypsy). More could be said about this gypsy imagery, which possibly alludes to Kafka's famous description of German Jewish literature as a "Zigeunerliteratur, die das deutsche Kind aus der Wiege gestohlen . . . hatte" (gypsy literature, which had stolen the German child from its cradle).[21] Here it may suffice to point out the irony that Biller, who generally champions the idea of ethnic authorship, ends his autobiographical sketch—and his *Deutschbuch*—by acknowledging both the instability of ethnic identity as well as its origins in external labeling or branding.

Since the turn of the millennium, German Jewish writers have continued to think through notions of Jewish authorship, and they have increasingly done so within their literary works.[22] Edgar Hilsenrath's 2006 novel *Berlin . . . Endstation* (Berlin . . . Final destination), for example, can be read as a fictional biography that reveals the psychic reality of its German Jewish author.[23] Another intricate take on Jewish authorship is Benjamin Stein's novel *Die Leinwand*, which was widely perceived as a novelty on the German literary scene upon its publication in 2010: a successful German novel about Orthodox Jewish life, written by an observant Jew. In the next chapter, I analyze the usage of paratext in the book, especially the intriguing interplay between the identity of one of its narrators and the author's identity as presented in the jacket copy, an interplay that potentially undermines the authenticating function of the jacket copy. Stein stakes out a new authorial position—that of an Orthodox Jew who writes German literature—while exposing and questioning the paratextual strategies that identify an author as Jewish. *Die Leinwand* is a great example of an author's self-reflexive engagement with the conditions under which Jewish literature is produced and consumed.

In this chapter I focused on a slightly earlier moment of German Jewish writing in order to illustrate the *simultaneity* of authorial self-fashioning and the creation of a new German Jewish literature. I identified three strategies by which the prose collections of Biller, Dischereit, and Honigmann, which appeared around 2000 and include texts from the 1990s, define, perform, and produce Jewish authorship: they create contiguous webs of references to other Jewish authors, assert a spatial distance from non-Jewish German audiences, and narrate the development of their authors into consciously Jewish writers. Overall, the collections dramatize the tension between declared and ascribed Jewishness—or between an author's self-identification as Jewish and his or her external identification by publishers, journalists, and audiences. They show that the rise of a new Jewish literature in postreunification Germany owes much to the German fascination with things Jewish and the ensuing marketability of Jewish authors but that it cannot be reduced to the logic of the market. Rather, the prose collections develop their notions of Jewish authorship in explicit confrontation with the classification mechanisms of the literary market and the literary public. They claim an authorial label while exposing, questioning, and ultimately disrupting the very process of labeling. In that sense, they are indeed part of the broader phenomenon Sedlmeier calls, in an adaptation of Hollinger's term, the *postethnic literary*. In order to subsume contemporary German Jewish literature under this term, however, we will need to rethink the *post-* in *postethnic* (or *post-Jewish*) so that the prefix no longer connotes succession, as it still does in Hollinger and Sedlmeier, but rather helps us recognize simultaneity.[24]

2

PLAYING WITH PARATEXT
Benjamin Stein's Die Leinwand

SHORTLY AFTER THE PUBLICATION OF HIS 2010 NOVEL *Die Leinwand* (*The Canvas*), Benjamin Stein said in an interview with the German weekly *Die Zeit*:

> Für mein Judentum . . . brauche ich keinen Zionismus und keinen Holocaust. Das spielt zwar eine Rolle, kommt aber von außen. Wenn sich jemand an mich wendet, weil er seine jüdische Identität sucht, dann sage ich ihm: "Versuche doch mal, Schabbes-Kerzen anzuzünden, und schau, was das mit dir macht."[1]
>
> For my Judaism . . . I need no Zionism and no Holocaust. These certainly play a role, but they come from the outside. If someone turns to me because he is searching for his Jewish identity, I tell him: "Try lighting Shabbat candles, and see what that does to you."

In many ways, this quote captures the essence of Stein's literary project, which seeks to broaden the range of Jewish identities, and especially religious identities, that can be expressed in German-language literature. Indeed, *Die Leinwand* reintroduces into German literature the possibility of representing and affirming Orthodox Judaism as a way of life, as the book's protagonists are two observant Jews from different cultural backgrounds. Within contemporary German Jewish fiction, Stein's novel is unique in its emphasis on the ways the Halacha, or Jewish law, structures the everyday life of observant Jews and sets them apart from non-Jews.[2]

The opposition Stein establishes in the quote between an embrace of religion and a focus on the Holocaust is nevertheless puzzling given the actual plot of his novel. For *Die Leinwand* can be read as a commentary on the Wilkomirski affair, the scandal that erupted in 1998 after Binjamin Wilkomirski's widely acclaimed Holocaust memoir, *Bruchstücke: Aus einer*

Kindheit 1939–1948 (1995; *Fragments: Memories of a Wartime Childhood*), was exposed as a fake. The formation, fabrication, and transmission of memories make up the central theme of *Die Leinwand*, which exemplifies the nexus between Holocaust remembrance and contemporary German Jewish writing. Indeed, it is interesting to note that the German Jewish author who most emphatically seeks to stake out a new authorial position—that of an Orthodox Jewish writer whose Jewishness is not primarily defined by the Holocaust—does so by thinking through questions of Holocaust testimony. This connection indicates that Holocaust remembrance is still widely seen as the principle task of contemporary German Jewish writers.

In this chapter I argue that Stein's most salient contribution to contemporary German Jewish literature is his creative use of paratext. I define paratext with Gérard Genette as the texts and images that surround the published literary text and control its meaning, including book titles, jacket copies, illustrations, prefaces, and afterwords.[3] The significance of such elements in *Die Leinwand* becomes apparent as soon as we realize that the book has two covers, each of which can serve as the starting point of our reading. Other features of the book, such as the glossary and datelines, further draw our attention to the margins of the literary text. As I show here, Stein's self-conscious use of paratext in *Die Leinwand* raises questions about authorship and authority that have a bearing on both German Jewish writing and Holocaust testimony. Through the interplay between author biography and narrator identity, for instance, the novel challenges the notion of contemporary German Jewish authors as ethnic authors. Stein also engages with the phenomenon of the fake Holocaust memoir on the level of paratext—for example, by highlighting the ways authorial gestures such as datelines serve to verify an author's ability to tell the story of his or her life. If Stein questions the paratextual conventions that classify an author as Jewish and a work as testimonial, this does not mean that he seeks to abolish these conventions. Indeed, I suggest that the proliferation of paratexts in *Die Leinwand* can be read as an alternative to the collapse of paratextual distinctions in Wilkomirski's *Bruchstücke*. My claim is that Stein alerts us to the power of paratext at a moment when the range of German Jewish identities is expanding and the Holocaust is turning from memory into history.

Constructing the Author Paratextually

Benjamin Stein belongs to the new generation of German and Austrian Jewish authors that began to emerge during the late 1980s and whose members self-identify as Jewish in interviews and other public forums. How are they identified and characterized in the books they publish? The jacket copies and blurbs show that attribution of a Jewish author identity often occurs indirectly. In books by Maxim Biller, Esther Dischereit, Barbara Honigmann, Doron Rabinovici, Rafael Seligmann, and Robert Schindel—and by older authors who were still publishing after 1990, including Edgar Hilsenrath and Angelika Schrobsdorff—the jacket copies usually identify the books quite clearly as Jewish but almost never the authors as such. The jacket copies tend to characterize the authors as Jewish in an indirect manner, either by connecting them to the content of their books—often by emphasizing the autobiographical character of the work—or by displacing the adjective *jüdisch* (Jewish) onto other aspects of their life, work, or family. For instance, the book description on the front flap of Barbara Honigmann's 2004 *Ein Kapitel aus meinem Leben* (A chapter from my life) includes the sentence: "Barbara Honigmann wurde berühmt durch *Eine Liebe aus Nichts*, die Geschichte ihres Vaters, mit der sie die Geschichte ihrer jüdischen Familie zu erzählen begann" (Barbara Honigmann became famous through *A Love Made Out of Nothing*, the story of her father, with which she began to relate the story of her Jewish family).[4] The author profile on the back flap of Edgar Hilsenrath's *Gesammelte Werke* (Collected works) identifies neither him nor his family as Jewish but displaces that attribute onto the ghetto to which they were moved during the Second World War: "kam die Familie in ein jüdisches Ghetto in der Ukraine" (the family was sent to a Jewish ghetto in Ukraine).[5] The indirect attribution of a Jewish author identity in German paratexts likely results from the tension between sociocultural taboos, on the one hand, and marketing pressures during a time when many Germans are fascinated with things Jewish, on the other hand.

The paratextual representation in which authors are never called "Jewish" but are described as such metonymically—via references to a place, a genealogy, or a literary work—positions contemporary German Jewish writers as "ethnic authors" within the "paradigm of communal and cultural representativeness."[6] As explained earlier, this paradigm proceeds from the assumption that ethnic writers write primarily about their own ethnic culture and identity and that they do so in an authentic and representative manner, opening a window into the lifeworld of an ethnic minority. Thus, the book description inside the front cover of Maxim Biller's *Wenn ich einmal reich und tot bin* (1990; Someday when I'm rich and dead) begins: "Der junge Autor Maxim Biller führt uns in seinen Erzählungen eine Welt vor Augen, von der wir wenig wissen: Die Welt der 30.000 in Deutschland lebenden Juden, für uns bislang ebenso exotisch und entfernt wie vor kurzem noch Isaac Bashevis Singers jüdisches Lodz, Warschau oder New York."[7] (The young author Maxim Biller shows us in his stories a world about which we know little: the world of the thirty thousand Jews who live in Germany and who are as exotic and distant for us as were Isaac Bashevis Singer's Jewish Lodz, Warsaw, or New York until recently.)

While this description does not call Biller himself Jewish, it treats him as a representative of contemporary German Jews. It endows Biller the author with a special knowledge about the world he describes, positioning him as the expert narrator of a world set apart from that of the readers. Of course, he could theoretically be writing from the perspective of an anthropologist or investigative journalist, but the comparison with Isaac Bashevis Singer, a well-known example of Jewish ethnic authorship, implies that Biller writes representatively about a world to which he himself belongs. This jacket copy is from 1990, when what has since been called "young German Jewish literature" (Nolden) had just emerged as a new literary phenomenon. Now that Jews have once again become a more integral presence in German public life, editors are less likely to assume so blatantly that "we"—the publishers and readers of German literature—are not Jewish. Yet this is still the backdrop against which Benjamin Stein's *Die Leinwand* has to be read. If the novel stakes out a new Jewish authorial position within German literature, it at the same time it unsettles such classifications altogether.

The first thing to note about *Die Leinwand* is that it draws attention to the paratext as a threshold—a device that defines the boundaries of the literary text and sets the stage for its reception and transmission. The book consists of two parts, each with its own narrator. In one part, Amnon Zichroni, who was born into a Haredi (or "ultra-Orthodox," although that term is now considered somewhat pejorative) family in Jerusalem but later became a psychoanalyst in Zurich, relates his ability to see, feel, and experience the memories of others. Zichroni befriends a man named Minsky, who believes himself to be a child survivor of Majdanek and Auschwitz. Zichroni then helps him articulate his fragmentary childhood memories—as a friend, it should be noted, not as a therapist. When the memoir Minsky resolves to write is later shown to be a fabrication, both he and Zichroni are devastated. (The parallels to the Wilkomirski affair are quite obvious here.) In the other part of the book, Jan Wechsler, an author and editor who lives as a modern Orthodox Jew in Munich and believes he grew up in the GDR, gradually finds out that he adopted a radically new identity about ten years ago, when he was the journalist who exposed the identity fraud of Minsky. Each part ends openly, indeed enigmatically, with (a memory of) the encounter of the two different narrators in Israel.

It is up to the reader to decide which part to read first, for the book has two covers. These covers are identical in the upper right and bottom of the page, which contain the author's name, the book's title, and an announcement that the book can be read in several ways. But other parts of the covers are not exactly alike. In the middle of each cover, we find a name—set off in italics and the colors red or blue, respectively; we soon learn it is the name of the narrator of that part of the book, Amnon Zichroni or Jan Wechsler. Next to the narrator's name is a photograph of an object particularly important to him, and right below that are the first lines of his part of the book. How do we decide where to begin our reading? There are some powerful paratextual signals that point in different directions. For instance, the flap inside the front cover typically contains a book description or an excerpt from the book. The flap inside a book's back cover typically provides some information about the author and often includes a photograph of him or her. If we follow that convention, we will begin reading *Die Leinwand* with the Wechsler part, for it is here that we find the book summary in the front and the author profile plus photograph in the back. However, the book summary itself first describes the Zichroni part and then the Wechsler part, which is also somewhat logical, since Zichroni is older than Wechsler and his narrative reaches further back into the past—all of which suggests the opposite sequence of reading: first Zichroni, then Wechsler. One effect of Stein's use of contradictory paratextual signals is that it alerts the reader to the presence and power of paratext. I suspect many readers will find themselves, as I did, holding the book in their hands, turning it around and around, first looking for paratextual signals and then pondering which ones to follow. The double mode of entry into the book also hints at the duality of German Jewish identity, since the book can be read not only from left to right—as in German—but also from right to left—as in Hebrew and Yiddish.

Another paratext likely to confound the reader's expectations is the glossary that concludes each part. The glossary is identical in both parts of the book, although neither of the narrators uses all the terms, so it is truly a glossary of the book as a whole. Consisting mostly of Hebrew terms with a religious meaning (and a few Yiddish, Aramaic, and Arabic words and Hebrew words with a secular meaning), the glossary creates the impression that Judaism constitutes a realm of its own into which non-Jewish readers first have to be initiated. Indeed, the duplication of the glossary and its location in the middle of the book reverse the usual spatial relationship between text and paratext. If Genette defines the paratext as the *threshold* that allows the reader to enter the literary text, Stein turns the literary text into the threshold of, or entry into, the paratext—namely, the glossary that forms the core of the book. All these unexpected paratextual elements—the covers, jacket copies, and glossary—make the reader highly aware of the book as the material carrier of the literary text. It is also noteworthy that the very center of the book is a single page with the publisher's information and a reference to Stein's literary blog *Turmsegler*.[8] This page reminds us that the book is also an occasion for an author's—potentially infinite—electronic commentary on his or her own work.

The most interesting interplay between text and paratext in *Die Leinwand* is that between the presentation of the author in the jacket copy and the construction of Wechsler the narrator in the literary text. At an important juncture, Wechsler realizes that he is "nichts mehr als eine literarische Figur" (nothing more than a literary figure) he himself created after exposing the identity fraud of Minsky, the pretend survivor of Majdanek and Auschwitz.[9] Wechsler's new biography, which he initially made up in a novel that appeared around the same time as Minsky's memoir, roughly corresponds to Stein's biography as presented in the author profile. Both Wechsler and Stein grew up in the GDR and now live in Munich; both previously worked as custodians (W, 136/111) and now as publishers. Other facts about Wechsler—that he was a rower in the GDR (W, 105/85) and that his great-grandfather was murdered by the Gestapo (W, 31/22)—correspond to things Stein mentions on his literary blog *Turmsegler*, which is, of course, an important paratext of its own. Furthermore, the clothes Wechsler wears during his visit to Israel are quite similar to what Stein is wearing on the photograph in the dust jacket. Zichroni describes Wechsler as follows: "Er kam in schwarzem Anzug mit Weste, weißem Hemd und Krawatte, auf dem Kopf einen jeschiwischen Hut. Er sah aus wie ein Frommer." (Z, 189–90/155; He was wearing a black suit with a vest, a white shirt, and a tie, and a yeshivish hat on his head. He looked frum [pious, KG].) Wechsler himself describes his attire as "schwarzer Anzug mit Weste, weißem Hemd und einer großen Kippa aus schwarzem Samt" (W, 192/158; a black suit with a vest, a white shirt, and a large black velvet kippa). Wechsler adds that Israelis tend to mistake him for a "Haredi" (W, 192/158)—that is, for more strictly orthodox than he actually is—because of these clothes. The photograph inserted in the jacket copy shows the author Stein in a similar garb, with a white shirt, a tie, and a large black velvet kippah (the vest and jacket are missing, though).

In other words, the *paratextual* construction of the *author* Benjamin Stein considerably overlaps with the *made-up* identity of the *narrator* Jan Wechsler. While Wechsler gradually reconstructs the ways he fashioned a new identity for himself—apparently out of guilty feelings about his role in the Minsky scandal—the reader is invited to ponder the connections between Wechsler's adopted identity and Stein's actual identity. This interplay between text and paratext highlights and potentially undermines the function of the author profile in the cover flap. Such profiles typically offer some information about the author and thereby verify the author's existence, which is also the function of the author's name on the book cover. In addition, the profile often invests the author with a special authority to write about the subject at hand. As I have argued, the paratext often positions contemporary German Jewish authors as ethnic authors who are metonymically linked to the world they narrate and therefore capable of describing this world with greater authenticity, or at least legitimacy, than those who do not belong to it. But how sure can we be about an author's identity if it is presented in the paratext of a novel that is all about a literary character's delusional adoption of a very similar identity? The interplay between text and paratext in *Die Leinwand* invites the reader to contemplate the function of the author as the guarantor of the text, as the one who can claim rightful ownership of and take responsibility for it.[10]

Testimonial Authority

This question of authorship and authority—of how to lay claim to an experience and its transmission through writing—is also at the heart of Stein's reflections on the fake Holocaust memoir. *Die Leinwand* contains many allusions to the scandal that erupted when it was discovered that Binjamin Wilkomirski, the author of the celebrated Holocaust memoir *Bruchstücke*, was not a Jewish child survivor but the out-of-wedlock child of a Christian mother and the adoptee of a wealthy Swiss family.[11] At first glance, Stein's novel passes a surprisingly lenient verdict on a very similar figure called Minsky, a pretend survivor of the death camps who now builds musical instruments. The campaign launched against Minsky after the discovery of his identity fraud comes across as a cruel and destructive act that is in some ways more problematic than the fraud itself.[12] Ultimately, however, *Die Leinwand* does not so much condone the Holocaust impostor as unhinge the problem of false memory from that figure. Minsky remains a subsidiary character in a book that focuses on Zichroni and Wechsler, both of whom are shown to engage in acts of sympathetic identification or memory fabrication. Zichroni puts his special gift—the ability to experience the memories of others—to therapeutic usage, but he also ponders the ethical dilemmas involved in accessing the minds of others, especially without their permission (Z, 88/70). Wechsler, who throughout his narrative struggles with the unreliability of his memory, gradually finds out that he has committed an offense similar to Minsky's—that is, he has assumed a false identity. After the Minsky scandal, he invented for himself a new life story and a new family genealogy modeled on a novel he wrote earlier, and from a letter by his publisher we learn that he is in the habit of ransacking the memories of others to compose his fiction (W, 55/43).

Rather than indict the fake Holocaust memoir, Stein examines the mechanisms of transmission that make it possible. In so doing he is in tune with one subset of scholarly responses to the Wilkomirski case. Several scholars have argued that Wilkomirski, who seems to have truly believed he spent his childhood in the camps, has important lessons to impart about the transmission of traumatic experience and the conceptualization of such experience in contemporary theory. Amy Hungerford points out that *Bruchstücke* was published at a time when the Holocaust memoir had become a genre in its own right and trauma studies had become an established academic field. Both the Holocaust memoir and trauma studies presume a specific "relation between language and experience," a relation "that ultimately asks us to understand *Bruchstücke* not so much as a fraud, but as the epitome of the very assumptions that underlie trauma theory's analytic discourse."[13] Hungerford cites Shoshana Felman's notion that the stories told by survivors can have a traumatic effect on readers or listeners. During her tenure at Yale University, the literary critic Felman taught a class on literature and testimony that included screenings of videotaped testimonies of Holocaust survivors. In the hours and days after the screening, Felman became aware that her students went through a crisis in which they reenacted the disorientation and loss of language experienced by the Holocaust survivors they had watched. Hungerford suggests that something similar may have happened when Bruno Dössekker—the real name of the Swiss man who later called himself Binjamin Wilkomirski—immersed himself in the study of Holocaust materials: "He absorbed the accounts of camp life, the stories of extreme violence, the testimonies and histories and photographs, and they finally became him, finally made him Binjamin Wilkomirski."[14]

In this reading, Wilkomirski's deluded identification with a child survivor of the Holocaust is not so much identity fraud as the by-product of a process of transmission otherwise seen as inevitable and legitimate, even necessary, to pass on the memory of the Holocaust. Indeed, *Bruchstücke* might be understood as an extreme example of what Marianne Hirsch calls, in her recent book *The Generations of Postmemory*, "affiliative postmemory." In contrast to familial postmemory, in which memories are transmitted vertically from parent to child, affiliative postmemory proceeds along horizontal lines and "makes that child's position more broadly available to other contemporaries."[15] Of course, Bruno Dösseker's identification with the victims of the Holocaust is on the extreme end of the spectrum of affiliative postmemory. (Hirsch herself, who always emphasizes the mediated character of postmemory, would perhaps be reluctant to apply the term here.) Yet his case still fits the paradigm in that Dösseker/Wilkomirski, who has neither direct experience of the Holocaust nor family members who survived, connects so deeply to the remembrances of survivors that he experiences that connection as a form of memory. The main vehicles of this kind of extreme identification are testimonial forms such as documentary films and written memoirs—and, to emphasize this again, many theorists claim that some degree of identification is a natural and even desirable response to testimony. As Hungerford points out, the widely shared notion that Holocaust testimony can—and perhaps should—produce in its audience a sympathetic identification with the victims and a vicarious experience of suffering rests on two assumptions: first, that memories can be severed from people and transmitted onto texts, and second, that texts can have the same effect on readers as real people.

If the case of Wilkomirski raises the question of what constitutes an appropriate affective response to Holocaust testimony, Stein engages with this question through his creative play with paratext. He highlights, and ultimately undermines, the paratextual mechanisms that enable an unreflecting identification with the survivor-witness. We can see these mechanisms at work in Wilkomirski's *Bruchstücke*. In Holocaust memoirs, the paratext often serves to confirm that the author testifies to his or her own life experience and that he or she is truly in a position to do so. The reception of *Bruchstücke* as a Holocaust memoir depended on what Pierre

Lejeune calls the "autobiographical pact"—that is, the implicit or explicit agreement by which readers are encouraged to read a text as an authentic representation of real-life experience.[16] Among other things, the autobiographical pact stipulates that the author, narrator, and protagonist of a book have to be identical. This identification is typically achieved through the interplay between the text inside the book and the paratext on its cover. The appearance of a proper name on the book cover (above or below the title) tethers the text to a person—the author—who is presumed to exist in the real world and is capable of assuming responsibility for the text. The use of that same name as the name of the book's narrator and protagonist, then, signals a commitment to autobiographical truth. This is emphatically the case in *Bruchstücke*, in which the narrator's name is not only identical with that of the author but also the source of particularly dramatic moments of recognition and revelation. It is during these moments, in which the narrator hears others calling him Binjamin or Binjamin Wilkomirski, that he begins to get a sense of the true identity of which he presumably has been robbed.[17]

Wilkomirski further confirms this identity in an afterword he added after rumors had reached his publishers that he was born in 1941 rather than in 1939 and in the Swiss town of Biel rather than in the Latvian city of Riga. In this afterword, which is titled "Zu diesem Buch" (About this book) and is thus clearly marked as a paratext, Wilkomirski seeks to explain the discrepancy between his childhood memories and his legal identity:

> Auch ich habe noch als Kind eine neue Identität erhalten, einen anderen Namen, ein anderes Geburtsdatum, einen anderen Geburtsort. Das Dokument, das ich in Händen halte—ein behelfsmäßiger Auszug, keine Geburtsurkunde—, gibt den 12. Februar 1941 als mein Geburtsdatum an. Aber dieses Datum stimmt weder mit meiner Lebensgeschichte noch mit meinen Erinnerungen überein. Ich habe juristische Schritte gegen diese verfügte Identität eingeleitet.
>
> As a child, I also received a new identity, another name, another date and place of birth. The document I hold in my hands—a makeshift summary, no actual birth certificate—gives the date of my birth as February 12, 1941. But this date has nothing to do with either the history of this century or my personal history. I have now taken legal steps to have this imposed identity annulled.[18]

Wilkomirski's explanation for the discrepancy between the birth date on the title page of *Bruchstücke* (1939) and the one on his birth record (1941) shows how skillfully he manipulates biographical information. In the jacket copy of a book, such a discrepancy would signal the at least partially fictitious character of the work. Here, however, it serves as further evidence of autobiographical truth. Wilkomirski notes that the 1941 birth date is recorded on a somewhat dubious makeshift document that he reads as an indication of the hostility of the society in which he grew up after the war. Much of the afterword is about society's attempt to silence the memories of child survivors of the Holocaust and impose on them a false identity. That is, if the text of *Bruchstücke* is about Wilkomirski's struggle to recuperate an identity that has been stolen from him, the paratext presents the legal document as further proof of the difficulty—and thus the reality—of his struggle. Indeed, the afterword of *Bruchstücke* invests the author with a remarkable power and authority. Wilkomirski insists that 1941 cannot be his birth date because it does not fit into his life story as he himself just told it. The man who began his account by describing how, as a child, he even lacked a language to process his experience now seems capable of producing an authoritative autobiographical narrative that can even disprove official documents.

If the afterword of *Bruchstücke* confirms the author's ability to write authoritatively about his own experience—to produce a valid *Lebensgeschichte* (life history/story)—the two endings of *Die Leinwand* have the opposite effect: they create an irreducible gap between experience and writing. The two parts of *Die Leinwand* mime autobiographical writing—Zichroni presents the story of his life in the past tense, and Wechsler describes the gradual retrieval of his memories in the present tense—and both have curiously open endings. Zichroni's part concludes with a scene in which he pushes Wechsler, whom he holds responsible for Minsky's downfall, back into the ice-cold water of an ancient mikvah they are visiting together at night. (The context here is that Wechsler has come to Israel as a tourist to complete his transformation into an observant Jew. He has a particular interest in the historical mikvah—a ritual bath used for purposes of purification. When Wechsler, by chance, arrives at Zichroni's house in the West Bank, he does not recognize Zichroni, but Zichroni recognizes him.)

> Während er sich so auf seine Tevila vorbereitete, zog ich meine Handschuhe aus. Dann holte Wechsler tief Luft und tauchte unter. Ich kniete mich auf den nasskalten Steinrand des Beckens und streckte die Arme aus. Als er wieder auftauchte und zitternd prustete, sah ich ihm direkt in die Augen und griff nach seinem Kopf. Ich hielt ihn wie einen Ball zwischen meinen Händen und drückte ihn langsam, doch so fest ich nur konnte, zurück ins Wasser.
> *Yerushalayim/Ofra*
> *Sh'vat—Av 5768* (Z, 193)

While he was preparing for his tevila, I took off my gloves. Wechsler took a deep breath and submerged. I knelt down at the cold, wet edge of the pool and stretched out my arms. When he resurfaced, huffing and shivering, I looked right into his eyes and grabbed his head. I held it like a ball between my hands and pushed it slowly, but as hard as I could, back into the water.

> Yerushalayim/Ofra
> Sh'vat—Av 5768 (Z, 158)

Wechsler's part ends about six months later than Zichroni's when he once again returns to Israel. There, an Israeli officer suspects Wechsler of having a role in Zichroni's mysterious disappearance and escorts him to the place where Zichroni was last seen, the ancient mikvah. Wechsler, who has reconstructed the memories of his last trip up to the scene at the mikvah, jumps into the pool in order to recover the last piece of the puzzle. Alas, he finds the mikvah empty:

Ich glaube nicht, dass Ben-Or mir erlauben wird, noch einmal hier unterzutauchen. Aber es gibt keinen anderen Weg, wenn ich zu mir selbst zurückfinden will. Also stoße ich ihn entschlossen zur Seite und nehme Anlauf. Ich halte den Atem an und springe. Gleich werde ich in das eiskalte Wasser sinken, und alles wird sein, wie es einmal war.

Aber ich sinke nicht. Ich falle.

Das Becken, in das ich stürze, ist leer.

> München/Jerusalem
> Februar–Oktober 2008
> (W, 203–4)

I don't think Ben-Or will allow me to immerse in this mikvah again. But there's no other way, if I want to get back to myself. So I push him aside, as hard as I can, and I start running. I hold my breath and jump. In a second I'll be sinking in the ice-cold water, and everything will be the way it was before.

But I don't sink. I fall.

The pool I'm plunging into is empty.

> Munich/Jerusalem
> February–October 2008
> (W, 168)

Both parts of *Die Leinwand* end on a moment of suspension, thus raising the question of how the struggle at the mikvah ends and what happens to the narrators afterward. These open endings are conspicuous, especially because the very last lines of each part inform us about the time and place of writing: Zichroni, who had been missing since his encounter with Wechsler in January of 2008, composed his memoir after his disappearance—namely, between January and August of 2008. The use of the Hebrew calendar and Hebrew place names further confirms that it was Zichroni who wrote these lines. Wechsler, whom we last saw in July of 2008 falling into the empty mikvah—literally suspended over a void—wrote his account in Munich and Jerusalem between February and October of that same year. As a paratext, the designation of the time and place of writing at the end of a literary text functions similarly to the author's name on the title page in that it verifies the author's existence outside the text. It is a signature of sorts. In *Die Leinwand*, these signatures create a conspicuous gap between text and composition, thereby raising a series of questions about the act of writing: When, where, and why did Zichroni decide to sit down and write up his recollections? How did Wechsler recover from his fall and complete his narrative about the retrieval of his past identity? And why does neither of them bring his story to some sort of a conclusion?

There is no direct line from experience to memory to writing in *Die Leinwand*. In fact, the novel's two abrupt endings create the impression that the narrators are disappearing as they are writing their texts. These endings highlight the severability of author, text, and memory on which the fake Holocaust memoir hinges and which, at the same time, it has to disavow, often paratextually. It is noteworthy that the cover flaps of Wilkomirski's *Bruchstücke* mix two types of paratexts that are usually printed separately: the book description and the author profile. This jacket copy, which runs from the front flap to the back flap, describes how Wilkomirski reclaimed his memory and identity while writing the book. The jacket copy thus completely collapses the distinction between text and author, creating the impression that the author is but the process of writing, the text but the author in action. The paratextual conflation of text and author makes possible what Hungerford and others stipulate: that written testimony can function as a stand-in for its author and can affect readers as if it were a real person. By detailing the process in which Wilkomirski purportedly retrieved his memories and turned them into a memoir, the cover flaps invest *Bruchstücke* with a testimonial authority typically only ascribed to human beings. Once text and author are completely fused—or confused—the text can indeed replace the author. Stein, in contrast, decouples writing from experience and thus prevents the text from taking over the function of the author.

The severability of author, text, and memory is especially relevant in our time, when the number of remaining survivors is dwindling and the memory of the Holocaust is becoming permanently severed from the people who lived through it. At such a time, both familial and affiliative postmemory take on a new significance but also raise new ethical questions. German-language authors, in particular, have to consider what happens when, as Hirsch puts it, "the lines of affiliation . . . cross the divide between victim and perpetrator memory."[19] It is no coincidence, then, that identification and memory transfer between the descendants of victims and perpetrators are such popular themes in contemporary German and Austrian Jewish literature. For example, the novels of Doron Rabinovici, whom I discuss in the next chapter, feature a number of characters who adopt the identities and memories of others. In *Suche nach M.* (1997; *The Search for M.*), the son of two Holocaust survivors compulsively confesses past crimes he has not committed and thereby helps remember those crimes and track down their perpetrators. In *Andernorts* (2010; *Elsewhere*), Rabinovici pokes fun at a non-Jewish scholar who searches for his father and is all too eager to find him in an Israeli businessman and Holocaust survivor. As I have shown, Stein engages with the ethical dilemmas arising from the transfer of memories and identities in a particularly intriguing way—namely, through his creative use of paratext. Through a *fictional inflation* of paratext and an emphasis on the gaps between text and paratext, Stein adds the layer of mediation that Wilkomirski's *Bruchstücke* so sorely lacks. By highlighting the defining power of paratext, Stein promotes a more responsible transmission of memories to new generations.

PART II
REMAKING MEMORY

3

MEMORY AND MOBILITY
The Novels of Doron Rabinovici

THE AUSTRIAN JEWISH WRITER DORON RABINOVICI HOLDS A PhD in history and has published a scholarly book about an aspect of the Holocaust, an abridged version of which appeared in English translation as *Eichmann's Jews: The Jewish Administration of Holocaust Vienna*.[1] As a public intellectual, Rabinovici has frequently spoken out against the repression of the Nazi past and the manifestations of antisemitism, racism, homophobia, and right-wing populism in contemporary Austria. He has also written three novels that take the lasting effects of the Third Reich and the Holocaust as their central theme: *Suche nach M.* (1997; *The Search for M.*), *Ohnehin* (2004; *Anyway*), and *Andernorts* (2010; *Elsewhere*). These novels are metamemorial works that both remember the past and reflect on the mechanisms—including the medial forms and neurobiological foundations—that enable the formation, organization, and transmission of memories. Interestingly, all three novels focus on mechanisms that actively reshape rather than simply preserve the memory of the past. Indeed, Rabinovici seems to suggest that the displacement, decontextualization, conflation, fabrication, and even forgetting of memories are all feasible and valid ways of engaging with the past. And that is surprising. Why would someone who is so invested in the history of the Holocaust see something positive in the disruption—even the corruption—of memory?

Rabinovici's own reflections on the function of literature vis-à-vis historiography give us some hints. In an essay entitled "Wie es war und wie es gewesen sein wird: Geschichtsschreibung und Literatur zur Shoah" (How it was and how it will/would have been: Historiography and literature on the Shoah), he effectively reinterprets Aristotle's dictum that history recounts what has happened and poetry what may happen. In the case of the Holocaust, Rabinovici writes, even historians have to use their imagination—and its grammatical equivalent, the subjunctive—and ask not only "wie es einmal war" (how it once was) but also "wie es sein hätte können" (how it could have been).[2] This does not mean that historians are free to speculate about history or imagine alternative historical outcomes but rather that they need to be open-minded while exploring the uncharted territory of industrial genocide and must be possessed by a thirst for knowledge that time and again propels them toward historical documents and historical truth. In contrast, literature constantly adapts the memory of the past to the demands of the present and the possibilities of the future. What drives Rabinovici to literature is the wish to find out "wie es gewesen sein wird" (how it will/would have been), a phrase that invokes the two different usages of the future perfect tense in German: to make a conjecture about the past and to refer to a completed event in the future. According to Rabinovici, literature both speculates about the past and envisions the future usage of its memory. Moreover, literary texts can render memory fluid and thus counteract the ritualization of remembrance that may occur in commemorative ceremonies: "Literatur bietet die Chance jeweils neuer Fortschreibungen. Gegen das Zeremoniell wird jeweils neu angeschrieben. Ihre Kraft liegt jenseits von Ritual und Dogmen." (Rabinovici, "Wie es war," 28; Literature always offers the chance of new rewritings. Something is always being newly written against the ceremonial. Its power lies beyond ritual and dogmas.)[3]

In this chapter, I read Rabinovici's first three novels as such rewritings of and creative interventions in Holocaust remembrance. Around the turn of the millennium, the disappearance of the eyewitness generation and the increasing mobility of Holocaust memory coincided with a paradigm shift in the field of memory studies from "sites of memory" (Pierre Nora) to "travels of memory" (Astrid Erll).[4] Rabinovici himself has been in dialogue with Nathan Sznaider, one of the authors of *The Holocaust and Memory in the Global Age*, which first described the emergence of a global or cosmopolitan memory of the Holocaust.[5] In this book, Levy and Sznaider argue that the forms and rituals of Holocaust remembrance—its iconic images, structuring narratives, and moral imperatives—have been used to represent other forms of exclusion, expulsion, and genocide and thus helped establish new political norms in the contemporary world. As I show here, Rabinovici's first three novels testify to this political productivity of Holocaust memory on the move. Each depicts a specific movement of memory across national, medial, or generational borders—the interpersonal transfer of memories in *Suche nach M.*, the lapses and displacements of memory in *Ohnehin*, and the transnational travel of memory discourses in *Andernorts*—while establishing connections to other forms of historical trauma, violence, and injustice. In an online version of his essay, Rabinovici describes how his own awareness of the Holocaust generates new comparative perspectives:

> Ich schreibe vom Umgang mit der Vertreibung, der Verfolgung und der Vernichtung. Ich spreche hier vom Umgang mit diesen Fragen, und meine nicht bloß die historische Auseinandersetzung mit der Shoah, sondern ebenso die aktuelle, die politische Handhabung von Flucht und Genozid in der Gegenwart. Dabei geht es mir keineswegs um eine Gleichsetzung dessen, was einst geschah, und was heute sich ereignet. Vielmehr will ich sehen, welche Parallelen sich uns aufdrängen und warum. Ich schaue mir an, was Menschen nun geschieht, im Lichte, nein, vielmehr im Schatten des Vergangenen, und ich rätsle, wie es gewesen sein wird.[6]
>
> I am writing about dealing with displacement, persecution, and extermination. I am talking about dealing with these questions and I mean not only the historical confrontation with the Shoah, but also the current, the political handling of flight and genocide in the present day. For me, this is in no way about an equation of what happened then and what is happening today. Rather, I want to see which parallels force themselves on us, and why. I am looking at what is happening to people now in the light, no, rather in the shadow of the past, and I am speculating about how it will / would have been.)

Even more than a "cosmopolitan memory" as defined by Levy and Sznaider, this passage evokes Michael Rothberg's idea of a "multidirectional memory." While Levy and Sznaider conceive of the globalization of Holocaust memory as a unidirectional movement by which the circulation of Holocaust signs and symbols enables the commemoration of other atrocities, Rothberg thinks of this movement as truly multidirectional. According to Rothberg, memory of the Holocaust has not only helped articulate other traumatic histories but itself has been shaped by other commemorative discourses and political movements, especially the decolonization processes of the 1960s.[7] Rabinovici's phrase "wie es gewesen sein wird" projects such an interaction of public memories into the future; it implies that Holocaust memory itself will change while it is brought to bear on other instances of flight, persecution, and genocide. Furthermore, his rejection of simple equation recalls Rothberg's idea of "differentiated solidarity," or the ability to pursue shared political goals in full awareness of historical differences. In what follows, I show how the memory movements in Rabinovici's novels indeed open up perspectives of multidirectionality and solidarity as they bring into view a broader range of cultures, ethnicities, and historical experiences. At the same time, these novels testify to the abiding power of binaries, boundaries, and divisions, which challenges the idea that the wider dissemination of Holocaust memories is automatically politically productive. Thematically, Rabinovici maintains a focus on the relationship between Jews and (non-Jewish) Austrians and on particularly fraught mnemonic movements, such as the memory transfer between victims and perpetrators and the circulation of memories between Austria and Israel. Stylistically, his texts create a most precarious balance between conflicting voices, modes, and discourses of memory. This lack of thematic and stylistic homogeneity, I suggest, may be precisely what opens up Holocaust memory to the future.[8]

Memory Transfers: *Suche nach M.*

Rabinovici's *Suche nach M.* is a novel about the repression of the Nazi past in Austria as well as the transmission of memories through psychological mechanisms of identification, empathy, and transference. The two main protagonists, Dani Morgenthau and Arieh Fandler, are children of Holocaust survivors who grow up in an atmosphere of trauma, guilt, and denial. Both live in Vienna in a society that has largely failed to prosecute the wartime atrocities and still engages in willful forgetting. Both have been raised in survivor families in which traumatic repression leads to physical and psychical symptoms, such as the chronic back pain of Dani's father, the repeated identity changes of Arieh's father, and the parents' emotional reactions to clothes reminiscent of the Nazi past. The presence of painful yet unspoken memories first occasions the transfer of memories: in the home of Dani's family, "schien die Luft geladen mit Erinnerung" (the air seemed heavy with memory).[9] Both Dani and Arieh respond to the eerie silences and memory gaps by accessing the thoughts, memories, and identities of other people. They develop special empathic abilities—similar to those of Zichroni in Benjamin Stein's *The Canvas*—that allow them to read the minds of offenders, impersonate them, and deliver them to justice. As a child, Dani compulsively admits to all sorts of pranks and offenses he has not committed; later, he morphs into the ghostlike figure of Mullemann, whose hallucinatory self-incriminations help procure confessions from criminals. As a schoolkid, Arieh first discovers his ability to track down people who wronged him by miming their behavior and appearance; as an adult, he puts his mimetic abilities and investigative skills to the service of the Israeli secret police. Dani and Arieh embody two different yet complementary ways of remembering past crimes and tracking down their perpetrators: Dani elicits confessions; Arieh takes revenge.

In *Suche nach M.*, the presence and circulation of repressed Holocaust memories at times open up larger questions of justice in a multicultural society. Significantly, the transformations of Arieh and Dani begin when they relate to members of other minorities—namely, the victims of a racist attack in a suburban bar and a Turkish German man wrongly accused of murder, respectively. These parts of the plot invoke the idea that Holocaust memory can inspire acts of transcultural empathy and political solidarity. Arieh decides to chase down the man who initiated the bar attack by shouting the anti-black slur "Negersau" (46/28; nigger bastard). Pretending to be a fellow racist, he gains the man's confidence and sets a trap to get him convicted of a hate crime. And as a juror in the trial of the Turkish German man, Dani is the only one aware of the complex psychological motives that induced Yılmaz Akan to confess to a murder he did not commit. Their shared predicament—of living between two cultures and experiencing social isolation—sensitizes Dani to the nuances of Yılmaz's testimony: "Solche Nebentöne konnte Dani Morgenthau ausmachen, denn in Wahrheit machten diese Dissonanzen ihn aus, lebte er im Zwieklang verschiedener Harmonien, kannte er die Weisen, die seinen Eltern im Kopf noch umgingen, genau so wie die Volkslieder des Alpenlandes." (76/49; Dani Morgenthau was able to make out such secondary intonations because he himself was made up of these dissonant combinations. He lived in the dual tonality of various harmonies. He knew the melodies which his parents still carried around in their heads as well as the folk songs of this alpine country.) However, such acts of transcultural empathy and understanding fail to forge a broader alliance against racism and xenophobia, at least in the proximate future. Arieh's plan to convict the racist offender falters as he inadvertently kills the man, which in turn forces him to flee to Israel. Dani votes with the rest of the jury against Yılmaz despite his knowledge that the murder verdict is false. Their subsequent transformations—Arieh's into an agent of the Israeli secret service and Dani's into a medium of memory called "Mullemann" (Bandage Man)—result, at least in part, from their inability to act in immediate solidarity with other minorities.

The figure of Mullemann illustrates both the perils and the possibilities of multidirectional and multifunctional Holocaust memory. Dani's empathetic identification with various offenders causes him to develop a painful rash—the somatic sign of the guilt he takes upon himself—and he covers himself up in layers of gauze bandages. Wandering the streets of Vienna as the ghost or phantom Mullemann, he articulates the guilt of others and stirs up much commotion. The surreal chapter that describes Dani's transformation switches back and forth between first- and third-person narration, an experimental style that reflects the contact between two people with telepathic abilities. It is never quite clear whether we hear the voice of Dani or that of Arieh Fandler, alias Arthur Bein, who as a secret service agent has killed several people and now listens to the Morse signals Dani sends through the hospital wall. The oscillation between narrative voices indicates that Dani splits off Mullemann as a double, detaching from his own mind and body as he gives voice to the memories of others. As Dani/Mullemann describes himself: "Zuweilen scheint mir, als wäre Mullemann ein Schmerzpaket zahlloser Tode, nichts als ein Erinnerungsbündel aus verschiedenen, zufällig verwobenen Mullrollen" (114/76; It seems to me at times that Mullemann is a clump of pains made of numerous deaths and nothing more than a commemorative bundle of various rolls of gauze accidentally woven together).[10] The chain of associations created by the name Mullemann—including Fritz Lang's famous film *M.* (233), the figure of the *Muselmann* (188), perhaps even the Messiah—further indicates that Dani is no longer a real person but rather a transpersonal medium of memory.[11] As such he becomes an object of media attention and public obsession in a city pervaded by guilt, whether in the form of the victims' survivor guilt or the perpetrators' stubborn disavowal of responsibility. Ultimately, the police learn to utilize Mullemann's capacity for empathetic identification to elicit confessions from criminals during their investigations.

As Doerte Bischoff has argued, the novel describes the appropriation of Mullemann by consumer culture and government institutions as problematic—since, in both cases, Mullemann is a product of projection and masquerade whose public celebration does little to help the real Dani—but also as productive. *Suche nach M.* exemplifies the new future-oriented memory culture described by Levy and Sznaider, which moves away from dichotomous conceptions of the Holocaust as either a Jewish catastrophe or a rupture in civilization toward a sense that Holocaust memory concerns everybody, yet in specific ways. In the novel, the displacement and globalization of Holocaust memory deflects attention away from questions of memory accuracy toward the interaction between memories, the ways such interaction sparks new dialogues, discourses, and communities. The commercialization, theatricality, and multifunctionality of Mullemann, who becomes a fashionable object in advertising and entertainment, is indicative of this shift. The figure of Mullemann invites spectators not so much to locate him or identify with him but rather to find new forms of living with him and to create diverse identities in reference to him.[12]

In *Suche nach M.*, the circulation, dissemination, and permutation of Holocaust memories through the spectacle of Mullemann opens up new forms of engagement with the past. Yet what does it mean that the novel first invokes and then dismisses the possibility that the transfer of memories might lead to solidarity with other minorities, such as the victims of the xenophobic crime and the Turkish German man wrongly accused of murder? If the novel stops short of depicting the actual emergence of a multiethnic alliance, empathetic identification turns out to be limited in other ways as well. Tellingly, the only perpetrator from whom Mullemann fails to extract a confession is a Nazi perpetrator, the retired *Ministerialrat* Anton Weilisch. It is not that Mullemann's empathic abilities fail when he faces Weilisch—on the contrary, he is able to describe the horrific atrocities in great detail—but that these descriptions do not move the perpetrator emotionally or awaken his conscience. Mullemann cannot get him to acknowledge his crimes, much less render justice to the victims. In the absence of a genuine *Vergangenheitsbewältigung* (coming to terms with the past) or a true cure for Dani (who at the end of the novel leaves the police force and may or may not begin to heal), we are left with some salient metamemorial reflections. Arieh, who has decided to quit his position with the Secret Service and now enjoins Dani to give up the role of Mullemann, casts true remembrance as an active process that involves forgetting: "Nicht in den Banden der Zeit eingelegt sein wie eine Mumie, allen Techniken der Konservierung eine Absage erteilen, die Schichten abstreifen, die Knoten aufdröseln, ihrer Verknüpfung nachgehen, die Knubbel ertasten, die Riemen umschnüren und ablösen, das ist Erinnerung." (259/180–81; Not to be tied down by the shackles of time like a mummy, to reject all the techniques of preservation, to shed the layers, undo the knots, to go after the knotting together, to feel for the lumps, to unlace and remove the straps: this is the work of memory.) The dialectic of remembering and forgetting is one of the central themes of Rabinovici's next novel.

Memory Lapses: *Ohnehin*

If *Suche nach M.* depicts the process by which memories are decoupled from people and transferred onto others, the novel's focus is still on two protagonists who serve as containers of these memories. The horizon widens in Rabinovici's next novel, *Ohnehin* (2004), which is concerned not only with the memories of individuals but also with institutional forms of memory and scientific research about memory. The novel's protagonist, Stefan Sandtner, is a young neurologist who comes across a particularly interesting case of Korsakoff syndrome (a disorder that causes severe memory defects) in a former SS officer. While he tries to restore the patient's memory with an experimental cocktail of medications, Stefan would like to shed some of his own memories—namely of his ex-girlfriend Sonja, whom he cannot forget despite his best efforts. This ironic clash between his professional commitment to retrieve lost memories and his private desire to forget first introduces the dialectic of memory and forgetting that is so central to the novel. In this section, I show that the story of the Korsakoff syndrome patient is one of several instances of memory lapses or malfunctions in the novel; other examples are the disturbance of a commemorative ritual and the repeated call for an end to Holocaust remembrance. As I argue, Rabinovici ascribes to such memory disruptions three kinds of productive effects: (1) they spark insights into the structure of memory itself; (2) they counteract the increasing ritualization of Holocaust remembrance; and (3) they establish connections to other episodes of historical trauma and violence.

Ohnehin engages with Holocaust memory most clearly through the family drama between the former SS officer, Herbert Kerber, and his children, Hans and Bärbl, who have to confront their father's past anew when he falls sick. Kerber, who lives in the house in which Stefan grew up, suffers from Korsakoff syndrome, a memory disorder caused by severe vitamin B deficiency that is usually a consequence of alcoholism. As a result, he has lost all his postwar memories and has become mentally stuck in the year 1945, when he returned from the Eastern Front eager to begin a new life. Much of the novel revolves around Bärbl's attempt, inspired by hope that the syndrome has eased her father's self-censorship, to find out what kind of crimes he committed during the Second World War. As Stefan explains to the siblings: "Er sagt nun, was er euch bisher verschwieg, weil er nicht mehr erinnert, woran er sich nicht mehr erinnern darf; weil er vergaß, was er vergessen machen wollte."[13] (He says now what he has thus far concealed from you, because he no longer remembers what he is not allowed to remember; because he forgot what he wanted to be made forgotten.) Importantly, the novel never really answers Bärbl's question; that is, it never reveals the truth about Kerber's wartime deeds. Despite the elaborate interrogation scenarios she creates, and despite her conviction that her father accurately remembers the time up to 1945, she cannot get him to divulge many concrete details, much less to express regret or acknowledge his guilt. *Ohnehin* undermines the idea that subsequent generations can find a new access to the past by unearthing its secrets, working through its traumas, and restoring a sense of meaning.

One effect of the stalled interrogation is a shift of narrative focus from the truth of the past to the concerns of the present. The reader learns less about what happened in the past than about what motivates various acts of remembrance and denial, such as Bärbl's almost manic attempts to force a confession from her father and the opposite wish of her career-minded brother to keep his father's past in the dark. In place of a confession or revelation, we get the drama of interrogation itself and a close look at the conflicting fears and desires that energize its participants, including Kerber's own persistent denial of his culpability. Perhaps even more important, the case of Kerber gives rise to some provocative thoughts, in the mind of Stefan Sandtner the neurologist, about the workings of memory. When he realizes that Kerber engages in confabulation to make up for his memory deficits—that Kerber fabricates memories by using clues provided by his interlocutors—Stefan muses that healthy people often do exactly the same thing. Pondering the meaning of the common phrase "daß ihnen irgend etwas . . . einfalle" (63; that something occurs to them), Stefan concludes that "mithin jegliche Erinnerung ein Einfall, eine Entdeckung, mehr noch, eine Erfindung des Augenblicks sei, eine Konstruktion, und deshalb . . . schillere eine Geschichte, leuchte sie jedesmal in einem anderen Licht und weiche von allen früheren Varianten ab, wenn sie wiedergegeben werde." (63; hence every memory is an idea, a discovery, even more, an invention of the moment, a construction. When it is retold, it therefore dazzles as a story; each time it shines in a different light and deviates from all previous versions.) This could be a motto for all of Rabinovici's novels, a comment on the ways memory reconstructs the past from the point of view of the present, thereby distorting the past but also opening it up to the future.

In essays and interviews, Rabinovici has repeatedly claimed that forgetting is the condition of memory, an idea shared by numerous thinkers from

Friedrich Nietzsche to Paul Ricoeur: memory can impose an order and bestow a meaning on the past precisely because it is selective.¹⁴ Lew Feininger, a Jewish friend of Stefan, advances a similar idea in *Ohnehin*: "Vielleicht ist jedes Gedenken, sind alle Rituale und Mahnmale immer Instrumente des Vergegenwärtigens und des Vergessens zugleich" (92; Perhaps every commemoration and all rituals and memorials are always instruments of making present and at the same time of forgetting). In reflections such as this, the novel reveals itself to be work of metamemory as Birgit Neumann defines it: "fictions of meta-memory . . . combine personally engaged memories with critically reflective perspectives on the functioning of memory, thus rendering the question of how we remember the central content of remembering."¹⁵ As seen in the previous quote, Stefan's musings about the workings of memory are even more radical than Lew's. Stefan posits that memory not only omits certain perceptions and experiences but also generates new ones in order to fill in the gaps thus created. The fact that he generalizes here from a case of pathological forgetting—a patient with Korsakoff syndrome—shows the productive force of memory malfunctions, which spark new insights, not so much into the events of the past but into the structure of memory itself.

The Kerber story, which is about an individual Holocaust perpetrator, intersects with other narrative strands that touch upon communal memory and the commemoration of victims. This happens because Stefan Sandtner, who is interested in several forms of memory, acts as the novel's focalizer. Because he believes that Judaism attaches particular importance to memory (91), Stefan at one point asks his friend Lew to take him to a series of events that commemorate the victims of the Holocaust and past Jewish life in Europe. The depiction of these events as well-established rituals that confirm the views people hold anyway—one friend calls them a form of "Schlafen gegen Faschismus" (101; sleeping against fascism)—suggests that what Aleida Assmann claims about German memory culture also applies to Austria: that the injunction to remember the Holocaust began as a leftwing critical demand but turned into an affirmative, *staatstragend* (state-supporting) element of official politics during the 1990s.¹⁶ And it is in this context that we find a second example of productive memory disruption in *Ohnehin* in a scene in which the smooth functioning of such a commemorative ritual suddenly falters.

This happens during a symposium on Eastern European antisemitism, when a non-Jewish student mistranslates an account of the Warsaw ghetto uprising given by a survivor of the ghetto, an Orthodox rabbi who is speaking Yiddish. Instead of conveying the rabbi's critique of the uprising's leaders as not focused enough on the preservation of Jewish life, the translator praises those leaders for their exemplary courage and heroism. This mistranslation disturbs neither the Orthodox Jews (who listen only to the rabbi) nor the non-Jews (who listen only to the translator), but some secular Jews notice the discrepancy between original and translation and react with discomfort and/or amusement. One of them, a professional translator, gets upset and tries to intervene, but she departs from the scene a bit later. The commotion caused by the mistranslation does not truly change the flow of the ritual or the reaction of the audience: "Jede Gruppe hörte etwas vollkommen anderes, doch vielleicht schienen alle ebendeshalb in ihren Anschauungen gleichermaßen bestätigt" (100; Each group heard something completely different, but perhaps it was precisely for that reason that they all appeared equally validated in their views). However, its narrative elaboration in the text has a very different effect. Rather than impart a clear message or moral to readers—or confirm their preexisting views—the text alerts them to the existence of radically divergent interpretations of the Warsaw ghetto uprising.

What confuses the translator is not only the unexpected content of the rabbi's speech but also his use of the Yiddish double negative in sentences such as "diese Jungen wären gar keine Helden nicht gewesen" (98; these boys had not been no heroes). While Yiddish allows and often requires a double negative to express negation, this usage no longer exists in modern German, which uses the double negative only to signify a qualified affirmation. In other words, the mistranslation both results from and amplifies a real grammatical difference between Yiddish and German. The translator's performance produces a "Dissonanz, ein Knirschen, als drohe ein Zug aus den Schienen zu springen" (99; dissonance, a crunching, as if a train threatened to jump the rails) between the Yiddish original and the German translation. This dissonance between German and Yiddish and the clash between different mnemonic perspectives prevent the formation of a new memory community at the symposium on Eastern European antisemitism. The scene is emblematic for *Ohnehin*, which juxtaposes the memories of victims and perpetrators—and their offspring—without reconciling them. Thus Herbert Kerber's "stuckness" in the past is mirrored by that of the Holocaust survivor Paul Guttmann, who is still haunted by nightmares about his wartime experience; yet despite the fact that they are neighbors, the two never connect in any meaningful way.

This disconnect also applies to more recent experiences of flight and persecution. Generally speaking, *Ohnehin* is the most multicultural among Rabinovici's novels. It takes place in 1995, during the height of the civil war in former Yugoslavia, which Stefan encounters not only on TV news but also in the person of filmmaker Flora Dema, a refugee from Kosovo with whom he begins a love affair. The novel is partly set on the Naschmarkt, a large food market and multicultural gathering place in Vienna, and it features a panoply of people from different ethnic, religious, and national backgrounds. Stefan's friends and acquaintances trace their origins back to Cyprus, Turkey, the Congo, Israel, and other countries. However, as in *Suche nach M.*, these people from different ethnic backgrounds prove unable to form an alliance based on shared memories or an understanding of each other's history. Thus, Stefan never truly grasps the existential worries of his new girlfriend, Flora, and nobody in the group of friends who regularly meet at the Naschmarkt seems to care about Goran Bošković, a deserter from the Serbian army who ends up being deported back to Serbia, where he will face a military court and possibly death. At one point Goran accuses Lew Feininger, the Jewish scholar who devotes his work and life to the memory of the Holocaust, of being unable to connect to other traumatic histories, such as his own experiences with state-sponsored violence and a refugee existence. Goran says to Lew: "Was weißt du? Von Flucht? . . . Du machst eine Ausstellung über Kriegsverbrechen? Ich habe eine eingehende Führung erhalten, Ausstellung? Jede Nacht gehe ich durch meine persönliche Ausstellung. So eine Ausstellung wie meine wird dir nie gelingen." (83–84; What do you know? About flight? . . . You are organizing an exhibition about war crimes? I've taken a detailed guided tour. Exhibition? Every night I walk through my own personal exhibition. You will never succeed at organizing an exhibition like mine.)

Rather than narrate a process of rapprochement or mutual understanding, *Ohnehin* combines different mnemonic perspectives in a way that invites the reader to compare historical experiences without equating them. One might say that the novel establishes multidirectional connections between the past and the present on the level of the text rather than the level of the plot. Set in 1995, the year that marks the end of the Yugoslav wars as well as the fiftieth anniversary of the end of the Second World War, *Ohnehin* connects the collective traumas associated with these different historical moments through the repeated image of "Leichenberge" (mountains of corpses) and, especially, through the sentence "Einmal muß Schluß sein"

(At one point there must be an end to it). This sentence, which punctuates and structures *Ohnehin* throughout, has multiple extratextual references. It evokes the longing for a *Schlusstrich* (closure) to the critical investigation into the Nazi past, a widespread public sentiment expressed, for example, in a controversial speech by literary author Martin Walser in 1998, a few years before the publication of *Ohnehin*.[17] Furthermore, Jörg Haider, an Austrian politician and right-wing populist, had used the phrase in a 2001 discussion about compensation payments to Jews who had suffered under the Nazi regime.[18]

The line "Einmal muß Schluß sein" is the first sentence of the novel and is subsequently reiterated by different people in different contexts. This repetition with variation has two distinct effects. On the one hand, it splits the sentence into different meanings that at times directly contradict each other. The first chapter begins with the free indirect speech of Stefan Sandtner, who is evidently trying to find a TV station that does not show images of atrocity: "Einmal muß Schluß sein. Genug der Leichenberge, fort mit Krieg und Verbrechen. Der Finger streicht, bestimmt schon zwanzigmal, über den roten Knopf der Fernbedienung." (7; At some point there must be an end to it. Enough of the mountains of corpses, away with war and crimes. The finger strokes, surely for the twentieth time, the red button of the remote control.) Since the novel is set in August of 1995, this is likely a reference to TV news of the massacre of Bosnian Muslims in Srebrenica in July of that year. Stefan's train of thought evinces his disgust with the violence and his hope that there will be an end to it—or perhaps only his desire to stop seeing its images. The phrase "Einmal muß Schluß sein" appears again three pages later, this time spoken simultaneously by a tabloid journalist (on TV) and by Stefan (in his living room), who is tired of the journalist's slogans (10). The chapter ends on the utterance of the phrase by Kerber, who is mentally stuck in the year 1945 and desperately wants to absolve himself of the crimes he committed during the war. That is, in the first chapter alone, "Einmal muß Schluß sein" expresses at least five different intentions that are potentially at odds with another: the outrage at current genocidal terror, the wish to block out its images, the populist appeals of an Austrian journalist, the desire to cut his speech short, and the wish to forget one's complicity in the Nazi past.

On the other hand, the repetition of the sentence establishes connections between the most disparate memories: private and public, of wars and heartbreaks, of victims and perpetrators, of the Holocaust and other atrocities. One example of multidirectional memory is the use of the sentence in the story of Goran Bošković, the refugee from former Yugoslavia who lives illegally in Austria and works in a photo shop. When Goran's boss refuses to pay him his full salary and he starts to complain, he is fired with the line "Einmal müsse Schluß sein" (144), an expression that links the boss's desire to put an end to the refugee's complaints to Kerber's plea to forget the atrocities that happened during the Second World War. The linguistic echo between the former SS officer and the present-day boss establishes a connection between two historically distant acts of oppression. Even more important, it turns the original meaning of "Einmal muß Schluß sein"—the wish to put an end to Holocaust remembrance—into its opposite, an occasion for new acts of memory. It is telling that in the Goran scene, the text switches into the subjunctive I ("müsse"), which in the immediate context marks the sentence as a quotation and asserts some distance from it. More generally, the use of the subjunctive I indicates that the line "Einmal muß Schluß sein" has become a citable fragment, which can be taken out of one linguistic context and circulated in others. This unmooring from a context, this new fluidity of the phrase, helps generate a new memory—namely, of the oppression of a Serbian refugee. The ironic reversal of the line that calls for an end to Holocaust remembrance thus points in the same direction as the stories about an SS perpetrator's pathological lying and a mistranslation of Holocaust testimony. These three narrative strands of *Ohnehin* illustrate the paradoxical experience that it may be precisely when memory falters or fails altogether that we can generate new meanings out of the past.

Memory Travels: *Andernorts*

Rabinovici's next novel, *Andernorts* (2010), describes yet another form of memory mobility—namely, the de- and recontextualization that follows from the transnational travel of memory discourses. At first glance, the novel's thematic range is narrower than that of *Ohnehin*, as it focuses once again on the fraught relations between Jews and non-Jews, and between Israelis and Austrians, and refrains from representing the fuller range of ethnicities in contemporary Austria. Indeed, several perceptive critics have read *Andernorts* in terms of postmemory, family relations, and the "negative symbiosis" between Jews and Germans/Austrians.[19] The novel's protagonist, Ethan Rosen, a Jewish sociologist who divides his time between Tel Aviv and Vienna, gets embroiled in a public controversy with Rudi

Klausinger, his professional rival and the son of a non-Jewish mother; Rudi grew up with a vague conception that his father might be a Jewish Holocaust survivor. In an obituary for Dov Zedek, Ethan's fatherly friend, Rudi criticizes the Auschwitz trips for Israeli youth that Dov used to organize. In support of his views, he cites a Hebrew-language article by a well-known intellectual who later turns out to be Ethan himself. Ethan, who initially does not recognize the quotes from his own article in the obituary, writes a sharp rebuke, declaring the critique inappropriate in the country that gave birth to Hitler and still engages in willful forgetting. Things get even more complicated when Rudi shows up in Israel because he believes he has found his long-lost father in Felix Rosen, Ethan's father, who acknowledges the paternity in order to preserve another family secret—namely, that Ethan is the biological son of Dov Zedek. The truth comes out after a rabbi, who believes Ethan is a relative of the Messiah who was killed in his mother's womb during the Holocaust, conducts some genetic testing. Despite these revelations, Rudi appears to belong to the Jewish family in the final scene of the novel, as he delivers the eulogy at the funeral of Felix Rosen, a symbolic gesture that conjures an idea of family not as a closed biological unit but as an inclusive group based on acts of recognition, respect, and love.

While *Andernorts* evokes—and at times parodies—the genre of the family novel, it is also a work of metamemory that reflects on the transnational travel of commemorative practices, rituals, and discourses. The novel's protagonist and antagonist are both theorists and practitioners of transculturality. An academic who works on questions of cultural hybridity, Ethan Rosen is perfectly bilingual in Hebrew and German and moves back and forth between Vienna and Tel Aviv; his father once called him a "verkehrtes Chamäleon" (reverse chameleon) that always stands out against his environment.[20] Likewise, Rudi Klausinger is a social scientist who is fluent in multiple languages and professionally committed to cultural relativism, a "Verwandlungskünstler" (69/52; quick-change artist) who easily adapts to changing environments. Even the form of their scholarship is marked by fluidity and transculturality. Rumors have it that Ethan translates one cultural discourse into another rather than offers his own original theory, and Ethan himself believes that Rudi tailors his writing to the imagined expectations of his changing audiences rather than thinks for himself. The transnational existence and transcultural activity of Ethan and Rudi allow commemorative discourses to travel across spaces and cultures, which becomes evident in the unfolding of the controversy related to the Auschwitz trip in different media, languages, and countries. Does the travel of memory discourses help "forge empathic communities of remembrance across national, cultural, or ethnic boundaries," which in this case would include people from victim and perpetrator countries?[21] Or does it, on the contrary, show the incommensurability of specific discourses and practices?

First and foremost, the controversy around the Auschwitz trips shows just how much public debates about memory practices depend on the context in which they take place; whatever is appropriate in one sociopolitical context is not necessarily so in another. In Ethan's original article, which appeared first in Hebrew in a liberal Israel newspaper and then in English on the Internet, he criticizes the state-sponsored Auschwitz trips as a misguided attempt to initiate Israeli youth into remembrance and politics. He claims that the trips foster an exclusionary collective identity based on prejudice and hostility to others and that the young people would be better off driving to the nearby occupied territories. Ethan's enraged response to Rudi's obituary, then, shows that the debates around commemorative rituals are just as situated and dependent on context as the rituals themselves. Whereas the critique of the Auschwitz trips may provoke a fruitful discussion about Jewish identity politics in Israel, the same critique may promote a further repression of the Nazi past in Austria: "Im Geburtsland des Führers, tippte er, kämen einem die Ausführungen irgendeines ungenannt bleibenden Israeli gerade recht, wenn es darum gehe, heimatliche Selbstvergessenheit zu beschönigen" (Rabinovici, 29/18; It is particularly fitting, he typed, for this writer to trot out, in the Führer's native country, an unnamed Israeli's arguments when the fundamental question is one of glossing over a nation's amnesia). Of particular interest is the fact that Ethan does not even recognize his own writing once it is removed from its original context and reproduced anonymously in Rudi's obituary. One of Ethan's friends explains this lapse in terms of the losses incurred in translation: "Michael meinte, auf hebräisch und in Israel klinge jedes Wort eben anders als auf deutsch und in Österreich. Ethan habe seine eigenen Zeilen nicht wiedererkannt, weil sie nicht mehr die seinen gewesen seien. Im anderen Kontext sei ihre Bedeutung ins Gegenteil verkehrt worden." (41/29; Michael maintained that every word sounds different in Hebrew and in Israel than it does in German and in Austria. Ethan hadn't recognized his own lines because they weren't his anymore. The different context had changed their meaning into the opposite.)

Rabinovici gestures here at something more radical than the well-worn idea that translations modify or even distort the originals on which they are based: he suggests that the transposition into a new context completely unhinges a text from its producer. Ethan does not recognize his own words, we have to infer, because the new context changes and co-opts these words in ways he cannot control. Rather than the author of a text, he is simply a relay station in a larger memory discourse, a fact that highlights the primacy of context over text. Nor are de- and recontextualizations always as productive as in Vienna, where Ethan's memory lapse, though unintended, triggers a lively debate that suits his own penchant for provocation.[22] That debate simply peters out after its next transposition into a new context—namely, at an academic conference in Los Angeles, where Rudi first reads a paper by Ethan (who had excused himself) that reiterates the points made in Israel and then uses his own paper to echo the opposite views Ethan expressed in Austria. This curious performance, in which the presenter offers contradictory opinions in two different voices, elicits from the audience first amusement, then uncertainty, and finally indifference, at which point the subject is simply dropped. Instead of new memory discourses or communal ties, the resolution of the dispute yields apathy: "Die ganze Auseinandersetzung, die in Österreich zwischen ihm und Ethan leidenschaftlich geführt worden war, konnte in diesem Rahmen niemanden erregen" (204/169; The discussion he and Ethan had so passionately held in Austria didn't get anyone here worked up).

If Ethan's critique of the Auschwitz trips fails to forge a new memory community on the level of the plot, the novel does indeed weave disparate memory discourses into a new entity on the level of the text. *Andernorts* promotes new transnational and transcultural connections by juxtaposing a range of voices, discourses, and perspectives of memory that clash at times and intersect at others. The text constitutes an assemblage of what one might call *voices from elsewhere* and thereby allows contradictory views to exist side by side. One of these voices belongs to Dov Zedek, who shortly before his death in Israel recorded an audiotape to which Ethan later listens in Austria. In his recorded speech, Dov grapples with his role as a public Holocaust survivor but also vindicates his work as an Auschwitz tour guide and laments the future disappearance of survivor testimony:

> Aber was, wenn wir nicht mehr sein werden? Wenn sie dann kommen, aus Dresden, Teheran und Tennessee, aus Wien oder Wilna, wird niemand von uns aufstehen, niemand mehr beglaubigen, was uns am eigenen Leib widerfuhr.

Nein, nicht um den eigenen Tod geht es mir. Hörst du? Für mich muß kein Kaddisch gesprochen werden. (51–52)

And what will happen when we're gone? When they come from Dresden, Tehran and Tennessee, from Vienna or Vilnius and not one of us will rise from the dead, no one will bear witness to what we went through. No, for me it's not about my own death. I don't need anyone to say Kaddish for me. (37, emphasis by translator)

The reader only gradually learns that these words are the product of a mechanical recording, spoken by someone who is now dead. Dov's is a disembodied voice from the grave that lingers on uncannily after his death, a voice that signals the most radical disjunction between speaker and speech—and that nevertheless has a strong presence within the text. In the German original, Dov's recorded speech is printed without quotation marks or narrative frame. It thus appears to be on equal footing with the text's third-person narration; all the while, its phatic qualities and direct address to Ethan give it a sense of immediacy and urgency. Dov's impassioned plea for the continued relevance of Auschwitz as a site of memory becomes part of a multifarious textual web that allows conflicting viewpoints to coexist and interact. Maria Roca Lizarazu arrives at a similar conclusion for two other contemporary Austrian Jewish writers, Vladimir Vertlib and Eva Menasse. Vertlib's 2001 *Das besondere Gedächtnis der Rosa Masur* (The peculiar memory of Rosa Masur), a novel about a Russian Jewish migrant who participates in a memorial project in Germany, stages a conflict between the German discourse of *Vergangenheitsbewältigung* and a Russian memory culture that emphasizes heroism while blocking out Jewish suffering during the Second World War. Vertlib's novel provides a corrective to overly optimistic visions of transnational memory, as it shows how national frameworks may persist and hinder the development of transcultural empathy and solidarity. Yet the text itself, which Roca Lizarazu characterizes with Mikhail Bakhtin as polyphonic and dialogical, creates new transcultural and transnational connections by interweaving a variety of voices, modes, and perspectives of memory.[23]

Perhaps more so than any other contemporary German or Austrian Jewish writer, Doron Rabinovici focuses on the new mobility of Holocaust memory around the turn of the millennium. As I showed here, each of his first three novels offers metamemorial reflections on one form of mobility or fluidity: on memory transfers (*Suche nach M.*), memory lapses (*Ohnehin*), and memory travels (*Andernorts*). I also argued that Rabinovici views displacements and distortions of memory, even egregious ones, as a source of new comparative perspectives in an age of global Holocaust memory. However, Rabinovici only gestures toward the possibility of new transcultural and transnational communities of remembrance without picturing their actual emergence. Instead, he highlights the rifts and divisions between different memorial discourses and communities. In the next chapter, I suggest that Katja Petrowskaja's *Maybe Esther* identifies *similarity* as another principle that establishes connections between diverse memories without concealing the fault lines between them.

4

MEMORY AND SIMILARITY

Katja Petrowskaja's Vielleicht Esther

Perhaps no other recent German Jewish writer has received as much immediate and positive critical attention as Katja Petrowskaja. In 2013, when Petrowskaja read the section "Vielleicht Esther" (Maybe Esther) in the city of Klagenfurt, she won the prestigious Ingeborg Bachmann Prize. When the book of the same title appeared the following year, critics were unanimous in their praise of the author's ability to distill the universal from the individual, to weave a whole out of fragmentary stories, and to maintain a tone of warmth and lightness in the depiction of war and atrocity. However, in all its focus on historically significant experience, Petrowskaja's *Vielleicht Esther* challenges the idea that we can reconstruct a historical epoch by narrating the fate of an extended Eastern European Jewish family. The narrator initially believes that the description of her colorful set of relatives can capture the full range of twentieth-century historical experience— "und schon hat man das ganze zwanzigste Jahrhundert in der Tasche" (all that was needed to conjure up the entire twentieth century)—and lists some facts to prove her point: her ancestors lived in Warsaw, Kyiv, Odessa, Vienna, Paris, and other cities; they were working as physicists, farmers, poets, and, above all, teachers of the deaf; and they included a war hero and an assassin as well as numerous victims of persecution and murder.[1] However, it soon becomes clear that the family genealogy will not lead to a panoramic overview of history. Instead, it yields a highly self-reflective literary work that comments upon its poetics of multilingualism, its vacillation between fact and fiction, its lack of narrative cohesion, and its dependence on various memory media. The book's German subtitle, *Geschichten*, hints at the fragmentation and fictionalization of the genre of the family memoir.[2]

Born in Kyiv in 1970 and a native speaker of Russian, Petrowskaja has been living in Germany since 1999. She began to learn German and started to write for news media, including as a columnist for the *Frankfurter Allgemeine Zeitung*, before she published *Vielleicht Esther*. Her literary debut reflects the shifts in German and German Jewish memory cultures around the turn of the millennium. At that time the remaining eyewitnesses were passing and the Holocaust was turning from memory into history and Germany was seeing an influx of Russian Jewish migrants with a different historical experience. Whereas most Jews living in the Federal Republic in the immediate postwar era were of Polish origin and remembered the war as a time of victimization, ghettoization, and systematic annihilation, Soviet Jews tended to be less directly affected by the Holocaust and remembered the war from the perspective of the eventual victors. When the quota refugees brought this perspective to Germany—for example, by appearing in their decorated military uniforms on May 9, the Soviet holiday of the victory over fascism—they often met with skepticism in their local Jewish community. As Karen Körber writes, the post-Soviet migrants found themselves torn between two different cultures of memory, between the celebration of military victory in the Soviet Union and the focus on Jewish victimhood during the Holocaust in Germany. They responded to this cultural clash by fashioning new figures of memory, such as that of the Jewish Red Army soldier who fought for the liberation of his people, or by highlighting forms of female Jewish survival. In this way the quota refugees who became literary authors have expanded, and continue to expand, collective Jewish memory.[3]

German writers of Russian Jewish origin often engage in what Michael Rothberg terms *multidirectional memory*—that is, they bring into view other atrocities, war crimes, and genocides that had gone largely unnoticed in their new country. Thus, Vladimir Vertlib and Lena Gorelik draw attention to the German siege of Leningrad in the early 1940s, which was staged with the explicit intent to starve its population and caused the death of more than a million residents.[4] Olga Grjasnowa's novel *Der Russe ist einer, der Birken liebt* (2012; *All Russians Love Birch Trees*) connects the personal trauma of the narrator—whose boyfriend unexpectedly dies after a soccer injury—to the violent ethnic conflicts she witnessed years ago in Azerbaijan and also, more indirectly, to the Armenian genocide of 1915.[5] At first glance, Katja Petrowskaja differs from these writers in that she refocuses attention on the Holocaust, and especially on the mass shootings of Jews at Babi Yar. However, as I argue here, Petrowskaja develops her own poetics of multidirectionality as she explores the foundations of transcultural witnessing and remembrance. If multidirectional memory means to establish new memorial connections between historically and geographically distant events, Petrowskaja achieves this through forms of remembrance that are based on *similarity*.

In recent years, *similarity* has emerged as a new paradigm among scholars such as Anil Bhatti and Dorothee Kimmich, who seek to go beyond the binary of identity and difference. As a theoretical attitude, *thinking in similarity* calls into question the dichotomy between self and other. This dichotomy is at work not only in all racisms—which are paranoid about the revelation of similarities, opposed to fraternization with the racial "other," and so on—but also in postcolonial studies, which in all its emphasis on difference is still indebted to identitarian concepts. Thinking in similarity does not eliminate the category of difference altogether but rather exposes the ideological underpinnings of the talk about opposites, differences, and clashes. Because it blurs clear boundaries and distinctions, thinking in similarity is especially appropriate in an increasingly pluralist world of global entanglements. Compared to notions of purism and authenticity, "considerations of similarity place more emphasis on the tentative, the transitory, the unclear – on fluid borders, nuances, minimal deviations, *fuzziness* and vagueness – and define such terms using flexible and polyvalent language."[6] At the same time, thinking in similarity also means to be skeptical about dialogical models, which, as the example of colonialism shows, can be part and parcel of oppression. The political goal is not understanding each other but getting along with each other.

Thinking in similarity is not only a theoretical attitude but also a lived experience past and present. Historians who work in the paradigm often focus on neighborhoods, in which spatial proximity fosters the contact and interaction necessary for the perception of similarities.[7] Petrowskaja likewise emphasizes, in the Babi Yar chapter of *Vielleicht Esther*, the role of Ukrainian *neighbors* who witnessed the notorious massacre of Jews carried out by German forces during the Second World War. As I argue, the chapter raises the question of what makes transcultural witnessing possible— and provides an answer by citing a famous poem in which the non-Jewish speaker relates to Jewish victims by means of a simile and other strategies of tentative identification. I also show that, much like the novels of

Doron Rabinovici, *Vielleicht Esther* is a work of metamemory—namely, one that reflects on the mediated character of memory. Throughout the book, Petrowskaja portrays memory media as a wellspring of similarity: analog media such as records, films, and photographs appeal to the mimetic faculty of humans while digital memory media such as Internet platforms and search algorithms establish correspondences between distant events and users. Finally, I examine Petrowskaja's poetics of similarity—that is, the way she creates additional similarities through literary techniques of poetic expansion and fictive approximation.

Similarity, Proximity, and Transcultural Witnessing

The question of how to recognize and commemorate the victims of the Holocaust is at the core of *Vielleicht Esther*. Arguably, the central chapter of the book is the chapter on Babi Yar, which includes the section that won Petrowskaja the Ingeborg Bachmann Prize and later provided the title of the book. A ravine in the Ukrainian capital of Kyiv in which the narrator grew up, Babi Yar was the site of one of the largest massacres carried out by German troops during their invasion of the Soviet Union. Over the course of two days, on September 29–30 of 1941, special German forces there killed more than thirty-three thousand Jews by shooting. In the following two years, they targeted other groups, including Soviet prisoners of war, partisans, Roma and Sinti, and finally the Ukrainian nationalists who had initially collaborated with them. In *Vielleicht Esther*, the narrator revisits Babi Yar sometime after the turn of the millennium and faces a conundrum. Although she lost two great-grandmothers and a great-aunt in the killings, she would like to speak about her visit "als ob es möglich wäre zu verschweigen, dass auch meine Verwandten hier getötet wurden, . . . als abstrakter Mensch, als Mensch an sich und nicht nur als Nachfahrin des jüdischen Volkes, mit dem mich nur noch die Suche nach fehlenden Grabsteinen verbindet." (184/164; as if it were possible to keep silent that also my relatives were murdered here, like a person in the abstract, a person per se, and not just as a descendant of the Jewish people to whom my only connection is the search for missing gravestones.) Yet while walking over the completely reconfigured terrain, it becomes clear that the narrator cannot sustain the universal human perspective to which she aspires. Rather, she feels disconnected from other visitors of Babi Yar who appear to move on "verschiedenen Leinwänden. . . . Warum sehen sie nicht, was ich sehe?" (186/166; on different screens. . . . Why don't they see what I see?).

The tension between the narrator's family connection to the Holocaust and her desire for a shared human memory animates the quest for new forms of remembrance. She critiques the commemorative politics of the Soviet Union and its successor states before invoking several acts of transcultural witnessing as an alternative. After the war, the Soviet Union under Stalin effectively continued the memory-killing tactics of the Nazis, who had forced POWs to erase all traces of the killings at Babi Yar. The Soviet state suppressed the memory of the anti-Jewish massacre, failed to establish a memorial at the killing site, and launched antisemitic campaigns that silenced potential witnesses: "Dem Töten folgte das Schweigen" (189/168; Killing was followed by silence). The monument finally built at the ravine in 1976 was dedicated to Soviet heroes and did not even mention the Jews of Kyiv. However, the memorials erected at Babi Yar after the dissolution of the Soviet Union leave the narrator just as dissatisfied. In view of the ten separate monuments nowadays dedicated to different victim groups, she contemplates: "Zehn Denkmäler, aber keine gemeinsame Erinnerung, sogar im Gedenken setzt die Selektion sich fort. Was mir fehlt, ist das Wort Mensch. Wem gehören diese Opfer? Sind sie Waisen unserer gescheiterten Erinnerung? Oder sind sie alle—unsere?" (191/171, emphasis by translator; Ten monuments, but no shared memory; even in commemoration, there was no end to *selection*. What I am missing is the word *human*. Who do these victims belong to? Are they orphans of our failed memory? Or are they all ours?). In other words, neither the Soviet ideal of socialist humanism nor the post-Soviet practice of memorial pluralism are able to express the unique sufferings of Holocaust victims in shared forms of human memory. Against this failed remembrance—and against the sense of disconnection she herself experienced earlier—the narrator sets a hesitant "unsere" (ours) tethered to a question mark.

At this point the narrator invokes two non-Jewish Soviet writers who spoke on behalf of the Jewish victims of Babi Yar and, in so doing, moved beyond the dual impasses of particularization and generalization: Yevgeny Yevtushenko and Anatoly Kuznetsov. Yevtushenko's 1961 "Babi Yar" marked a turning point in the commemoration of the Babi Yar killings, especially after Shostakovich in 1962 set the poem to music in his Thirteenth Symphony. The poem indicts not only the German atrocity but also its Soviet misrepresentation—that is, the concealment of its anti-Jewish character—as well as the long history of antisemitism in Russia, Europe, and beyond. The poem's speaker identifies with a series of Jewish figures from ancient history to the Holocaust: the Jewish people during the Exodus, Jesus Christ, the French Jewish officer Alfred Dreyfus (who was wrongly accused of treason in 1894), an unnamed boy from Bialystok (where more than eighty Jews were killed during a pogrom in 1906), the iconic Holocaust victim Anne Frank, and, finally, every old man and every child shot at Babi Yar. These acts of identification are based on the construction of similarity rather than identity. The poem's speaker makes himself similar to various Jewish victims while never glossing over the fact that these acts of assimilation to another's experience are imaginary, transitory, and fragile.

Paul Celan's German translation of the poem, from which *Vielleicht Esther* cites, draws special attention to relations of similarity. The poem's speaker initially relates to the Jews by means of a simile—"Ich bin alt heute, / so alt wie das jüdische Volk"—and then tentatively identifies with them: "Ich glaube, ich bin jetzt / ein Jude" (189/169; *Today I am as old in years as all the German Jewish people / Now I seem to be a Jew*; emphasis by the translator).[8] Celan's translation of the poem subsequently uses the literary device of prosopopoeia to intensify the identification; the speaker speaks directly for the fleeing, tormented, or murdered victims of anti-Jewish violence. The use of the present tense and the depiction of sensory impressions help conjure up vivid scenes, and the repetition of the word *jetzt* (now) further elides the gap between the dead and the living, between the past of the Jewish victims and the present of the author and the reader. However, despite this blurring of boundaries, the poem's speaker never fully impersonates the dead or appropriates their otherness. Rather, the very seriality of the figures draws attention to the acts of identification, all while the threefold repetition of the expression "ich glaube" highlights their tentative character. Time and again, the speaker makes himself similar to a Jewish victim while reminding us that these connections are tenuous and transitory.

Toward the end of the poem, when the speaker zooms in on the victims of Babi Yar, there is a tendency toward reduction and abstraction—for example, through enjambments (which in *Vielleicht Esther* are represented through slashes): "Jeder hier erschossene Greis / ich. Jedes hier erschossene Kind / ich."[9] These severed lines and the lack of predicates raise the question of what exactly is the relationship between the speaker and the dead. Has the speaker's identification with the Jewish victims become a stable and absolute equation or, on the contrary, a fragile and fleeting connection?

Interestingly, there is no more prosopopoeia here—that is, the speaker does not speak in the voice of those murdered in Babi Yar. He rather relates to them indeterminately in a way that epitomizes the poem's ethical stance. The disjunctions of enjambment, the stammers of repetition, the cutting of predicates, the seriality of figures, and the recurrent formula "ich glaube": all these stylistic devices announce an otherness that can neither be disavowed nor fully appropriated—it can only be tentatively, hesitantly adopted.

As mentioned earlier, thinking in similarity often involves spatial proximity. The one can give way to the other—for example, when the juxtaposition of two objects allows us to perceive the correspondences between them. This connection between similarity and proximity explains Petrowskaja's interest, in *Vielleicht Esther*, in neighborly relations and the actual sites of destruction. In the Babi Yar chapter, in particular, there is much emphasis on the role of neighbors as bystanders of the past and witnesses in the present. Thus, the (presumably non-Jewish) domestic servant Natascha initially accompanied the narrator's great-grandmother Anna and great-aunt Ljloja on their way to the killing site. And the neighbors of the narrator's other great-grandmother (who is given the peculiar name "Vielleicht Esther" because the narrator's father cannot recall her name with certainty) first warned her about the danger awaiting her at the hands of the Germans—"Gehen Sie nicht!" (210/187; "Don't go")—but eventually helped her out of her apartment and toward the killing site: "Die Nachbarn müssen ihr geholfen haben, wie sonst?" (211/188; The neighbors must have helped her; how else could she have done it?). It is interesting in that regard that the narrator mentions Jan Gross's pathbreaking book, *Neighbors*, on the complicity of non-Jewish Eastern Europeans in the Holocaust.[10]

Vielleicht Esther emphasizes not so much the collaboration between Germans and non-Jewish Ukrainians but rather the *presence* of the latter as the events of the Holocaust unfolded, the way that their proximity to the killing sites positioned them as quintessential witnesses. The narrator surmises that there were hundreds, even thousands, of people who saw the Jews move through the city to the killing site. Among them she names Anatoly Kuznetsov, the other major non-Jewish writer-witness mentioned in *Vielleicht Esther*. Kuznetsov, who grew up not far from the ravine and later published a documentary novel about the massacre, would guide visitors through the ravine, "um zu zeigen, dass es nichts mehr zu zeigen gibt, nur zu erzählen" (191/170; to show that there was nothing more to show—only to tell). The fact that one of these visitors is Yevgeny Yevtushenko—whose poem "Babi Yar" was actually published several years before Kuznetsov's documentary novel on the subject—shows the significance of spatial proximity: *Vielleicht Esther* suggests that Yevtushenko was able to identify with the Jewish victims in his poem only because Kuznetsov had first shown him the physical site of destruction.

The emphasis on neighborly relationships in *Vielleicht Esther* goes hand in hand with a critique of othering, especially through language. The narrator believes "dass es keine Fremden gibt, wenn es um Opfer geht" (184/164; that there are no strangers among victims), and she recognizes the danger of othering the victims of the Babi Yar massacre through the very word *Jew*: "Ja, man nennt diese Opfer für gewöhnlich Juden, aber viele meinen damit nur die anderen. Das ist irreführend, denn die, die da sterben mussten, waren nicht die anderen, sondern die Schulfreunde, die Kinder aus dem Hinterhof, die Nachbarn, die Omas und die Onkel." (185/165; Most people talk about these victims as Jews, often meaning simply "the others." That is misleading, for those who had to die were not the others; they were, rather, friends from school, kids next door, neighbors, grandmas and uncles.) By choosing words such as *friends*, *neighbors*, and *kids next door*, the narrator describes the victims of the Babi Yar massacre in terms of their *relationships* to their non-Jewish neighbors. That is, she reinvests the word *Jew* with connotations of proximity and similarity and thereby restores to the victims the status of neighbors.

It is also telling that the narrator self-consciously introduces the word *Jew*—"lassen Sie uns Juden sagen" (218/194; let's say Jews)—in another passage that directly addresses her readers and critically engages their historical knowledge—or rather, their willful ignorance. This passage, which contemplates the fate of those Jews who, in contrast to her father, stayed behind in the city of Kyiv, is particularly hesitant and long winded. After finally stating that the remaining Jews were shot, the narrator ambiguously assures the (presumably German) reader: "Aber das wissen Sie bestimmt. Kiew ist von hier genauso weit entfernt wie Paris." (218/194; But you surely know that. Kiev is just as far from here as Paris.) The assurance cannot but sound hollow, considering that the section began by invoking a Berlin librarian who clearly did not know what happened in Babi Yar (183/163). An important part of the project of *Vielleicht Esther* is to raise the readers' awareness of their own participation in historical forgetting and practices of othering.

As I have argued, the literary works by Yevtushenko and Kuznetsov occupy a central place in *Vielleicht Esther* because they are quintessential acts of transcultural witnessing. The narrator herself engages in such acts when she conjures in her mind her relatives' non-Jewish neighbors and, in at least one instance, imaginatively adopts their viewpoint. In the "Vielleicht Esther" section, the narrator recounts her great-grandmother's march to the ravine in a highly protracted fashion, as if trying to stave off her killing, before visualizing the murder by imagining herself in the place of a hypothetical, non-Jewish witness. After describing how a German officer casually and callously shot the old woman who asked him for directions to Babi Yar, she reflects on her own position: "Ich beobachte diese Szene wie Gott aus dem Fenster des gegenüberliegenden Hauses. Vielleicht schreibt man so Romane. Oder auch Märchen." (221/196; I observed this scene like God out of the window of the building across the street. Maybe that's how people write novels. Or fairy tales.) Although the narrator compares her position here to that of God, she later attributes it to a human witness. She ponders the origins of her knowledge about her great-grandmother's story and realizes that there were indeed witnesses—who have all disappeared, except for one. The last lines of the chapter reveal that the narrator has put herself imaginatively in the place of the non-Jewish superintendent who *maybe* witnessed her great-grandmother's last moments: "Mein Großvater Semjon suchte lange nach jemandem, der etwas über Babuschka wusste. Es war der Hausmeister des nicht mehr existierenden Hauses, der ihm alles erzählte. Es scheint mir, dass an diesem 29. September 1941 jemand am Fenster gestanden hat. Vielleicht." (223/198; My grandfather Semion spent a long time looking for people who knew something about Babushka. The superintendent of the building that was no longer there told him everything. I think that on this twenty-ninth of September 1941, there was someone standing at the window. Maybe.)

As shown here, *Vielleicht Esther* seeks to expose the blind spots of Soviet memory, especially the ideologically motivated forgetting of the Jewish victims of the Holocaust. The clear thematic focus on the Holocaust positions the book within German memory culture and might explain its critical success in Germany. Compared with other post-Soviet Jewish writers such as Gorelik and Grjasnowa, Petrowskaja seems less interested in bringing previously unnoticed atrocities or genocides into view. To be sure, she mentions the persecution of several other groups, the siege of Leningrad, and the sufferings of Soviet POWs during the Second World War as well as the hardships Soviet citizens endured under Stalin, including the mass starvation caused by agricultural collectivization in the Ukraine. Yet her true innovation concerns the formal principles of remembrance: her appeal to the mimetic faculty and her penchant for picking out analogies—however minor, arbitrary, or difficult to recognize—from which she construes new and meaningful connections. As seen in the story of the great-grandmother's death, this often involves a degree of spatial proximity. As she tries to picture the murder of Vielleicht Esther from a house on the opposite side of the street, the narrator imaginatively assumes a position—"am Fenster" (at the window)—that is both *contiguous with* and *similar to* the one from which the superintendent may or may not have witnessed the scene.

One example of the connection between diverse historical traumas in *Vielleicht Esther* is a passage that suggestively links the siege of Leningrad to the Holocaust. In the spring of 1942, the narrator's grandmother Rosa was charged with establishing an orphanage in Southern Ural for two hundred half-starved child survivors of Leningrad. The narrator interweaves this story with that of Janusz Korczak, a physician and pedagogue who led a Jewish orphanage in the Warsaw ghetto and voluntarily accompanied the two hundred children under his care to the Treblinka death camp in 1942. The juxtaposition of these two episodes is based on seemingly random correspondences and analogies. The narrator speaks of "die Rochaden des Schicksals . . . die Zufälle in Raum und Zeit" (70/60; the twists and turns of fate . . . chance occurrences in space and time) and frequently uses words such as *auch* (also) and *ebenfalls* (likewise) to establish parallels between Rosa and Janusz, including their addresses in Warsaw and Kyiv, the number of orphans entrusted to them, and the "Kriegsbefehl" (70/60; wartime command) on which they both acted. True to the principle of similarity, which makes it possible to behold identity and difference simultaneously, the narrator ends the comparison by taking note of the fundamental difference—namely, that her grandmother and the children under her care did, in fact, survive. Had her grandmother's family returned to Warsaw during the First World War, as Korczak did, they would have been neighbors of his, "mit allen folgenden Adressen" (71/61; with the further destinations that this implies)—that is, they would have perished in the Holocaust. Yet despite the differentiation, there is no hierarchy of victims or a sense that one experience of suffering is worse than the other. The narrator holds the comparison in suspense, without judgment or conclusion, and simply goes on to tell the story of how her grandmother and the orphaned children of Leningrad managed to survive despite hunger, grief, and illness. The principle of similarity allows her to bear witness to two kinds of historical atrocities: those her relatives experienced and those they escaped.

Similarity, Mediality, Digitality

As Dora Osborne has pointed out, *Vielleicht Esther* is a prime example of the "archival turn" in Holocaust memory, or the moment when historical documents become the sole means of preserving and transmitting memories.[11] The quest for the past truly begins when the death of an aunt forces the narrator to realize the meaning of the word *history*: "Geschichte ist, wenn es plötzlich keine Menschen mehr gibt, die man fragen kann, sondern nur noch Quellen. Ich hatte niemanden mehr, den ich hätte fragen können, der sich an diese Zeiten noch erinnern konnte. Was mir blieb: Erinnerungsfetzen, zweifelhafte Notizen und Dokumente in fernen Archiven." (30/22–23; History begins when there are no more people to ask, only sources. I had no one left to question, no one who could still recall these times. All I had were fragments of memory, notes of dubious value, and documents in distant archives.) While critics usually emphasize the problems incurred at this moment—the fragmentation, mediation, and fading of memories—Petrowskaja also sees new possibilities for re-remembrance, in part because the archival turn coincides with the digitization of Holocaust memories. Like other third-generation family memoirs and family novels written around the turn of the millennium, *Vielleicht Esther* features a protagonist who gathers documents, visits archives, and travels to historical sites in order to reconstruct the past. Well-known examples of this genre are Monika Maron's 1999 *Pawel's Briefe* (*Pavel's Letters*, 2002) and Daniel Mendelsohn's 2006 *The Lost*. Yet, more clearly than these authors, Petrowskaja highlights the role of electronic media and digital platforms in the search process and, in particular, the random findings and fortuitous encounters generated by the space of the Internet. In what follows here, I show that digitization turns out to be another wellspring of similarity.

Throughout *Vielleicht Esther*, the narrator is reconstructing her family history with the help of memory media, both analog and digital. The analog media she mentions—the phonograph record, the silent movie, and the photograph—are not only metonymically connected to the period she reconstructs, the early and mid-twentieth century. They also illustrate the role of mimesis, or what Walter Benjamin calls the "mimetic faculty," in the process of remembrance.[12] For example, during her trip to Warsaw, the narrator purchases an old record with Yiddish tunes that she later plays in Kyiv to her Warsaw-born grandmother, Rosa, who begins to sing along and dance. This bodily enactment of the melodies opens up a window to a forgotten past, both for Rosa, who reconnects with her childhood in Warsaw, and for the narrator, whose mnemonic movement imitates her grandmother's clumsy bouncing: "Dann hüpfte auch ich komisch und ungeschickt, wie eine Nadel auf einer abgespielten Platte, übersprang den ganzen Krieg wie ein Gebiet, das meinen rettenden Phantasien nicht unterstellt war, und landete in den siebziger Jahren meiner Kindheit." (77/66; Then I, too, skipped about comically and clumsily, like a needle on a worn record, skipped over the whole war like a realm not subject to my liberating fantasies, and wound up in the 1970s setting of my childhood.) In another passage, the narrator compares her own mental reenactment of her mother's wartime memories to a silent movie, a simile that shows how the images that traumatized the mother have been etched into her child's memory: "Wieder und wieder setzt sich der Zug in Bewegung, und ich sehe die aufgerissenen Münder, die lautlosen Schreie, wie im Stummfilm, als hätten sich alle Sinne in Bewegung verwandelt, als gäbe es nur noch etwas zu sehen und nichts mehr zu hören." (83/71; Again and again the train starts moving, and I see the mouths open wide, the mute screams as in a silent movie, as though all senses have been transformed into movement, as though there was only something to see and nothing to hear.)

A third analog medium, photography, is present in the book through the inclusion of a number of black-and-white photographs. Though indexical in origin, these photographs, I argue, were chosen primarily because of their iconic qualities—that is, their presumed resemblance to the represented object and their ability to visualize what may otherwise be forgotten. Thus, the portrait of Aunt Lida shows her beautiful appearance, which the narrator praises but Aunt Lida herself "verschwieg" (34/26; kept . . . to herself), and the photograph of Rosa testifies to the expressiveness of her gestures mentioned in the text (62–63/53–54). Photographs play a special role in a couple of situations in which empathy fails, as in the case of the narrator's enigmatic great-uncle, Judas Stern, an assassin whose political background and motives remain opaque. Possibly inspired by Monika Maron's *Pawel's Briefe*, *Vielleicht Esther* includes here a series of images consisting of a photograph and its enlarged details, as if offering that photograph up for close examination. While the narrator concedes that she is unable to understand her great-uncle because he killed another human being, the photographs invite the reader to scrutinize his face, perhaps for signs of madness: we first see a close-up of Judas's face (158/139), then the photograph from which the face section was cut and enlarged (162/143), and finally a differently sized face section from that same photograph (170/150).[13] The reproduction of the photograph and its cutouts has the effect of bringing someone who otherwise eludes comprehension somewhat closer to the reader. As the narrator becomes aware of the limits of empathy, the photograph offers an alternative way of approaching her great-uncle imaginatively—and just like the acts of transcultural witnessing described earlier, this form of remembrance never fully grasps or appropriates the other.

What makes *Vielleicht Esther* stand out among recent third-generation family novels is its focus on the transition from analog to digital memory media. Petrowskaja writes at a moment when analog media such as records, films, and photographs can be digitized and distributed through the Internet, and she depicts this transition as nonlinear and multidirectional. Her book lends evidence to Amanda Lagerkvist's existential approach to media studies, according to which we encounter the virtual world of the Internet as fully embodied subjects. We must therefore "start from the realization that our lives have become increasingly digitized but that they remain, like all forms of life, marked by regression, hesitations, tensions, and other hiccups."[14] In a similar vein, the narrator of *Vielleicht Esther* can be said to hesitate at the threshold of digitization as she alternates between the virtual space of the Internet and more traditional research that requires movement in real space. The interdependence of these two modes of research points to new possibilities for Holocaust remembrance in an age of digitization. For example, when the narrator travels to a brick-and-mortar institute in Warsaw, the Jewish Genealogy & Family Heritage Center, the staff helps her locate the death records of two relatives, Zygmunt Krzewin and Hela Krzewina, on the web pages of Yad Vashem, the World Holocaust Remembrance Center in Jerusalem. Marveling at the virtual connectivity that provides the information about their death dates and places, the narrator nevertheless highlights the personal contact with a staff member of the Warsaw institute: "Vielleicht bin ich nur deshalb nach Warschau gefahren, um diesen Internet-Fund aus Annas Händen entgegenzunehmen" (107/94; Maybe I had traveled to Warsaw for the sole purpose of accepting this Internet discovery from Anna's hands). Later Anna shows her a website of old Warsaw that features the street in which her relatives lived, and

Anna's colleague Jan gives her a photo of the relatives' house that he procured through eBay.

Above all, in *Vielleicht Esther* the Internet is a source of seemingly random similarities and connections that turn out to be deeper correspondences. Grappling with the tension between contingency and necessity in her web searches, the narrator tends to privilege the latter. When she verges on despair because her attempt to reconstruct the past with the help of the Internet strikes her as arbitrary and accidental, she surmises that all these blind movements might have stirred up the "Geister der Vergangenheit" (84/72; ghosts of the past). She also recalls an episode in which her mother, who had been reconstructing the history of her school in Kyiv, was contacted by a former neighbor who had found out about the project through Facebook and now provided moving details about the impact the mother's family had on her. The whole episode illustrates the narrator's remark about the "Geister der Vergangenheit" arising from the Internet and suggests that her own web browsing might similarly help restore important connections. But what exactly is the deeper logic or necessity the narrator sees at play here? Would she agree with recent media historians who argue that the human *connectedness* initially made possible by Web 2.0 has given way to a technical and profit-oriented *connectivity*?[15] Or does she rather—more optimistically and more mystifyingly—suggest that the omnipresence of the Internet and the increase of global connectedness help us retrieve forgotten facets of the past? Her penchant for depicting Google as an anthropomorphic entity that can think, plan, and communicate certainly speaks to a sense of agency on the part of the Internet. And the operating principle behind that agency is neither sameness nor difference, but similarity.

The book's prologue shows how the Internet brings like-minded people together, an effect the narrator initially views critically as a mere by-product of technology but later affirms as the expression of a deeper necessity. In the first scene, she meets Sam, an American Jew of Iranian descent, at the central station in Berlin, where they are both struck by the seeming aggressiveness of a *Bombardier* advertisement.[16] She learns that Sam's wife searches for her family's Polish origins, just as she does, and that the couple already found, on the Internet, important facts about the Belarusian village from which the wife's family hails, "Google sei Dank" (11/5; thank Google). Sam marvels at the fact that, in the narrator, he encounters someone who looks like the Iranian women of his childhood, who takes the same train to Warsaw, and who has the same goal as he and his wife, and he views these correspondences as a "Schicksalsfügung" (11/5; twist of fate). The narrator, however, disagrees and attributes their encounter rather to the search algorithm of Google, which appears here as a godlike authority bent on reinforcing a user's established preferences: "Google wacht über uns wie Gott, und wenn wir etwas suchen, dann gibt er uns nur unsere Reime darauf.... Gott googelt unsere Wege, auf dass wir nicht herausfallen aus unseren Fugen, ich treffe ständig auf Menschen, die das Gleiche suchen wie ich." (12/5–6, translation changed; Google watches over us like God, and when we search for something, it gives it rhyme and reason.... God googles our paths, so we don't fall out of our fugal tracks, I always meet people who are searching for the same thing I am). It is surely no coincidence that these sentences both invoke artistic principles of similarity. Rhyme is a poetic device that strings together two or more words of similar sound, thereby creating new syntactic and semantic relations between them. According to Roman Jakobson, rhyme is an important element of the poetic function of language, which "*projects the principle of equivalence from the axis of selection onto the axis of combination.*"[17] And the German word *Fuge*, which normally denotes a fissure between two building components and here evokes a path of life, can also refer to the fugue—that is, the composition technique that works with polyphony and imitation and introduces a musical theme by repeating it at different pitches. If the narrator eventually appreciates Sam's sense that the encounter of like-minded people through the Internet is *Schicksal*, this may very well be because she redefines these correspondences as a form of artistic creation.

Thanks to complex ranking systems and the increasing personalization of searches, Internet algorithms tend to confirm the biases and preferences of a given user—that is, they produce results that are *similar* to the outcome of other searches. For example, Google's PageRank algorithm not only gives weight to the history of a page and the number and place of keywords but also takes into account the user's electronic device, current location, and search history. The narrator of *Vielleicht Esther* notices the adaptation of her search results to the outcome of her previous searches. When she searches for the stalag (a camp for prisoners of war) in which her Ukrainian grandfather had been interred, her initial results are geared toward tourists seeking recreation, making it difficult for her to find the information she seeks: "ich führte einen ungleichen Kampf mit dem Internet und seinen Ferienangeboten" (242/215; I waged an unequal battle with the Internet and its vacation packages). Subsequently, however, the search engine remembers her preferences and shows results involving catastrophes even when she wants to read about churches and museums. One may say that these personalized web searches make the narrator similar to herself, lending support to her earlier assessment of Google as a similarity-producing machine. But similarity is not identity. Just like rhymes repeat certain sounds with slight variations, any given web search expands upon and diversifies earlier searches.

In *Vielleicht Esther*, the space of the Internet allows for the perception and construction of similarity: between users, between search terms, between an individual's past and present selves. However random and/or subjective, these similarities have the power to create meaning and identity. For example, it may be pure coincidence that the color yellow, which Google uses to highlight search terms, is also "die Farbe des Judentums" (52/43; the color of Jewishness). Yet the perception of this similarity allows the narrator to construe a connection between Judaism and the word *taub* (deaf), for which she searches because many of her ancestors were teachers of the deaf, and to turn the Internet search into a constructive moment in her own quest for a Jewish identity: "Jede Geschichte mit dem gelben Taub wurde zu einem Baustein meiner Vergangenheit, meines Internet-Judentums" (52/43; Every story with the yellow *deaf* became a building block of my past, of my Internet Jewishness).

Internet algorithms also generate results by matching a new search with earlier searches by other people, thereby projecting the interests of past users onto the current user. In at least one instance in *Vielleicht Esther*, this form of similarity reveals a truth that was forgotten, repressed, or never present to begin with. This happens when the narrator traces the Krzewin branch of her family and notices that all her Internet searches generate links to the Warsaw ghetto. She initially finds it unnerving that even searches for people who lived in Warsaw before 1940 lead her back to the ghetto. Ultimately, however, the Internet's repeated references draw the narrator's attention to aspects of the past she never fully acknowledged. She suddenly remembers two sentences she used to hear her mother say without registering their meaning: "Als Ozjel 1939 starb, haben wir seiner Mutter in Warschau nichts gesagt, sie war schon einundneunzig. Und dann leuchtete noch einer auf. Wir haben Pakete nach Warschau geschickt, noch 1940, später wurden sie nicht mehr angenommen. Wie viele Jahre steckten diese beiden Sätze in mir, bis ich sie hörte?" (102/89, translation changed; When Ozjel died, in 1939, we never told his mother in Warsaw, who was already ninety-one. And then another sentence flashed up. We sent packages to Warsaw, even in 1940; after that they were no longer accepted. How many years did I bear these two sentences within me until I heeded them?) The implication is that the narrator finally takes in the reality of her Warsaw relatives, their life under German occupation, and their eventual confinement in the ghetto. The similarity enforced by the Internet, which makes the narrator view her family's Polish past through the lens applied by other users—the Warsaw ghetto—in the end enables her to fully grasp her mother's words. Thrown into the virtual neighborhood of those who browse the Internet for details of Warsaw's past, the narrator moves from initial irritation to a new openness. This is one example of re-remembrance made possible by the digitization of Holocaust memory. Throughout the book, the narrator's hesitation at the threshold to digitization and her combination of web browsing and traditional research enable her to retrieve meaningful correspondences while eschewing the empty homogeneity produced by the Internet.

A Poetics of Similarity

Throughout this chapter, I have argued that similarity is for Petrowskaja what mobility is for Rabinovici: a mnemonic principle that allows for a conscious re-remembrance when Holocaust memory is undergoing profound changes due to the disappearance of the eyewitness generation and the globalization, hypermediation, and institutionalization of memory. In *Vielleicht Esther*, similarity undergirds both the connectivity of memory media and the possibility of transcultural witnessing, in which one relates to the ethnic, cultural, or religious other as neither identical nor entirely different. I further argue that Petrowskaja differs from many other contemporary Soviet-born Jewish authors in that she opens up new comparative perspectives not so much on the level of the plot but on the level of style—a style that builds on the principle of similarity. There is a distinctly poetic quality to Petrowskaja's prose, with its streams of associations, webs of literary allusions, and puns across different languages. According to the famous definition by Roman Jacobson cited earlier, poetry creates syntagmatic chains out of words that *resemble* each other in sound or meaning and potentially can substitute for each other. Petrowskaja often achieves this by combining words from the different languages that play a role in her family's life past and present, including German, Russian, Polish, Yiddish, Hebrew, and English. This poetics of multilingualism wrests new meanings from words and helps her maintain a playful tone despite a thematic concern with persecution, deportation, and genocide.[18] Two other textual strategies in *Vielleicht Esther* are based on the principle of similarity and aid the reconstruction of the family history: *poetic expansion* and *fictive approximation*.

Poetic expansion occurs, for example, when the narrator construes correspondences between the dead and the living, building a web of associations that extends the presence of the murdered family members into the present. At times these correspondences are disconcerting, as when the physical clumsiness of the seventeen-year-old narrator reminds an aunt of a relative killed at Babi Yar and the narrator is too anxious to even ask what the comparison means (201/179). At other times, the correspondences create new meanings and even seem capable of undoing some of the destruction wrought by the Holocaust. And at one point, the narrator mentions that their identical birthdate connects several of her relatives who otherwise have very different fates and backgrounds, including a woman who was killed as a Jew even though she no longer felt as a Jew and the son of a family that returned to Judaism (203/181). The text also construes correspondences between the narrator and her relatives through the repetition of key phrases and symbolisms. For example, the remark that the narrator was "sieben Jahre alt" (194/173; seven years old) when she watched the slow and agonizing death of her grandmother Rita, who herself had witnessed the killing of a brother in a pogrom when she was "sieben Jahre alt" (195/174; seven years old), connects the two women through the age at which they were first confronted with death. Beyond these correspondences between the dead and the living, the narrator builds on the principle of similarity to expand the kinship structure beyond her biological family. While contemplating her relatives who were killed at Babi Yar, her mind wanders to all the others who were shot there, conjuring an image of equivalent victimhood: "Anna und Ljolja, die in Babij Jar liegen, und *alle anderen dort*" (19/12, my emphasis; Anna and Lyolya, who died in Babi Yar, and *all the others there*). In another scene, the narrator is haunted by a list of names of lost and dispersed relatives, which she then expands to include unrelated people bearing the same surnames as her relatives. The fact that one of them is Itzhak Stern—the Jewish protagonist of Steven Spielberg's blockbuster film *Schindler's List*, though the narrator omits the title and simply speaks of "einem Film" (28/21; a movie)—shows that popular media are very much part of the expanding field of equivalences she creates.

Fictive approximation is another strategy that utilizes the principle of similarity to reconstruct the family's history. In an interview, Petrowskaja describes how she supplements facts with conjectures, a procedure she distinguishes from poetic invention: "In this book, I tried not to *make up* [*erdichten*] anything. I worked a lot with documents and various testimonies. When you're not certain, you try to include all versions. And also this vague *presumption* [*Vermutung*]. That is possibly the only opportunity to go in the direction of truth: knowing the facts, bases, and retellings, and also proceeding with *presumptions*."[19] I argue, however, that the distinction between *erdichten* and *vermuten* is more difficult to uphold than Petrowskaja's interview suggests. The narrator of *Vielleicht Esther* repeatedly and openly engages in acts of fictionalization that come very close to invention. In the prologue, she reacts to the discomfort she and Sam feel in front of the violent-sounding word *Bombardier* by spinning a story about an alleged French musical of that same title, and she offers an intriguing self-explanation: her storytelling is not exactly a lie but a way of moving forward—indeed, it is a form of flying.[20] The narrator's reconstruction of her family history, which she begins to relay to Sam "mit dem gleichen Schwung, als würde ich das nächste Musical verurteilen" (9/3; with the kind of verve I might use to excoriate some other musical), is throughout the book imbued with a certain fictiveness, as indicated by the frequent use of the subjunctive and words such as *Legenden* (17/11; legends). These allusions to the presence of fiction do not so much cast doubt on historical reality as draw attention to the similarity *and* the difference between the events and the stories told about them. Storytelling becomes a creative way of approaching a reality that can never be fully recaptured.

In Holocaust studies, the concept of postmemory has been introduced in part to explain the peculiar creativity required of those born later, who fill in gaps of knowledge by conjuring scenarios of what *maybe* occurred in the past.[21] As covered in the two previous chapters, contemporary German Jewish writers push the boundaries of this concept by widening the range of fictions that are potentially of interest because they tell us something new about the workings of memory. In *Die Leinwand*, Benjamin Stein does not outright condemn the fake Holocaust memoir but rather invokes the phenomenon to interrogate the material conditions and (para)textual mechanisms that enable the transmission of Holocaust testimony. And in Doron Rabinovici's *Ohnehin*, the confabulations of a former SS officer suffering from amnesia afford an opportunity to contemplate the constructive nature of *all* memory. Petrowskaja contributes to this metamemorial turn by exploring the principle of similarity, with its "emphasis on the tentative, the transitory, the unclear—on fluid borders, nuances, minimal deviations, *fuzziness* and vagueness."[22] The signature word of her book—*vielleicht*—epitomizes similarity thus defined. The passage that explicitly adds *vielleicht* to the name of the father's grandmother—"Ich glaube, sie hieß Esther, sagte mein Vater. Ja, vielleicht Esther." (209/186; I think her name was Esther, my father said. Yes, maybe Esther.)—echoes the tentative "ich glaube" in Celan's translation of the poem "Babi Yar," a paradigmatic act of transcultural witnessing. The word *vielleicht*, which serves throughout the book as the great-grandmother's epithet, is another reminder of tentativeness, and a highly conspicuous one. For, in contrast to other epistemic adverbs such as *mutmaßlich* (presumptively) and *vermeintlich* (supposedly), *vielleicht* may only be used adverbially, never attributively. By creating a compound structure that stretches this grammatical rule, and by using *Vielleicht Esther* as the title of the book, Petrowskaja turns approximation into a literary program. Speaking in the mode of *maybe*, her narrator approximates a reality she can never entirely know. As she imaginatively expands the circle of her relatives, makes up stories to fill in the gaps of knowledge, and conjectures in the mode of *maybe*, writing itself turns into a form of thinking in similarity.

PART III
CLAIMING PLACES

5

RETURNING

*Diasporic Place-Making in
Barbara Honigmann*

"A LS JUDE BIN ICH AUS DEUTSCHLAND WEGGEGANGEN, ABER in meiner Arbeit, in einer sehr starken Bindung an die deutsche Sprache, kehre ich immer wieder zurück."[1] (As a Jew I left Germany, but in my work, in a very strong attachment to the German language, I return again and again.) Thus Barbara Honigmann captures the complex relationship between departure and return in her life and work. Honigmann left East Germany, the country to which her parents had moved in 1946 after years of exile in London, in 1984. Her mother, Alice Friedmann (née Kohlmann, known as Litzi Friedmann), was a Viennese communist of Hungarian Jewish origin. Her father, Georg Honigmann, was a German Jew who worked as an editor, journalist, film producer, and cabaret director after his return to Germany. While Judaism in a religious or cultural sense seems to have played no role in her parents' home, in the 1970s Honigmann herself began what she described as a "Suche nach einem Minimum jüdischer Identität in meinem Leben" (search for a minimum of Jewish identity in my life).[2] She started learning Hebrew, got married in a Jewish ceremony, and finally moved to Strasbourg, a French city with a thriving Jewish community and a rich Jewish history.[3] In 1986 she published her first collection of prose texts, *Roman von einem Kinde* (Novel of a child) to critical acclaim. Honigmann went on to describe her migration from Germany and her decision to live a more consciously Jewish life in several literary and essayistic texts. One of the main motives of her oeuvre, one may say, is the birth of writing from the spirit of departure.

This duality—of rebuilding a Jewish life in France and returning to Germany in writing—informs much of Honigmann's work, both in style and content. In her own understanding, she continues the project of her German Jewish ancestors in a new language—a language that recycles and recharges everyday words.[4] And while some of her texts are set in Strasbourg, many are thematically oriented toward Germany, drawing on her own experience in the GDR, the itinerant lives of her parents, and the German Jewish past more generally. The effect of this relatively narrow range of themes is cumulative. In contrast to Benjamin Stein, for example, who stakes out a new authorial position in a single literary text, throughout her work Honigmann revisits certain core experiences and retells them with slight variations. One of these recurrent themes is the profoundly displaced life of her parents, especially her father, who figures prominently in books from *Eine Liebe aus nichts* (1991; *A Love Made Out of Nothing*) to *Georg* (2019). In what follows, I read Honigmann's representation of her parents' return to Germany together with two other spatial motifs frequently encountered in her work: visits to Jewish cemeteries and her own resettlement in Strasbourg. The overall effect of these interrelated movements is one of diasporic place-making as defined in the introduction to this book. As Honigmann's narrators rethink the meaning of *return* and reconnect to the Jewish past, they create new places, make new homes, and strike new roots in the diaspora.

Honigmann's work hovers between history, autobiography, and fiction in a way that marks it as *autofiction*, a term that has been applied to her work by critics and by the author herself. Autofiction is a form of autobiographical writing that emerged toward the end of the twentieth century at a time when postmodern aesthetics had called into question the unity of the self and the stability of linguistic reference. Honigmann used the term in a 2002 lecture in which she criticized the attempt to reduce her literary work to her biography and emphasized the at least partially fictitious character of all autobiographical writing:

> *Autofiktion.* Das autobiographische Schreiben liegt irgendwo in der Mitte zwischen Tagebuch und Roman, und es ist nicht nur deshalb Fiktion, weil alle Verwandlung von Wirklichkeit in Schreiben Fiktion ist, sondern auch, weil sein Projekt der Selbsterforschung, Selbstentdeckung und Selbstoffenbarung mindestens in dem gleichen Maß immer auch Selbstinszenierung, Selbstfiktionalisierung, Verwandlung des Lebens in einen Roman, manchmal sogar Selbstmythologisierung ist. In diesem Sinn kann autobiographisches Schreiben romanhafter sein als ein Roman.[5]

Autofiction. Autobiographical writing lies somewhere between diary and novel. It is fiction not only because every transformation of reality into writing is fiction but also because its project of self-examination, self-discovery, and self-revelation is to at least the same degree always also self-staging and self-fictionalization, a transformation of one's life into a novel, sometimes even a self-mythologization. In this sense autobiographical writing can be more novelistic than a novel.

The historian Yfaat Weiss has suggested that Honigmann's autofiction allows for the constant variation of a life story that has historical significance and that the genre enables the author to wrest her stories away from the specific historical context and give them a universal meaning.[6] In this chapter, I continue this line of thought and argue that as Honigmann narrates experiences that are, at their core, historical but not tied to a single meaning, she elaborates new possibilities out of the concepts of departure, return, and settlement. She offers her own unique vision of what it might mean to return to Germany and to rebuild Jewish life—on French territory, to be sure, but also in German literature and culture.

Rethinking Return

The decision of her parents—communists and refugees from Nazism—to move to East Germany and help build a new socialist state after the Second World War is an important reference point throughout Honigmann's work. She repeatedly criticizes the blind spots and self-delusions that informed this decision, which ultimately left her parents with an exacerbated sense of displacement. Her own development into a practicing Jew and a German-language author living in France emerges as an alternative to her parents' precarious settlement in East Germany. In pitting her own departure against her parents' return, I argue, Honigmann ends up reworking the very meaning of return.

The dialectic between departure and return plays out in early works such as *Eine Liebe aus nichts*. The book's narrator, a young Jewish woman working at a theater, leaves the GDR for Paris in the hope of gaining new experiences and perspectives. But she soon finds that by going to Paris, she involuntarily repeats the journey of her parents, who were persecuted both as Jews and as socialists and were forced into Parisian exile during the Third Reich. The book never fully resolves the tension between these two different conceptions of exile—of exile as a grand awakening to new possibilities and of exile as the result of persecution and expulsion—leaving the reader with a peculiar sense of circularity and "stuckness." As the narrator states at one point: "Mehr als von allem anderen bin ich vielleicht von meinen Eltern weggelaufen und lief ihnen doch hinterher."[7] (Perhaps more than anything else, I've been running away from my parents and yet still go on trotting along behind them.) Only at the very end does the narrator stand a certain chance of breaking the cycle of repetition. After attending her father's funeral in Berlin, she departs a second time for Paris, and while sitting on the train, she closes the window curtains because she cannot endure seeing the scenery "noch einmal" (106/76; again). Significantly, the narrator's refusal to reenact her parents' past "again" coincides with the beginning of her own writing. Among the belongings of her deceased father, she had found a notebook he had kept after the end of the war, and now, while leaving Germany for good, she decides to fill the remaining empty pages with her own entries.

Throughout the book, the narrator suggests that her parents' return to Germany did not lead to a more settled life but rather created a sense of permanent displacement. Thus, they moved in social circles composed of former emigrants and kept their distance from most Germans, yet they did not identify with Jews and Judaism in any positive way. At one point she speculates that her parents, who escaped Nazi persecution during the war yet afterward were haunted by images of the Holocaust, suffered from survivor's guilt and desperately sought to distance themselves from the past:

> Das muß eine schwere Last gewesen sein, so schwer, daß sie immer so taten, als hätten sie damit gar nichts zu tun gehabt. . . . Und schließlich waren sie nach Berlin gekommen, um ein neues Deutschland aufzubauen, es sollte ja ganz anders werden als das alte, deshalb wollte man von den Juden besser gar nicht mehr sprechen. Aber irgendwie ist alles nicht geglückt, und eines Tages mußten sie sich sogar für das Land ihres Exils rechtfertigen, warum es ein westliches Land war und nicht die Sowjetunion. (34)

> That must have been a heavy burden—so heavy that they always acted as if they hadn't had anything to do with all that. . . . And in the end, they'd come to Berlin to build a new Germany. It was supposed to be entirely different than the old one, and for that reason, one preferred not to even speak about the Jews anymore. But somehow things didn't work out and the day came when they even had to justify their choice of the country where they'd spent their exile—why was it a Western country and not the Soviet Union? (24, trans. changed)

The use of the indefinite personal pronoun *man* in this passage creates some ambiguity. To whom does the *man* refer? That is, who no longer wants to talk about the Jews? While the narrator appears to refer to her parents' desire for a radically new beginning, *man* also alludes to the GDR at large, which glorified the political resistance to Nazism and eschewed a commemoration of the Jewish victims of the Holocaust.[8] The mention of subsequent discrimination against remigrants from Western countries vaguely evokes the ideological opposition between political and so-called racial refugees. Beyond survivor's guilt and public silencing, there are additional reasons for her parents' persistent sense of displacement. Her mother never felt at home in Berlin because she was not from Germany to begin with (in the novel she is from Bulgaria; in reality Honigmann's mother was born in Vienna to Hungarian Jewish parents). Her father's rather abrupt adoption of a communist worldview and identity intensified his sense of displacement and disorientation, of which his multiple failed marriages seem to be a corollary. As he states: "eigentlich weiß ich nicht, wo ich herstamme, weiß auch nicht, wo ich jetzt hingehöre" (35/25; actually I don't know where I'm from and don't even know where I belong now). As noted previously, the narrator both reenacts this model and distances herself from it. Ultimately, *Eine Liebe aus nichts* shows how the narrator becomes a writer while thinking through her parents' fraught attempt at resettlement.

Eine Liebe aus nichts is a prime example of autofiction. The book carries no subtitle or genre designation, yet its paratext helps establish what Philippe Lejeune has called the "autobiographical pact"—that is, it sets up readers' expectations that the events relayed in the text reflect the author's experience.[9] The jacket copy of the German paperback edition announces the book's autobiographical character—"Barbara Honigmann *berichtet* von *ihrer* Kindheit in Ost-Berlin" (Barbara Honigmann *reports* on *her* childhood in East Berlin)—and provides details of the author's background that correspond to the narrator's life as depicted in the literary text.[10] A closer reading, however, reveals some differences between the lives of author and narrator, suggesting the presence of other fictitious elements in the text. For example, in *Eine Liebe aus nichts*, the narrator's mother is from Bulgaria rather than Vienna/Hungary, the narrator moves to Paris rather than Strasbourg, and the narrator is single and childless rather than a married mother of two. The book also lacks a pivotal feature of autobiography—namely, the homonymy of author, narrator, and protagonist (who remains unnamed in *Eine Liebe aus nichts*)—which creates a further ambiguity about the autobiographical nature of the work. This ambiguity, I argue, sets into motion an experiment with various forms of settlement and displacement. In subsequent essayistic and autobiographical works, Honigmann elaborates the critique of Jewish emigrants returning to East Germany first advanced in *Eine Liebe aus nichts*.

Throughout her work, Honigmann adds new facets to the nonarrival of her parents. "Selbstporträt als Jüdin" (Self-portrait as a Jewish woman), for example, suggests the existence of a vibrant network of former emigrants in the GDR that constitutes the family's primary social circle. Yet this does not shield them from feelings of coldness and emptiness that result, the narrator suspects, from a pervasive sense of unbelonging:

> Vielleicht kam diese Kühle und Leere nicht nur davon, daß aus dem Sozialismus, den meine Eltern aufbauen wollten, nichts wurde, sondern auch davon, daß sie vollkommen zwischen den Stühlen saßen, nicht mehr zu den Juden gehörten und keine Deutschen geworden waren.[11]
>
> Perhaps this coolness and emptiness arose not only because nothing came of the socialism that my parents wanted to build, but also because they were caught in the middle: they no longer belonged to the Jews and had not become German.

The life trajectory of the narrator—who resettles in France, embraces her Jewishness, and intermittently returns to Germany through her writing—offers the alternative model of return cited earlier, that is, the idea that Honigmann's continued attachment to the German language allows her to imaginatively return to Germany in her literary works. One effect of these juxtapositions of her parents' return to Germany and her own departure to France is that the very concept of "return" undergoes a revision and redefinition. In another piece from *Damals, dann und danach*, for example, Honigmann imagines her emigration to Strasbourg as a form of return. To be sure, her remarks are a bit tongue in cheek—she admits that she has construed a legend—yet at least partially based in reality because she can potentially trace her family genealogy back to the Rhine valley:

> Für mein neues Straßburger Leben hatte ich mir eine Legende zurechtgelegt, nach der ich nämlich gar nicht her-, sondern vielmehr hierher zurückgekommen bin, da eine meiner Großmütter eine geborene Weil war, und ja jeder weiß, daß alle Weils in allen Schreibweisen aus dem Rheintal kommen, und ich also in dieser Linie meiner Familie von dort stamme.[12]
>
> For my new Strasbourg life I had concocted a legend according to which I had not come to but had rather returned to this place, since one of my grandmothers had been born a Weil and everyone knows that all the Weils, regardless of spelling, come from the Rhine valley, so that through this side of my family, I also come from there.

According to Honigmann, we do not necessarily return to a place in which we have lived before but to a place that allows us to retrieve, resume, or reimagine a strand of past experience. This new concept of return also helps explain the curious subtitle of another work by Honigmann, *Das überirdische Licht: Rückkehr nach New York* (The supernatural light: Return to New York). The book reflects on a period in the winter of 2006, which Honigmann spent as a writer in residence in Manhattan, where she relished the vibrancy of New York City and especially the manifold forms of Jewish existence therein. Why did she subtitle her report a "return"? On the one hand, the act of writing itself is a return to past experience, in fact perhaps the only form of connection to it, since Honigmann ended her residence by destroying all sorts of objects, receipts, and papers that could remind her of her stay in New York City.[13] On the other hand, this stay leads to a reencounter with multiple layers of the past, both personal and historical: While in New York City, Honigmann meets an old friend from the GDR who moved there decades ago and a distant relative she never knew in person. During her long walks through the city, she also frequently encounters traces of German Jewish immigration of the past. The idea that New York City is not so much a place of arrival but a place of return also echoes a statement made earlier in *Eine Liebe aus nichts*: "Ellis Island ist meine Heimat" (57/40; Ellis Island is my home).[14]

The conspicuous position of the word *return* in the subtitle of *Das überirdische Licht* raises a broader question. What does one need to find in a place—or what does one need to make of a place—so one's arrival there can be considered a form of return? Tellingly, in *Das überirdische Licht*, Honigmann revisits her father's profoundly unsettled life once more, inspired by a dream she had about him. She now locates the reasons for her father's unsettlement in the early losses he incurred in childhood, including the death of his mother and brother, to explain why his most natural environment is the hotel room. Even more importantly, she remembers a scene in which the father, after learning that his daughter was about to emigrate to France, enjoined her to go to America instead: "Nach Amerika mußt du gehen. Dort wirst du deinen Platz finden. . . . Geh weit weg. So weit weg wie möglich! Geh nach Amerika. Reiß dich los!"[15] (You have to go to America. There you will find your place. . . . Go far away. As far away as possible! Go to America. Break free!) Read in conjunction with the book's subtitle, this scene implies that in going to New York City, Honigmann belatedly responds to her father's injunction and finds her place there—or, more precisely, that she *returns* to a place of openness and possibility to which she has always already belonged.

Visiting Jewish Cemeteries

In several of Honigmann's works, a defunct Jewish cemetery serves to illustrate the dislocation and discontinuity of Jewish life. *Eine Liebe aus nichts* opens with such an image. The narrator's father, who never identified with Jews and Judaism, is buried in Weimar in a tiny Jewish cemetery that has been out of use for decades. (This is another instance in which Honigmann takes poetic license with reality: the real Georg Honigmann was buried in the Weißensee cemetery in Berlin, a pivotal place for Honigmann that I discuss in the following.) The funeral is depicted as a strange and jarring ceremony, which highlights the inner heterogeneity of Jewish culture and religion and undermines the sense that a religious ritual might restore a sense of home, tradition, or identity. Among other things, the narrator notices with dismay that the Saloniki-born cantor, who had to be brought in from another city, continues to mispronounce her father's German name with his Sephardic accent. When the narrator enters her father's room after the funeral in search of a memento, she finds that his clothes are lying around "verloren" (*Eine Liebe aus nichts*, 9/6; forlornly)—a word that connotes both loss and dispersion—which helps her realize "daß die Erinnerung aus den Dingen herausgefallen war" (9/7; that the memories had fallen out of those objects). In other words, even in his death the narrator's father cannot find a place. Nor do cemeteries establish a connection to the past at any other point in the story. When the narrator, en route to France, makes a stopover in Hesse to see the places where her father's German Jewish ancestors lived, she searches for the gravestones of her relatives in the local Jewish cemeteries—in vain, it turns out, not because the gravestones are gone but because there are too many similar names and she lacks the knowledge of her ancestors' lives and deaths that would enable her to identify them.

At the same time, the visits to Jewish cemeteries provide an impetus for the narrator to reconnect to the German Jewish past and restore a sense of place and continuity. A powerful imperative seems to issue from these cemeteries—an imperative to recover, to retrieve, to retell. In Honigmann's first prose collection, *Roman von einem Kinde*, the narrator recounts how she accompanied Gershom Scholem, the famous historian of Jewish mysticism, to his family grave in the Jewish cemetery Weißensee in East Berlin.

While standing at the grave, Scholem began to tell stories about his parents and brothers, summing up the life of each and ending on a moment of silence and a short prayer.[16] Scholem's visit to Berlin is a form of return that stands in clear contrast to the return of Honigmann's parents, among others: "Er hatte die Reise seines Lebens noch einmal zurückgelegt, noch einmal Berlin–Jerusalem retour."[17] (He had again retraced the journey of his life, once again Berlin–Jerusalem, in the reverse direction.) Scholem's is a temporary return that occasions acts of commemoration and reaffirms his commitment to Judaism. When he dies shortly later, an epitaph is added to the family grave, so he ends up having two graves: one in Jerusalem and one in Berlin. Scholem's visit leaves a deep impression on the narrator both because his writings on Jewish history and religion come alive for her and, we can infer, because his double grave exemplifies the duality she would ultimately choose for herself. *Roman von einem Kinde* further suggests that the encounter with Scholem marks a turning point in the narrator's development and that the older scholar's advice to immigrate to a country in which the teaching of the Torah is still alive motivates her own move to France, which is recounted in the last story of the collection.

The Jewish cemetery is the site where the differences between the first two generations of post-Holocaust German Jews crystallize: between the survivors who want to cut all ties with the past and their children who wish to reconnect to it. This becomes especially clear in a story entitled "Gräber in London" (Graves in London), which Honigmann included in her prose collection *Damals, dann und danach*. Nestled in this story about the narrator's visit to her grandparents' graves in London are memories of her earlier excursions to the Weißensee cemetery in East Berlin. At the time the narrator had a circle of friends who, though mostly of Jewish descent, were ignorant about Judaism before they collectively began to rediscover and reimagine the German Jewish past. During her lonely walks through the vast, overgrown, labyrinthine Weißensee cemetery, the narrator first gets an inkling of the existence of an extensive network of Jewish families that also encompasses herself. This recognition occurs not only because the names on the gravestones resemble her parents' names but also because she encounters something unfamiliar, even illegible—namely, Hebrew characters that she cannot decipher: "Auf die hebräischen Buchstaben, die ich nicht lesen konnte, starrte ich, als ob sie vielleicht eine geheime, sehr wichtige Botschaft für mich enthielten, durch die sich das Rätsel meiner Herkunft offenbaren würde und das Schweigen meiner Eltern gebrochen werden könnte."[18] (I stared at the Hebrew letters, which I could not read, as if they contained, perhaps, a secret and very important message for me, a message that would reveal the riddle of my origin and that could break the silence of my parents.) The text implies that the riddle posed by the Hebrew characters propels the narrator toward the rediscovery of Judaism, or what she calls "die Wiedereroberung unseres Judentums aus dem Nichts" (the recapture of our Judaism out of nothingness).[19] She begins to attend a synagogue, marries in a Jewish ceremony, and reads the Bible in Hebrew.

As in many of Honigmann's writings, the Jewish cemeteries depicted in this piece are bleak, forsaken places. If the narrator found neglect and overgrowth in Weißensee, she later encounters absence and emptiness in the Jewish cemetery in London. And yet, these cemeteries harbor a message that is all the more imperative because of its obscurity. "Gräber in London" begins with a 1942 letter in which the narrator's grandmother enjoins her daughter (the narrator's mother) to take care of the grave of her father (the narrator's grandfather). This letter is the only thing the narrator's mother, who throughout her life showed a marked disinterest in genealogical continuity, bequeathed to her daughter. Over the course of the text, it becomes clear that the narrator's mother had completely ignored the grandmother's request: she had buried her parents in London "wie Hunde, ohne Grabstein und ohne Namen" (like dogs, without tombstone and without names).[20] Why, then, did she pass the written request, this proof of her own failure, on to her daughter? Was the bequeathal an admission of guilt, a plea to the daughter to fulfill the request in her place? The narrator's visit to London can indeed be read as a response to her grandmother's request, an attempt to take care of the grave, not by saying the kaddish or erecting a gravestone but by telling the story of the absent gravestone and the unfulfilled request. That storytelling has this power becomes clear in the passages that reflect on the effect of the narrator's writing. Thus, she describes how the book she wrote about her father's life (*Eine Liebe aus nichts*, though the book's title is not mentioned in the passage) effectively restored a sense of continuity and belonging, as lost relatives from all over the world have begun to contact her: "Plötzlich waren nach dem Tod meines Vaters vergangene Generationen wieder auferstanden, die eine zusammenhängende Geschichte erzählten und den Zustand der völligen Unbehaustheit, den mein Vater mir hinterlassen hat, milderten."[21] (Suddenly past generations had resurrected themselves after the death of my father, generations that told a coherent story and that softened the state of total homelessness my father had bequeathed to me.)

Chronicling an Immigrant Street

As seen here, Barbara Honigmann describes her parent generation's return to East Germany as fraught with problems and her own visits to Jewish cemeteries as excursions that, while ultimately motivating her to reconnect to Judaism, initially reinforce a sense of loss and exile. Her own 1984 move to Strasbourg offers an alternative to the sense of displacement and rootlessness that characterized her parents' lives. Honigmann revisits her settlement in France in a recent work, *Chronik meiner Straße* (2015). The subject of the book is the Rue Edel, a rundown street in Strasbourg where new immigrants often move first but seldom reside for long. While the Rue Edel is, for most immigrants, a mere stopover on the route to better neighborhoods, the narrator still lives there thirty years after her arrival. In what follows, I argue that the narration of the Rue Edel and the lives of its residents in *Chronik meiner Straße* is a form of diasporic place-making: the text transforms a *space* of transition into a *place* of dwelling.

In *Chronik meiner Straße*, Honigmann seizes upon an existing chronotope—that is, a literary time-space configuration that organizes the narrative of a particular motif or genre. The chronotope of the street, which is closely related to those of the path and the road, has been a structuring principle of the Western novel since antiquity.[22] Its three most prominent features can still be found in *Chronik meiner Straße*: (1) The street signifies both physical movement and individual development. In fact, the one is often mapped on the other as the literary image of the street overlaps with the metaphor of the *Lebensweg* (life path). In *Chronik meiner Straße*, this meaning resonates in the social mobility associated with the Rue Edel, whose immigrant residents are in the process of assimilating to French culture and moving to fancier neighborhoods. Although never described in detail, these "better" neighborhoods are the vanishing point of the street, the horizon to which the immigrants are moving. (2) The street is a site of chance encounters, an opportunity to meet and interact with a wide variety of people. In the Rue Edel, immigrants and French citizens from different ethnic, religious, and cultural backgrounds find themselves as next-door neighbors. There is no plan behind these living arrangements; they just continue to evolve and shape the narrator's experience and narration. (3) Finally, even though it signifies movement and mobility, the street always leads through a homeland, describing a path that is already carved out and therefore familiar. As I argue, this sense of familiarity is an effect rather than a precondition of *Chronik meiner Straße*, which claims the Rue Edel as the narrator's own—not necessarily as her homeland in an emphatic sense but as a place of permanent residence and reassuring familiarity.

Any given street can be considered a place in the sense of Yi-Fu Tuan's famous distinction between place and space, on which Barbara Mann draws: "If we think of space as that which allows movement, then place is a pause."[23] A street is a segment of space that has been given a proper name and visible contours, that has been carved out of the infinite space of possibilities into something definite. Over the course of *Chronik meiner Straße*, the Rue Edel is gradually endowed with meaning and value in a way that makes it more fully a place in Tuan's sense. The first act of place-making is the choice of the possessive adjective *meine* (my) in the title of the book—and the plural form *unsere* (our) in the first chapter—which, in combination with a blurb on the jacket copy that encourages the text to be read as autobiographical, associates the street with Honigmann and establishes a relationship of belonging. The first chapter expands this gesture of appropriation into scenes of inhabitation. The narrator begins by emphasizing the street's state of neglect, its emptiness and desolation. Referring to the gardens, beautiful parks, and notable buildings that surround houses in fancier neighborhoods, she states laconically: "Von alldem hat unsere Straße gar nichts."[24] (Our street has nothing of all that.) Instead, the street features ugly houses, which were often built rather quickly to fill in construction gaps. At this point the narrator mentions how a friend of hers used to play ball as a child in just such a construction gap in the Rue Edel. The image of a child's play filling an empty space with activity is, I would argue, an allegory of the act of narration: the narrator's depiction of the street and the lives of its residents turns a space into a place by furnishing it with particulars and endowing it with significance.

The narrator initially bestows on the street a sense of particularity by providing specific geographical and historical information. Not coincidentally, the first of these facts is one that would matter to her personally—namely, the location of the Rue Edel on the eastern edge of Strasbourg and in close proximity to Germany. The nicknames the narrator's family has given to different elements of the street—such as a false driveway and a restaurant—that in some cases draw on their memory of buildings in East Germany further shows how they inhabit the Rue Edel by attaching a personal meaning to it.[25] If the first chapter positions the narrator at the center of the street, subsequent chapters extrapolate her bodily location, posture, and perspective onto the surrounding space. The chapters often begin with an explicit description of the narrator's location—at her desk, in the brasserie next door, on the balcony—before shifting to the things and people she sees from, or encounters in, that location, such as an errant tree, a Kurdish man from Turkey, a rabbi from Kaunas. At other times, the narrator's location is implied in deictic expressions by which she introduces her stories of others, expressions such as "im Nebenhaus" (51; next door) and "auf unserer Etage" (58; on our floor). It is her own presence and orientation in the street that determines what comes into view and enters the narrative.

The text further creates a sense of particularity by oscillating between plural and singular, between groups and individuals. The narrator initially focuses on the different *Völker* that inhabit the Rue Edel—that is, she subsumes the individuals in the ethnic groups to which they belong: "Viele Völker wohnen in unserer Straße, und man hört sie in vielerlei Sprachen sprechen" (9; Many peoples live in our street, and one hears them speaking in many languages). Whether she registers the chaos of languages on the street or the separateness of different ethnic groups who actively avoid each other, she creates an impression of deindividualized multitudes. However, the focus on ethnic groups (which often borders on stereotypes) gradually gives way to stories of individual people and families. By resting her gaze on a specific site and her memory on a specific ritual, the narrator enables the individual to emerge from the group and a particular life story from the street's general history. Witness the story of the Kurdish man who owns a store where people from different ethnic backgrounds meet and interact. The narrator highlights the man's exceptional status—he is unassimilated, speaks poor French, and disregards the Sunday rest order—and it is perhaps for this reason that he serves as a cultural mediator and also the first resting place of the narrator's gaze. For the narrator, this man triggers memories of two Kurdish brothers who had previously operated the store and offered her special deals, which finally leads her to reflect on the regular rhythm by which the store changes owners and the chain of Kurdish relatives, of which the current owner is only one link. The effect of this oscillation between the general and the particular is that the street appears inhabited by particular people, its chronicle filled with life stories.

The place-making in *Chronik meiner Straße* culminates in an account of how the narrator's husband, Peter, erects a sukkah in their courtyard to celebrate the Jewish holiday of Sukkoth. This is a quintessential example of diasporic place-making. The temporary hut in which Jews are traditionally required to eat and sleep during the seven or eight days of Sukkoth is, by definition, a transient, porous, open place—more precisely, it superimposes in one specific site several real and imagined places, including the land of Israel and the presence of God. If celebrated in the diaspora, the sukkah engages in various ways with the non-Jewish environment. It may incorporate elements from local architecture and its three-walled structure may offer a view into the non-Jewish surroundings.[26] The celebration of Sukkoth marks a place as temporarily Jewish while exposing its participants to the gaze, or sometimes even the attacks, of their non-Jewish neighbors—as the narrator of *Chronik meiner Straße* remembers from her first Sukkoth in Strasbourg, when rotten tomatoes were thrown through the permeable roof of the sukkah. Over the course of the text, the sukkah becomes a signifier of openness as such. The narrator contemplates the function of the structure as a reminder of fragility and porousness:

> Daran sollen die Juden wohl gemahnt werden... an die Zerbrechlichkeit und Unsicherheit ihrer Existenz, die sie durch Zähigkeit und Anpassungsfähigkeit kompensieren müssen, wie damals, nach dem Auszug aus Ägypten, als sie in Hütten in der Wüste wohnten, diesem leeren, unbestimmten Ort, wo die neuerworbene Freiheit hauptsächlich darin bestand, daß keiner wußte, wohin jetzt, was tun und wie es weitergehen wird. (136)

> It seems that the Jews should be reminded... of the fragility and uncertainty of their existence, for which they have to compensate with tenacity and adaptability, just like back then, after the Exodus from Egypt, when they lived in huts in the desert, that empty and undefined place where the newly acquired freedom meant mostly that nobody knew where to go, what to do, and what was next.

What is particularly striking about the sukkah built in the Rue Edel is the extent to which it is a discursive event. The erection of the sukkah is preceded, accompanied, and followed by all sorts of speech acts, including Peter's lengthy explanations to the neighbors about the character and purpose of the sukkah (which are continued in the narrator's explanatory descriptions of the ritual, presumably for readers who are less knowledgeable about Judaism); the many letters Peter sends to the house management to request permission to build a sukkah; the narrator's quotation from the biblical book of Ecclesiastes that is read on Sukkoth; the slip of paper she and her husband attach to the sukkah to inform the neighbors of its purpose; and the anecdotes they exchange with other Jews after the conclusion of the holiday about funny and not-so-funny conflicts they had over the sukkah.

In *Chronik meiner Straße*, the sukkah is first and foremost an occasion for talking and writing, for a series of explanations, arguments, and contestations. This discursive dimension is one of the reasons I prefer to speak of *place-claiming* rather than of *place-making* alone. The erection of the sukkah, this act of engaging with a place and in that process laying a claim to it—however transient and nonexclusive—is a linguistic event even before its literary representation.

By the end of *Chronik meiner Straße*, the narrator's own environment is no longer as empty and undefined as the desert into which the Israelites escaped during the Exodus. The erection of the sukkah and other acts of place-making recounted throughout the text have endowed the Rue Edel with personal meaning and communal significance and thereby transformed it into a viable place of residence. The Rue Edel, the "Straße des Ankommens und Anfangens und des Hängenbleibens" (13; street of arriving and beginning and of getting stuck), does not necessarily become a final destination or a permanent home. Rather, it is a place in which the narrator can dwell in a state of preliminary permanence, fully aware of the other places from which people may hail and to which they may move. At the very end, she speaks of "den kleinen Weltraum unserer Straße, die nach überallhin offen und doch auch ein bißchen geschlossen ist" (152; the small cosmic space of our street, which is open in every direction and is also a bit closed off). As demonstrated here, this diasporic place-making is part of a larger project of reconstruction that also includes Honigmann's reconceptualization of return and her depiction of visits to Jewish cemeteries. *Chronik meiner Straße* once more combines these three motifs in one of its middle chapters, which relates the narrator's occasional returns to Berlin. During these trips, she generally feels alienated from the city; she never really loved it when she lived there, and it has dramatically changed since. At one point, however, a visit to her father's grave in Weißensee induces her to remember the traditions of Reform Judaism that originated in Germany, and the chapter ends on another instance of diasporic place-making: the narrator purchases for herself a grave in Strasbourg, the city to which she moved after she left Berlin "aus freiem Willen" (78; of my own free will).

A couple of decades ago, literary critic Andreas Kilcher distinguished between two forms of exterritoriality in contemporary German Jewish literature. Self-defined Jewish authors who reside in Germany or Austria (such as Maxim Biller, Esther Dischereit, Doron Rabinovici, and Robert Schindel) tend to deconstruct the German language from within and emphasize the difference between their own works and those of non-Jewish German and Austrian writers. In contrast, authors who have left Germany and write in German from a deliberate geographical distance (such as Chaim Noll and Barbara Honigmann) often situate their writing within German cultural traditions, especially of the *Goethezeit* (Age of Goethe), and choose a classical writing style marked by linearity and readability.[27] This chapter argues that Honigmann claims not only past traditions but also present-day places. In order to understand the dialectic between displacement and emplacement in contemporary German Jewish writers, I suggest that we need to pay attention to the literary places they claim or create while relaying their (often autobiographical) stories of exile and migration. In addition to the Rue Edel depicted in Barbara Honigmann's *Chronik meiner Straße*, such places include the ancient mikvah, or ritual bath, on which Benjamin Stein's *Die Leinwand* ends and the Viennese *Naschmarkt* on which Doron Rabinovici's *Ohnehin* is partly set. Another case in point is a work discussed in the next chapter, Vladimir Vertlib's *Zwischenstationen*, which recounts the journey of a Jewish family from Russia to Austria via several transit stations. What the family fails to achieve—firm establishment in a place—the novel itself accomplishes through its careful accumulation of descriptive and narrative detail, at least temporarily. Like Barbara Honigmann, these contemporary German Jewish authors engage in a literary place-making that allows displaced subjects to put down new roots in the diaspora.

6

TRANSITIONING

Migration Narratives in Vladimir Vertlib and Julya Rabinowich

THE CONTEMPORARY AUSTRIAN JEWISH WRITERS VLADIMIR VERTLIB AND Julya Rabinowich were born in Leningrad and came to Vienna with a wave of Russian Jewish emigration that began in 1970 and lasted for about a decade. The wave was preceded by decades of Soviet antisemitism and was enabled by a relaxation of Soviet emigration policy. The USSR opened its borders for a limited number of its Jewish citizens, who initially had to migrate to Israel via Austria, so that Vienna indeed became the "Drehscheibe der Ostemigration" (turntable of eastern emigration), as Vertlib writes in one of his novels.[1] This migration wave has to be distinguished from the more recent wave of Russian Jewish emigration that began with the disintegration of the Soviet Union in the late 1980s and eventually brought over two hundred thousand Jewish *Kontingentflüchtlinge* to Germany. While the quota refugees usually were able to sustain a relationship with their former homelands and even keep their old passports, the migrants of the previous wave had to contend with strong political reprisals and had virtually no opportunity to return once they had left the Soviet Union. In view of these differences, it is interesting that both Vertlib and Rabinowich began to publish literary texts only after the arrival of the quota refugees in Germany and that public interest in these refugees has always played a role in the reception of their works. Rabinowich herself has promoted this interest by calling herself, erroneously, a *Kontingentflüchtling* in articles and interviews.[2] Vertlib has addressed the fate of the quota refugees in several of his novels, especially in the widely acclaimed *Das besondere Gedächtnis der Rosa Masur*, and even some of his more autographical works give the protagonist a quota-refugee lineage. The publication and reception history of Vertlib and Rabinowich shows that literature can function as a resonance chamber of historical experience, in which earlier experiences of flight and exile can be rethought in light of new historical developments.

Indeed, the overall trajectory of these authors' work can be described as an expanding circle around the core experience of migration. Vertlib draws on the migration history of his own family most clearly in his first two books, *Abschiebung* (1995; Deportation) and *Zwischenstationen* (1999; Way stations) and returns to it in the multilayered novel *Schimons Schweigen* (2012; Schimon's silence), now framed by a trip to Israel where the narrator hopes to pick up the trail of his father's secret and where Vertlib himself spent two years as a child. Between 2001 and 2009, Vertlib published a trilogy of novels set in the fictional German city of Gigricht and featuring a number of different migrants, including Russian Jewish *Kontingentflüchtlinge*. And in Vertlib's most recently published novel, *Viktor hilft* (2018; Victor helps), the protagonist, a Russian Jewish immigrant who once again bears autobiographical traces, volunteers in a Salzburg transit camp for refugees from the Middle East. Julya Rabinowich's work similarly expands thematically from her own life experience to ever-new forms of flight and migration. Her literary debut, *Spaltkopf* (2008; *Splithead*), which depicts the emigration of a Russian Jewish family from Leningrad to Vienna, is very much modeled on the experience of her own family. *Die Erdfresserin* (2012; The earth eater) portrays a woman from the former Soviet Republic of Dagestan who works as a prostitute in Vienna, suffers a psychotic break, and embarks on a journey back home that ends in her complete psychical disintegration. In some of her theatrical plays and young adult literature, Rabinowich focuses on the traumas experienced by yet other migrants fleeing wars and persecution.

In this chapter I argue that much like Barbara Honigmann, Vertlib and Rabinowich engage in diasporic place-making—which, in their case, is focused on in-between spaces, on places of transit and moments of transition. It is, of course, important not to hypostasize the realm of the in-between that appears in their book titles as well as their metaliterary reflections. As Leslie Adelson has argued, the notion that migrants and their cultures exist "between two worlds" is widespread yet woefully inadequate because these worlds are usually "presumed to be originary, mutually exclusive, and intact, the boundaries between them clear and absolute."[3] In contrast, the concept of diasporic place-making involves a dynamic understanding of place and nation and relinquishes the idea of clear boundaries. Thus, in a 2006 lecture, Vertlib argues that the literature of migration does not enrich a national literature but rather helps constitute it and that the absence of migrant writing in contemporary literature would be a sign of lack and abnormality. The literature of migration creates a cultural "Zwischenbereich" (intermediary realm) well suited to the existential realities of a modern world in which "klar begrenzte Lebenswelten" (clearly delineated living environments) have become a rarity.[4] Vertlib's argument brings to mind James Clifford's claim that *routes* are not necessarily preceded by *roots* and that human places, cultures, and societies are first constituted through movement.[5]

This chapter analyzes acts of place-making under conditions of radical displacement. In their first book publications, both Vertlib and Rabinowich depict migration as a traumatic rupture and a cause of lasting uprootedness. In *Abschiebung*, Vertlib describes the deportation of a Russian Jewish family from the United States, and in *Zwischenstationen*, he portrays the seemingly endless series of stopovers on a migration route. Rabinowich is even more outspoken about the devastating effect of flight and migration, which she casts as a psychological trauma in *Spaltkopf*. However, in all their thematic focus on radical *dis*placement, both authors also devise new literary strategies of *em*placement. Their narrators imaginatively inhabit transitory, even hostile, places such as a deportation holding cell, the arrival zone of an airport, and dilapidated apartments on the urban fringe. The fact that Vertlib and Rabinowich conjure the possibility of lingering in transit, and of doing so productively, may explain the overall trajectory of their work—namely, their interest in ever-new forms of migration and their increasing embrace of global perspectives. In the final section of this chapter, I show how the authors, in their most recent literary works, intervene in the so-called European refugee crisis in distinct and paradigmatic ways: whereas Rabinowich invites her readers to empathize with a Muslim refugee girl, Vertlib alerts them to the limits of transcultural empathy.

Hostile Places: Vertlib's *Abschiebung*

Hardly any other contemporary German Jewish author so consistently thematizes emigration, exile, and diaspora as Vladimir Vertlib. This surely has to do with the biography of the author, whose childhood and youth resembled an odyssey: Vertlib was born in 1966 in Leningrad and emigrated with his family to Israel at the age of five. A year later, the family temporarily relocated to Austria. From there, they moved to Italy, then back to Vienna, to the Netherlands, a second time to Israel, to Italy again, back to Vienna, and then to the US. In 1981 the family was deported from the US to Austria, where they settled down once and for all. Vertlib used this emigration history most directly in his first two books, *Abschiebung* and *Zwischenstationen*. He labels these as fictions—the subtitles of the books are "story" and "novel," respectively—and also varies the emigration routes significantly. The story of the Russian Jewish family in *Abschiebung*, for instance, is played out entirely within the emigration triangle of Israel, Germany, and the US. Because Vertlib's first publications portray the experience of radical displacement, even placelessness, they present a challenge to the concept of diasporic place-making—that is, the idea that authors can create, define, or claim places in their literary works. The title of each of these books is a single noun that is not modified, not even by a definite or indefinite article, thus casting the phenomena described in the titles as absolute, life-defining experiences: *Abschiebung* centers around the moment of forced deportation, in which a migrant family is at the mercy of the partly indifferent, partly racist, partly sadistic bureaucrats; *Zwischenstationen* describes the structural interminability of a migration story in which each new city turns out to be a mere transit station. In what follows, I argue that despite the thematic emphasis on displacement and uprootedness in his early works, Vertlib also cultivates literary strategies of emplacement.

The subject of Vertlib's first publication, *Abschiebung*, is the expulsion and removal of a Russian Jewish family out of the US. The narrator, a fourteen-year-old Russian Jew, initially emigrated with his parents to Israel and then temporarily to Germany. When the mother loses her position at a German company, the family flies to the US on a tourist visa and spends a year trying to obtain an immigration visa, thereby becoming a plaything of the despotic and merciless bureaucracy. After numerous petitions and arguments with the American authorities—the last ending in a fistfight—the three are bundled off on a plane to Germany via London. The impression of disorientation and placelessness is further reinforced by the story's lack of a promise of happiness or even a realistic alternative to relocation in the US. The narrator's father—who, in response to the countless antisemitic reprisals he experienced in the Soviet Union, had become a member of an underground Zionist organization—has no desire to return to Israel following his severely disappointing stay there after first leaving the Soviet Union. The narrator, on the other hand, is afraid of returning to Germany, where he was isolated and bullied in school. Thus, the family has no hope of a peaceful arrival and stay anywhere in the world. In the last scene, we see parents and son in a plane descending into London.

The book is not only thematically focused on deportation but also structured around it. The narration begins on the morning of the deportation—which, as we discover later, takes place on a day in September 1980—and ends on the same evening with their actual removal. Between these moments, the story, told in nonlinear form, details the year in America, the preceding stays in Germany and Israel, and the parents' earlier experiences in the Soviet Union. In *Abschiebung*, we already see the structure of narrative interweaving characteristic of Vertlib's entire work, a structure generated by the embedding of text fragments—here, from the narrator's diaries and his parents' reports. The deportation provides the frame story, one effect of which is that the motif of deportation seems to determine the family's present, past, and future life. This impression is further strengthened by the violent confrontation between the family and immigration officers shortly before the evacuation. It is also interesting that we see the narrator sleeping at the beginning of the story and then see him waking from a dream at the end. Although these are two different periods of sleeping—in the morning, the narrator momentarily falls asleep in the office of immigration, and in the evening, he awakes on the plane to London—this narrative construction calls into question everything that is told in between these instances, as if the family's past life and visions of the future were only a dream.

Thematically and structurally, the narrative is thus centered entirely around the failure of immigration and the moment of deportation. Nevertheless, the book leaves the reader with the impression that the narrator not only visits but also inhabits the new places he encounters. The clearest example of this is the office of immigration, a place the family regularly visits during their last months in the US. The very first sentences of the story address the waiting room of this office: "Da saßen wir nun im stickigen, etwas schäbigen, durch und durch verrauchten Warteraum. Aus dem Nebenraum drang das monotone Klappern zahlreicher Schreibmaschinen, deren von geübter Hand erzeugte Gleichmäßigkeit mich bald einschlummern ließ."[6] (There we sat, in the stuffy, somewhat shabby, thoroughly smoke-filled waiting room. The monotone clatter of a great number of typewriters penetrated from the next room, and the metronomic sound produced by practiced hands made me doze off.) A waiting room is always a transition space in which one only stops temporarily—and in this case, as the reader learns shortly, it is simultaneously an embodiment of bureaucratic despotism, unpredictability, and inhumanity. Nevertheless, our first impression is of the narrator's physical presence in this place. The narrator directs his attention to the concrete, physical details of his surroundings: the stuffy air, the shabby decor, the cigarette smoke. He takes these impressions in with all his senses. The clattering of typewriters that he hears apparently has a calming effect, since it is this sound that allows him to quickly fall asleep—and the expression "to doze off" specifically accents the almost homeyness of this place. The beginnings of the sentences—the deictic "there" and the adverbial phrase "from the next room"—give particular grammatical emphasis to the physical presence of the place. The literary description of this place becomes a form of imaginary claiming, which manifests itself in a familiarity with the building, as the narrator explicitly says in one passage (8), as well as in a particular intimacy with those working there, as shown by the erotic fantasies of the pubescent narrator. These fantasies revolve around an employee of the immigration office, whom he actually finds repulsive but whose repulsiveness he integrates into his fantasies.

Due to the embedded, nonlinear narrative style, the reader only later discovers what led to this familiarity—namely, a whole string of petitions to and hearings at the office of immigration, leading to a quasi-occupation of the office. Of central importance here is a scene described in the last third of the book. The family appears at the office of immigration's department of deportation with a firm demand: either to receive an immigration visa or be shunted off at public expense as quickly as possible because the parents have hardly any money left and do not want to work illegally. If necessary, the family even plans to go on a hunger strike to enforce their demand. The family initially sits down comfortably in the office in a manner tantamount to an occupation. In this scene, exclamations in direct speech and third-person plot descriptions alternate, giving the impression that these are consequences of each other, as if the protestations had a performative power and could anchor the characters to the spot: "'Ich rühre mich nicht vom Fleck!' sagte mein Vater.... Wir machten es uns im Wartesaal bequem. Mutter zog sogar die Schuhe aus und begann etwas zu nähen.... 'Wir bleiben jetzt da', ließ mein Vater durch mich übersetzen.... also blieben wir sitzen." (162–63; "I won't budge!" said my father.... We made ourselves comfortable in the waiting room. Mother even took off her shoes and began to sew something.... "We're staying here," my father had me translate.... so we stayed sitting.) Even when the family finally leaves the office under the increasing pressure of the authorities, the gesture of anchoring or place-making remains.

A very similar act of anchoring oneself to a place that actually forbids it occurs on the very day of the deportation—that is, at the moment the father protests the planned surrender of their passports to the British officials. He does this out of fear that the family's deportation will be recorded in England and that it will thus become impossible for them to ever settle there— and it should be noted here that one of the father's few positive visions of the future is of their immigration to a European country that does not speak German. What follows is an argument and a fistfight with the officials, and father and son are thrown in a holding cell. Here, looking at the rage-filled graffiti that other prisoners have inscribed on the walls of the cell, the narrator experiences a momentary feeling of solidarity with all the deported: "Die Texte spendeten Trost. Sie stellten ein unsichtbares Band her zwischen mir und denen, die vor mir drinnen waren und nach mir kommen sollten." (184; The texts offered consolation. They created an invisible bond between me and those who were here before and those who will come after me.) The narrator's addition of his own graffiti a little bit later is a further expression of protest that goes hand in hand with a claiming of the space. The narrator makes the walls of the cell his own, in the truest sense of the word, when he gives expression to his rage and frustration: "Es ist alles nicht wahr! . . . Du liegst am Strand, und all die Schweine, die dich umgeben, sind schon längst zu Wurst verarbeitet worden!" (184; None of it is true! . . . You're lying on a beach and all the pigs surrounding you have already been made into sausage!) These last two scenes, in the department of deportation and the holding cell, are better captured by the concept of *place-claiming* than by *place-making*. *To claim* has connotations of self-assertion, demanding, and protesting that are noticeable and likely even essential in the situations of extreme displacement and endangerment described in *Abschiebung*.

Way Stations: Vertlib's *Zwischenstationen*

If *Abschiebung* describes how people trying to immigrate seek to occupy precisely those places that embody their own powerlessness and vulnerability— namely, the office of immigration and the deportation holding cell—Vertlib's next book deals with the claiming of another kind of transition place, as the title signals in apodictic brevity: *Zwischenstationen*. Whereas the Russian Jewish family in *Abschiebung* moves entirely within the emigration triangle of

Israel, Germany, and the US, here the family makes additional stops on their trip through the West—namely, in Italy and the Netherlands. But these remain way stations in exactly the same way as the many transition places where the narrator and his parents stop: in the boundary spaces of buildings (corridors, waiting rooms), in transportation vehicles (trains, streetcars, elevators), and in spaces intended for travelers and those seeking help (hotels, the YMCA, Jewish charities). The rundown apartments the family inhabits lie mostly in decentralized areas like "Little Odessa" in New York; the "Kischlak" in Israel; Ostia in Italy; and an old apartment block in Vienna where Jewish emigrants wait for permission to return to the Soviet Union. As one critic aptly formulates, all these are "counter-places to the autochthonous ... ephemeral transit spaces in which a multitude of territorial significations are overlaid or only briefly intersect."[7] The narrator in *Zwischenstationen* describes the experience of spaces folding over each other—for example, of images recalled from Russia and Israel superimposing themselves over the image of his room in Vienna— in the following way: "die Welt war wie eine Anzahl von Schachteln aufgebaut, die ineinanderpaßten" (31; the world was built like a number of boxes that fit inside each other).

The novel *Zwischenstationen* evokes routes as defined by James Clifford and Barbara Mann: migration routes that are more or less fixed and on which others have already moved and thereby created places of residence.[8] Although the young narrator is dragged to a new country by his parents again and again—usually without knowing about it beforehand— he feels a certain familiarity in each place of residence, in some cases even something like security. Even in the US—which in *Abschiebung* is portrayed as a distinctly hostile country where the narrator has no right to stay anywhere—he now finds refuge in the public library, where he obtains a library card by means of a lie and the help of a well-meaning librarian. One condition for this lingering on migration routes is the conscious surrender of utopian hopes. At times, both the narrator, a teenager who loses himself in the world of ancient Greece, and the parents, who have sought an ideal country their entire lives, indulge in utopian images of a "Land des Glücks" (257; land of happiness). The narrator's father, in particular, conjures up such a country in detailed monologues and hours of reading maps. However, the narrator himself ultimately parts ways with such fantasies as his love for a schoolmate prompts him to return to the realities of Austria, his family's final place of residence. Overall, this novel, written from the perspective of a child and teenager, imparts a sense of place that is opposed to that of a utopia. As the narrator perceives each of the way stations where his family stops in all their concrete, physical details, his conscious lingering in places of transit replaces utopian wishful thinking.

An important means of emplacement involves the beginnings of chapters, which almost invariably situate the narrator firmly in a place. The abruptness and apodictic tone of the short introductory sentences serve to postulate the reality of these places. Stylistic techniques such as specific descriptions of places, highlighting minute details, and using definite articles for previously unknown objects and people reinforce this effect of reality setting, however strange and alienating this reality may be: "Die orangefarbenen italienischen Busse hatten ihre Auspuffe auf dem Dach" (132; The orange-colored Italian buses had their exhaust pipes on the roof) begins the first sentence of the chapter about Ostia. "Das Lamm hatte ein weißes Fell" (105; The lamb had a white fleece), the narrator begins the chapter about his second stay in Israel before adding a more precise description of the lamb: "Nur auf seiner Stirn war ein schwarzer Fleck etwa von der Größe einer Münze" (105; Only on its forehead, there was a black spot around the size of a coin). Many chapter beginnings in *Zwischenstationen* situate the narrator in scenes that are rich in physical details, imparting clear contours to the places and the people, animals, and objects found there. In other chapters, the use of the present tense helps immediately set the narrator in a specific scene in order to highlight his physical presence in that place. The first sentences of the chapter about the US begin this way: "An einem Augustmorgen des Jahres 1980 wache ich früh auf. Die Jalousien sind hochgezogen, und die Sonnenstrahlen blenden mich." (187; On one August morning in the year 1980, I wake up early. The curtains have been raised, and the sun's rays blind me.)

It is astonishing how often the beginnings of chapters produce a certain feeling of familiarity, despite—as we learn later—how much the narrator suffers from being dragged, once again, to a new country by his parents. Following the description of the lamb, for instance, is a description of how the narrator finds the lamb on the steps of his house, hugs it, and sticks his nose into its fleece. This charming scene is surprising in a chapter that not only reports the slaughter of that very lamb but also many other disturbing events, including a terrorist attack in Israel and a revenge campaign against an Arabic guard that consequently lands the narrator in the police station. Similarly, in the chapter about Amsterdam, which describes the family's increasingly hopeless efforts to get a work visa for a western European country, the city itself is initially described very positively:

> Es waren aber nicht nur die freundlichen Frauen, deren Brüste auf den Fenstersimsen ruhten, die mir diese Stadt sympathisch machten. Ich mochte das Wasser, die unzähligen Kanäle, auf denen viele Menschen ihr ganzes Leben lang in Hausbooten lebten, die sogar an das Stromnetz angeschlossen waren. Mir gefielen die schmalen Häuser mit ihren vornübergebeugten Fassaden, reichverzierten Giebeln und Zugbalken an den Dächern. (78–79)
>
> But it wasn't only the friendly women resting their breasts on the windowsills that made me like the city. I liked the water, the countless canals on which many people lived their whole lives in houseboats that were even connected to the power grid. I liked the narrow houses with their forward-slouching façades, richly-ornamented gables, and tie beams on the rooftops.

In other chapters, the first sentences describe an encounter with someone or someone's gesture that means something to the narrator, and these help him feel safe and in good hands. The second chapter starts like this: "Jemand zog mich am Ärmel. Ein kleiner Junge, etwa so alt wie ich, stand neben mir." (25; Someone tugged me on the sleeve. A young boy, about the same age as I, stood next to me.), with the verb *to stand* calling particular attention to the physical presence of the boy. As we learn later, this boy named Viktor is the narrator's best friend during his first stay in Israel. Initially, however, he just stands there. Right after that, the stasis of this scene is broken by the evocation of movement. Viktor had moved from Ukraine to Israel, and he now encourages the narrator to run away from preschool by leaping over the fence and escaping into the hills.

Scenes such as this indicate the dynamic understanding of space advanced by Doreen Massey, one of Barbara Mann's theoretical inspirations. Massey emphasizes that places are always social constructs. Places do not provide a clear framework for the social relations, interactions, and acts of claiming taking place there but rather emerge from them. A correlate of this view that human action constitutes places is a particular attention to their malleability and permeability. Massey may not explicitly name Yi-Fu Tuan's distinction between space and place—according to which space enables movement and place constitutes a pause in that movement—but she does express a very similar idea when she describes places as "particular *moments* constructed, laid down, interacted with one another, decayed and renewed."⁹ And because places are nodes in a network of social relations, they are always connected to other places, making them permeable to the experience of other places. This view allows for an "extroverted" feeling of place and a new understanding of the interplay between the local and the global. Massey calls upon the reader to imagine the world as if from a satellite and explains:

> If one moves in from the satellite towards the globe, holding all those networks of social relations and movements and communications in one's head, then each "place" can be seen as a particular, unique, point of their intersection. It is, indeed, a *meeting* place. Instead then, of thinking of places as areas with boundaries around, they can be imagined as articulated moments in networks of social relations and understandings, but where a large proportion of those relations, experiences and understandings are constructed on a far larger scale than what we happen to define for that moment as the place itself, whether that be a street, or a region or even a continent.¹⁰

This dynamic understanding of places also characterizes Vertlib's *Zwischenstationen*. What the narrator perceives as places are constituted first by movements, whether by the family's walks through Amsterdam, which make the city so familiar to him that he soon knows every corner of it, or by the movements in his head, where memories of places he already visited or visions of places he would like to visit superimpose themselves on the impressions of the present. It is further revealing that the places evoked at the beginnings of chapters are often related to transportation, like the train station in Saint Petersburg or the buses in Ostia, and that the teenage narrator is particularly engrossed by construction sites in Vienna (163). After all, at a construction site, a place is visibly transformed into something new: "Es faszinierte mich, wie die Stadt ihr Gesicht veränderte und wie die düsteren Mietskasernen der Kraft von Abbruchmaschinen weichen mußten" (163; It fascinated me how the city changed its face and how the gloomy tenement blocks had to give way to the power of demolition equipment). In *Zwischenstationen*, places crystallize as moments of standstill in the middle of constant change and movement. While the novel as a whole is about continuous displacement, the beginning of each chapter evokes, describes, or posits a new place.

As argued here, the apodictic chapter openings, the detailed description of spaces and gestures, and the use of short sentences and definite articles all help create a sense of place in *Zwischenstationen*, however precariously. The episodic structure of the novel—in which each chapter resembles a short story with a central motif, abrupt beginning, open ending, and climax or turning point—further enhances a sense of dwelling in transition places. In a different context, Brigid Haines notes that the spatial character of Vertlib's texts undermines the narrative closure conventional realism otherwise promises: "*Abschiedung* and *Zwischenstationen* are structured in terms of space rather than time, thus working against any sense of arrival which their endings might imply."[11] In my reading, the spatialization of narrative gives more weight to each of the places; it is part and parcel of a literary place-making in the diaspora. In what follows, I suggest that Julya Rabinowich's novel *Spaltkopf* deploys a very different style—one that is fragmentary, elliptical, and associative—to a similar effect: to create a sense of lingering in transit, of having not quite arrived in a new country.

Not Quite Arrival: Rabinowich's *Spaltkopf*

In her 2008 novel *Spaltkopf*, Julya Rabinowich represents migration as a traumatic event that permanently disrupts the migrant's life. This may very well reflect the historical circumstances of the 1970s, when prospective Soviet emigrants were subject to recriminations, often kept their plans secret from their children, and eventually settled in host countries that were far less than welcoming. It is also possible that Rabinowich, who had received training in psychotherapy, deliberately drew on psychoanalytic notions of trauma and repression to depict the identity formation of a migrant child. Mischka, the protagonist and narrator of *Spaltkopf*, finds herself suddenly and irrevocably uprooted at age seven, when her parents and grandmother take her, without prior announcement, from Leningrad to Vienna. Subsequently Mischka breaks off all contact with friends and family in the Soviet Union, rebels against her parents even more than the average adolescent, and assimilates to the culture around her to a point that she develops a hatred of ethnic minorities. Torn between an Austrian environment that requires her to adapt to a new language and culture and a Russian family that seeks to maintain its traditions, she develops a range of psychological and psychosomatic symptoms, including anxiety attacks, an eating disorder, and bouts of drug abuse. Her marriage to a gay man who wants her only as a cover for his homosexuality remains predictably unfulfilling. It is only when she gives birth to a daughter and, around age twenty-five, pays a visit to her former homeland that she begins to find some peace.

The term *trauma* adequately describes Mischka's experience because her behavior can be traced back to the secrecy, silence, and repression that shrouded many of her early formative experiences. Take Mischka's discovery of her Jewishness. After first arriving in Vienna, Mischka expresses her excitement about the West in letters to Schenya, her best friend and childhood crush in Russia, whom she lost so abruptly and now misses intensely: "Er fehlt mir, als ob jemand ein großes Stück aus meinem Körper gebissen hätte, und ich halte diese erste Wunde zu, stopfe die hervorgellenden Erinnerungen zurück."[12] (I miss him, as if someone had bitten off a large piece of my body, and I hold this first wound together, staunching the flow of memories.) We learn that these memories are from scenes in Russia that Mischka could not fully comprehend at the time: Why did Schenya's father stare at her so disapprovingly after she and Schenya had a wonderful time dancing at a New Year's Eve party? Why did Schenya a short time later cancel their plans to go to the cinema with the explanation, "Ich darf nicht mit Juden spielen" (61/58; I'm not allowed to play with Jews)? It turns out that Mischka neither knows what a Jew is nor that she herself is one, and when her mother informs her about that fact, her mother ends up concealing more than she reveals. At this point a second narrative voice tells us that Schenya's father is an obedient party member and his mother is eager to prove her ideological conformity, so we can infer that by avoiding Jews such as Mischka, they pay tribute to Soviet antisemitism. Young Mischka, however, remains unaware of these implications of the word *Jew*: "*Noch kann das Kind keine Verbindung zwischen diesem seltsamen Wort und den seltsamen Erlebnissen herstellen, die es schon gesammelt hat, und die Großen wollen die ihren nicht mit ihm teilen.*" (62/60, emphasis in original; *The child still cannot connect the strange word to the strange experiences she has already had, and the adults will not share theirs with her.*) It is through her writing that she belatedly establishes these connections and renders them meaningful.

Spaltkopf not only depicts traumatic losses but also mimes the disjunctive rhythm of traumatic memory. It is an experimental work that consists mostly of brief scenes and memory fragments and proceeds via ellipses, associations, flashbacks, prolepses, and different modes of speech.[13] One effect of this disjointed style is the *Nachträglichkeit*, or deferred understanding, that ever since Freud has been seen as a defining feature of trauma. For example, the novel begins with a prologue consisting of four brief *Lektionen* (lessons), of which individual sentences are later repeated and elaborated, so that the reader initially glimpses an idea and gradually adds new facets of understanding. The novel's most conspicuous stylistic device, the use of a second narrative voice, has a similar effect of deferred understanding. Interspersed with Mischka's first-person narrative are cursive passages that comment upon the family's life from a different perspective. These passages are initially very difficult to understand both because they relate events without context and because we do not know who is speaking. Only gradually do we learn that the speaker is the eponymous *Spaltkopf*, or splitting head, an imaginary figure who has access to everything the family relegates to silence. This strand of the narrative focuses on the story of Mischka's maternal grandmother, who, as a young child, witnessed the killing of her father in a pogrom and subsequently numbed all her emotions and denied her Jewish heritage—among other things, she changed her name from Rahel Israilowna to Ada Igorowna. The sentence fragment "*Igor. Nicht Israil*" (*Igor. Not Israil*) runs like a leitmotif through the passages spoken by the *Spaltkopf*. The *Spaltkopf*, then, is a figure of traumatic dissociation by which the grandmother splits off important parts of her experience, memory, and identity.

If *Spaltkopf* is a trauma narrative, it is also story of transformation and—to some extent—arrival. Toward the end of the novel, there are signs that Mischka is healing from the wounds she suffered when she was abruptly taken from her place of origin. She revels at the sight of her young daughter, who has grown the roots and senses the firm ground under her feet Mischka herself has been missing (180/189). Mischka also recently found an apartment in Vienna and hopes this will help her confront her childhood anew and cure her "Spiegelsucht" (183/192; craving for mirrors). And now that the Iron Curtain has fallen, she decides to visit Leningrad, once again called Saint Petersburg, where she is able to face the *Spaltkopf* head-on and overcome her trauma-induced narcissism. In an act of inner liberation, she destroys the *Spaltkopf* by directly looking at its appearance in a reflective window glass, which in turn renders her capable of taking in the plain view of the houses around her: "Ich nähere mich [dem Spaltkopf] vorsichtig, bis Nase und Stirn die kühle Scheibe berühren und ich durch ihn in die St. Petersburger Hinterhöfe tauche und nur noch die Häuser ringsum zu sehen sind." (203/212; I approach him [the Splithead] carefully, until my nose and forehead touch the cool glass. I dive through him into the courtyards of St Petersburg. I no longer see anything but the surrounding houses.) This sentence, the closing sentence of the book, suggests that the return to the childhood home is a form of working through, that returning to Saint Petersburg will enable Mischka to truly arrive in Vienna at some point in the future.

The novel's prologue already gestures at this possibility of arrival. The four rather cryptic "lessons" that make up the prologue reenact Mischka's various travels—a journey from Ireland to Scotland, her family's migration from Leningrad to Vienna, her father's trip back to Russia, and an excursion to France—before culminating in a peculiar scene of arrival:

> Wenn ich die Wahl zwischen zwei Stühlen habe, nehme ich das Nagelbrett.
> Ich bin müde.
> Ich bin nicht daheim.
> Ich bin angekommen. (12)
>
> Faced with a choice between two chairs, I take the bed of nails.
> I am tired.
> I'm not home.
> I have arrived. (7, trans. changed)

What do we make of these last lines of the prologue, which cast arrival as the opposite of being home? In an interview, Rabinowich diminishes the jarring effect of this opposition by explaining the difference as follows: *ankommen* means that one has become fully familiar with a place and can participate in its society while remaining in a state of heightened (self-)consciousness; in contrast, *daheim sein* signifies a state of belonging that feels so natural that it can be completely unconscious.[14] While this distinction is useful, I maintain that the terse, provocative formulation in the prologue changes the meaning of arrival in a more radical fashion than Rabinowich suggests in the interview. The prologue of *Spaltkopf* fragments and condenses the event of arrival in such a way that *ankommen* comes to signify a state of uncertainty, exhaustion, and in-betweenness. When the phrase "I have arrived" reappears toward the end of *Spaltkopf*, it captures a brief moment of recognition at the Saint Petersburg airport: after landing, Mischka hears an aunt joyfully exclaim her name and thinks to herself "Ich bin angekommen" (185/194), fully aware of the transience of the moment and the fact that her stay in Russia will be just another stopover on the journey that is her life. Furthermore, the airport on which she conceives this thought is a quintessential transit zone, so that the verb *to arrive* comes to signify the ability to inhabit a transition place for a limited time.

The overall effect of the "I have arrived" in the prologue's last line is one of suspension rather than irony. Rather than invert the meaning of arrival,

Spaltkopf renders it ambiguous, polyvalent, and open ended. There is a tension between the emphatic positioning of the phrase "I have arrived" in the prologue—as the last line, it is the lesson to be taken away from the book—and the disappearance of its connotations of finality, completeness, and purposiveness over the course of the book. In the end, the statement "I have arrived" becomes a mark of pure possibility, devoid of concrete content. In the next chapter, I analyze several arrival stories by post-Soviet Jewish migrants that are similarly open ended and that are structured around emphatic scenes of arrival while redefining what it means to arrive somewhere. For the moment, I want to hold on to the insight that in *Spaltkopf*, arrival signifies yet another form of lingering in transit. In what follows, I suggest that this lingering in transit gives rise to new comparative perspectives in Vertlib's and Rabinowich's subsequent works. Both authors have continued to write about different forms of flight and migration—most recently, about experiences related to the so-called refugee crisis in Europe.

Comparing Migrations? Vertlib and Rabinowich on the "Refugee Crisis"

In the past few years, Vertlib and Rabinowich have intervened in the debates around the European refugee crisis through their literary writing as well as through their civic and professional engagement. Rabinowich has worked for several years as an interpreter in therapy sessions with traumatized refugee children, and Vertlib has volunteered in a transit camp for refugees near the Austrian city of Salzburg. These experiences have inspired at least two of their recent works—Rabinowich's 2016 young adult novel *Dazwischen: Ich* (In-between: I) and Vertlib's 2018 novel *Viktor hilft*—which, as I show here, offer two paradigmatic ways of comparing historically and geographically different forms of migration. Rabinowich's *Dazwischen: Ich* adopts the perspective of a refugee girl, whose specific cultural background and social experience remain oddly vague, to represent migration as a universal experience with which everybody can empathize. In contrast, Vertlib's *Viktor hilft* invokes the figure of the enigmatic young migrant to call into question the possibility of empathy across cultural, religious, and experiential boundaries.

In *Dazwischen: Ich*, Rabinowich draws on the generic conventions of young adult fiction, which tends to focus on universal problems such as first love, family issues, and struggles with authority, to render the experience of trauma and migration relatable. The novel is written from the perspective of Madina, a fifteen-year-old Muslim girl who witnessed the killing of her best friend in a bombing attack and later fled with her family from her war-stricken home country, which remains unnamed. Her story is not so different from the one Rabinowich told earlier in *Spaltkopf*—it is the story of a refugee who is able to inhabit places of transit and dwell in the in-between. The family currently lives in a refugee shelter, but Madina looks forward to the new apartment where they plan to live after receiving asylum. She serves as her family's translator with school and government administrations and as a cultural mediator. While her parents fear the loss of their traditions, Madina envisions a future in the new country and begins to question traditional customs such as the preferential treatment of boys.

A major factor in Madina's ability to adjust to the new country is her friendship with her classmate Laura. This friendship seems to be based on the "Geheimnisse" (secrets) both girls harbor—certain traumatic, incomprehensible, shame-inducing experiences they are reluctant to share with others.[15] In Laura's case, it is the circumstance under which her father left the family (he once injured her mother in a violent fit) that ostracized her in the past and now enables her to establish a bond with Madina the refugee. In Madina's case, these "secrets" include the story of her enigmatic and reclusive aunt Amina, who had married against the will of her family and whose husband was murdered during the war. Amina holds Madina's father responsible for her sufferings and seeks to avenge herself through all sorts of meanness. She is both a victim and a perpetrator, just as Madina's father, a professional nurse who treated the wounded of both sides during the war, might indeed be guilty of bigotry and betrayal. Interestingly, Amina's husband was named Amir, which is a multilingual and multinational name that derives either from the Arabic word for "prince" or from the Hebrew word for "treetop," suggesting that Amina's marriage might have crossed religious lines. Madina grasps the significance of Amina's story, which reveals the rifts within the family and confounds the line between friends and enemies, without getting to the bottom of it. *Dazwischen: Ich* suggests that such unspoken family secrets are the foundation of a friendship across ethnic, cultural, and religious boundaries.

The novel's conspicuous lack of cultural, historical, and geographical references can be read as an attempt to foster such transcultural empathy on a different level—namely, by communicating the experience of flight and migration to readers from a variety of backgrounds. In the absence of place names, the reader neither knows where Madina came from nor exactly where she is now. This ignorance reflects Madina's own lack of understanding of the political situation in her home country. She recalls overhearing conversations in her hometown—"Sie nannten Namen von Ländern, die ich nicht kannte" (94; They mentioned the names of countries I did not know)—and remembers social conflicts in similarly vague terms: suddenly there were odd rifts between people, some neighbors were no longer greeting her, and others began to disappear. The inward turn toward the end of the book, in which Madina imaginarily traverses a forest, reaches the sea, and embarks on a ship, further deterritorializes her story, as do the allusions to fairytales at the very beginning: "Ich komme von Überall. Ich komme von Nirgendwo. Hinter den sieben Bergen. Und noch viel weiter. Dort, wo Ali Babas Räuber nicht hätten leben wollen. Jetzt nicht mehr. Zu gefährlich." (7; I come from Everywhere. I come from Nowhere. From behind the seven mountains. And even further away. There, where Ali Baba's thieves would not have wanted to live. Not anymore. Too dangerous.)

What *Dazwischen: Ich* depicts on the level of the plot—a cross-cultural friendship based on family secrets that are never fully explained—is reinforced through its narrative style and reader engagement. By bracketing the cultural and geographical specificity of migration, Rabinowich invites readers from different backgrounds to empathize with a refugee child. In contrast, Vertlib invokes the figure of the refugee child to a different end—namely, to mark the limits of transcultural empathy. In his 2018 novel *Viktor hilft*, he once again draws on his own experiences with migration, both as a child immigrant in Vienna and as an adult volunteer in a refugee camp, to call into question the idea that we can fully understand the experience of others.[16] The novel is prefaced by a poem titled "Die Grenze" (The border), which depicts the impossibility of truly knowing other people: "Aber ich kenne / die Anderen nur so / wie man ein Haus kennt / an dessen Toren man vorübergeht / das Leben ahnend / aber nicht begreifend // Die Worte / reichen wir uns / wie Schüssel / Sie passen nicht / und schließen nichts auf."[17] (But I know / The others only the way / One knows a house / The gates of which you pass by / intuiting its life / without comprehending // We hand each other / Words / Like keys / They do not fit / And unlock nothing.) The author of this poem, Tamar Radzyner, was a Polish Jewish poet who survived Auschwitz and migrated with her family to Vienna in 1959 to escape Polish antisemitism. Her similes of others as closed houses and of words as ill-fitting keys return several times in Vertlib's text, casting doubt on Viktor's ability to alleviate the plight of Middle Eastern and African refugees in the transit camp, where he helps them cross the border from Austria to Germany. Even the first pages of the novel, which alternate between the perspectives of Viktor the child and Viktor the adult, suggest that the memories of his own arrival in Vienna do not help him access the inner life of a refugee child to whom he offers treats. His perspective remains purely external when he observes "wie die Wangen und Ohrenspitzen des Kindes rot anliefen" (9; how the child's cheeks and ears turned red).

Throughout *Viktor hilft*, child and teenage migrants come to embody the limits of transcultural empathy. The most important of these is the South Sudanese teenager Arok, an illiterate who speaks only his native language and a few phrases of English and Arabic and is therefore even more isolated than the other refugees. Viktor first provides him with clothes in the transit camp near Salzburg and later meets him again in a refugee shelter in Germany, where Arok's face brightens as he points to the coat he earlier received from Viktor. He gives Viktor a seashell, apparently out of gratitude, and begins to speak in his native language, but at this point, Viktor quickly goes away (203). At the end of the novel, Arok tries to take his own life by jumping from the roof of a newly built home for asylum seekers that burnt down during a right-wing demonstration. He survives, but rather than rush to help, Viktor once again realizes his own limitations:

> Erst jetzt löst sich Viktors Gliederstarre. Er überlegt kurz, ob er den Sanitätern folgen und sagen soll, dass er Arok kennt. Er könnte ihn in die Arme nehmen, könnte ihm gut zureden, könnte seinen warmen Wintermantel ausziehen und dem jungen Mann über die Schultern legen. Er könnte . . . Aber er kann nicht. (282)
>
> Only now the stiffness of Viktor's limbs passes. He briefly considers whether he should follow the paramedics and tell them that he knows Arok. He could take him into his arms, could encourage him, could take off his warm winter coat and place it around the young man's shoulders. He could . . . But he cannot.

In the end, Viktor's encounters with lonesome young migrants are an ironic refutation of the novel's title—*Viktor hilft*—by showing that Viktor can*not* do much to help them. This is not to say that people of different migratory backgrounds simply cannot understand or help each other in the novel. Rather, transcultural empathy emerges as a possibility in a protracted and nonreciprocal communication that requires an awareness of boundaries. Arok's seashell continues to sit on Viktor's desk, reminding him of the night in the Austrian transit camp when he first met Arok and, for a host of reasons, experienced intense feelings of shame and self-doubt. Yet rather than initiate a dialogue with Arok, the encounter ushers in a different kind of verbal exchange, one in which the boundaries between the speakers get increasingly blurred, namely between Viktor and the poet Tamar Radzyner. For the similes of the locked house and the ill-fitting word-keys from Radzyner's poem "Die Grenze" are resurfacing in this scene, not as citations but as thought fragments that are coursing through the head of Viktor, who is unsure about their origins. Viktor also subsequently uses the image of the keyless house in an autobiographical presentation at a cultural festival where he is expected to model successful integration, an instrumentalization of the migrant's experience that he evidently attempts to forestall with the image of the locked house (217). But again, this is a very different kind of cross-cultural exchange than that described and performed in Rabinowich.

These recent works of Vertlib and Rabinowich, then, offer two paradigmatic modes of comparing historically different forms of migration. In Rabinowich, the adoption of the child refugee's perspective and the reduction of cultural and geographical specificity work to universalize the experience of flight and migration. In Vertlib, the image of the other as a locked house and the inability of the Russian Jewish protagonist to access the African migrant's interiority tell a more cautionary tale about the possibility of transcultural empathy. Yet both writers engage in acts of comparison. Their reflection on the European refugee crisis is a logical continuation of the overall trajectory of their literary work, which began with depictions of their own migration experience, refracted through that of the quota refugees in Germany. I suggest that this expanding circle of concern around the core experience of migration owes much to the narrators' ability to dwell in the in-between and inhabit places of transit. If nationalist movements tend to erase histories of migration, the diasporic place-making in Vertlib and Rabinowich achieves the opposite: their fixation on states and places of transition keeps the memories of migration alive and connects them to the concerns of the present.[18]

7

ARRIVING

Arrival Stories in Lena Gorelik, Dmitrij Kapitelman, and Jan Himmelfarb

"MIGRATION IS A ONE WAY TRIP. THERE IS NO 'home' to go back to. There never was."[1] Thus writes Stuart Hall, the great postcolonial scholar who at age nineteen moved from Jamaica to Britain to become a diasporic intellectual, in a brief essay titled "Minimal Selves." He goes on to explain that one cannot be in transition forever: "The instant one learns to be 'an immigrant,' one recognizes one can't be an immigrant any longer: it isn't a tenable place to be."[2] According to Hall, migration entails an arrival, yet one that remains uncertain and ushers in a search for new identities. In his case, migration to Britain resulted in the discovery of his blackness, which he had rarely considered in Jamaica but now made a focal point of his political identity. In this chapter, I probe Hall's insight that migration means first and foremost to arrive somewhere for a group of contemporary German Jewish authors who share a biographical background as well as a publication history. Lena Gorelik, Dmitrij Kapitelman, and Jan Himmelfarb all migrated from Russia or Ukraine to Germany under the provisions of the German law for Jewish *Kontingentflüchtlinge*, or quota refugees, when they were children. They were thus part of a unique form of mass migration: relatively short lived, actively promoted by the German state, and transformative on many levels. As young adults, they debuted with what I term *arrival stories* that draw on their own migration experiences and delineate new possibilities: of linguistic mastery, the capacity for citizenship, or historical remembrance.

As Franziska Becker has shown, *arrival* is a complex political metaphor for migration processes. In official discourses, it is usually associated with a linear model of migration, according to which migrants shed their old identity and adopt a new one, and with a political imperative—namely, that migrants *should* do everything in their means to integrate into their new country as quickly and seamlessly as possible. The migrants themselves tend to use the term more vaguely to express a sense of stability and being at home.[3] As for the quota refugees, contemporary social scientists often take their arrival to be an accomplished fact—which is true in the sense that the post-Soviet Jewish migration to Germany came more or less to a halt after the introduction of Germany's new immigration act in 2005. In a recent snapshot of the contemporary German Jewish diaspora, Dmitrij Belkin emphasizes that the young adults who left the Soviet Union as children are nowadays postmigrants who no longer consider themselves quota refugees.[4] And in his 2018 *Desintegriert euch!*, Max Czollek mentions the quota refugees mainly to articulate his ideas about the concepts of integration and de-integration. Whereas *integration* is based on a myth of a homogenous national culture and a false dichotomy between natives and newcomers—the latter of which are expected to integrate into society—*de-integration* recognizes society itself as a site of constant change and radical diversity. According to Czollek, the recent migration from Eastern Europe has strengthened and diversified the Jewish population in Germany to a point that de-integration can indeed supplant integration.[5] One might say that, in his view, the post-Soviet migrants have indeed arrived and are now changing our conception of what it means to belong to a culture, a society, or a body politic. But if the post-Soviet migration has by now come to an end, why are arrival stories still such a popular genre among contemporary German Jewish authors from the former Soviet Union?

The three literary debuts discussed in this chapter appeared between 2004 and 2016, and they are all structured around the arrival of a protagonist of East European origin in postreunification Germany. As noted in previous chapters, other contemporary German Jewish authors also invoke *arrival* as an end point of migration—yet one that is tentative, dubious, or impossible to reach. In Barbara Honigmann's *Chronik einer Straße*, the narrator emphasizes the process of arrival by dubbing the street in which she and many other immigrants live the "street of arriving." Vladimir Vertlib's *Abschiebung* concludes with an image of the Russian Jewish family in an airplane on approach to London's airport, a mere stopover on the way to Germany; *Zwischenstationen* ends on the immigrant narrator's arrival in Salzburg, where he performs an ironic gesture of belonging: he buys himself a Tyrolian hat.[6] Finally, Julya Rabinowich's *Spaltkopf* features the line "I have arrived" in prominent places while stripping arrival of its connotations of finality and purposiveness.

In comparison to these complex and twisted tales, the arrival stories discussed in this chapter seem rather straightforward, programmatic, even declarative—especially those by Gorelik and Kapitelman. In Gorelik's *Meine weißen Nächte* (2004; My white nights), the narrator recounts her family's move from Saint Petersburg to Germany up to the point when they move into an apartment of their own and the narrator becomes fluent in German. In Kapitelman's *Das Lächeln meines unsichtbaren Vaters* (2016; The smile of my invisible father), the narrator, a *Kontingentflüchtling* with a Ukrainian passport, takes his father on a trip to Israel in the hopes of bringing out the father's suppressed Jewishness. But what actually happens is a profound change in the narrator himself, as he in the end embraces his German Jewish identity and decides to apply for German citizenship. Jan Himmelfarb's *Sterndeutung* (2015; Stargazing) complicates such clear and linear narratives as its story of a refugee family's economic success and social integration is interrupted by Holocaust memories that are haunting its protagonist. Yet *Sterndeutung*, too, culminates in a scene of arrival as the narrator embraces an idea of home defined as nearness to friends and family.

In analyzing these three works by post-Soviet German Jewish writers, I make two kinds of arguments. First, I suggest that the arrival story is a genre with distinct features. The etymology of the word is a good starting point. The English verb *to arrive* comes from Old French *ariver*, "to come to land," and from Latin *ad ripam*, "to the shore," and its original meaning was coming to shore after a (lengthy) sea voyage. Although the German word *ankommen* does not have the same connotations of a passage through water, it still conjures the image of an extended journey that precedes the moment of arrival. Arrival stories highlight this process character by depicting not so much the destination but the way toward it. In so doing they unfold additional layers of meaning of the word, such as the duality between outer movement and inner transformation. "I have arrived" can mean that I have reached a place and/or that I have attained a goal; it can imply destinations ranging from "my train has reached the final stop" to "I have found my purpose in life."[7] *To arrive* can also signal different degrees of finality, referring either to the moment someone first comes to a place or to the moment they have reached a final destination. The works discussed in this chapter unfold these dualities by splitting the process of coming to Germany into two arrivals: the migrants' initial arrival in the country, which typically lands them in a refugee shelter, and their true arrival—the moment they find a home, a vocation, or another sense of purpose. However, the duality of meanings persists, with the first calling into question the second: it is always possible that the place of "true arrival" is just another stopover on the way. The literary texts by Gorelik, Kapitelman, and Himmelfarb give expression to the peculiar open-endedness of arrival, thereby wresting the term away from official discourses that define migration as a linear process culminating in integration.

Second, I explore not only what the texts say—their tales of a protracted and uncertain arrival—but also what they do, the ways in which they create new modes of political belonging and cultural participation. Thus understood, the arrival story is another kind of founding gesture, a way of claiming a place in literature. Significantly, the works discussed in this chapter are all literary debuts, as were two of the works analyzed in the previous chapter, Vertlib's *Abschiebung* and Rabinowich's *Spaltkopf*. As such, they serve to establish their authors on the literary market or, to use Pierre Bourdieu's terminology, position them in the literary field.[8] A thematic concern with migration can help this positioning since it bestows on the author a certain symbolic capital, especially if he or she is also paratextually identified as a migrant, as is the case in all these books. Although they include a range of fiction signals, their jacket copies all mention the author's own migration background, with the implication that he or she can write about the topic representatively and authoritatively. But, of course, the label "migrant author" can just as easily serve to categorize and marginalize a literary work. Contemporary German Jewish writers are acutely aware of this possibility and frequently criticize the process of labeling. Thus, Rabinowich rejects the label altogether: "Migrant literature is the literature from the outside and it is defined, in my opinion, as the literature of the original defects, subsequently fortified by compensations. No literature, per se."[9] In what follows, I begin my argument by reading Lena Gorelik's *Meine weißen Nächte* as an attempt to counter such marginalization with the story of a migrant writer who has always already arrived, a story that seems to be shouting: "I am here!"

Arriving in Language: Lena Gorelik's *Meine weißen Nächte*

First published in 2004, Lena Gorelik's *Meine weißen Nächte* has been called a "quintessential immigrant success story," and for good reason.[10] The novel illustrates the seamless integration of a family of *Kontingentflüchtlinge* into the fabric of Germany society as they obtain paid work, a proper place to live, and, above all, proficiency in the German language. The text shuttles back and forth between the past—the family's life in the Soviet Union and their arrival in Germany—and the present—mostly the romantic dilemmas of the grown-up protagonist and narrator, Anja Buchmann. At age eleven Anja moved from Saint Petersburg to Germany, where her family initially stayed in a refugee shelter in Ludwigsburg. In a rather lighthearted manner, she relates their first experiences in Germany, from their fascination with Western consumer goods to their difficulties with German classmates, teachers, even a dentist. This strand of the narrative culminates in an emphatic scene of arrival as the family moves from the refugee shelter to a four-room apartment. Anja recounts the signs of successful integration: the parents have found work, the grandmother calls Germany her home, and Anja herself speaks an accent-free German and is comfortable enough to invite her classmates over.[11] Interspersed memories from the Soviet Union— for example, of the endless queues in front of stores—in retrospect further justify the family's decision to immigrate. And so does the other strand of the narrative, which is concerned with the present. Anja now studies in Munich, where she spends much time with her German boyfriend, Jan, and her best friend, Lara. Complications arise when her first love, the Russian Jewish immigrant Ilja, reappears in her life and still exudes an irresistible attraction for her. Anja is tempted to rekindle the relationship, especially when Ilja takes her on a trip to Paris, the proverbial city of love. However, in the end she chooses the rather unromantic and conventional Jan over flamboyant and adventurous Ilja, an amorous choice that appears to reaffirm her decision to become German.

  Meine weißen Nächte is unmistakably a work of middlebrow literature. Its literary style is fairly conventional, the narration moves smoothly from the narrator's voice to direct speech and back, and even the jumps between past and present pose no real challenge to the reader. The novel humorously comments upon intercultural differences. Like Gorelik's subsequent works, it has been very successful on the German book market—in fact, Gorelik has sometimes been called the female Wladimir Kaminer. As other scholars have noted, *Meine weißen Nächte* advances rather stereotypical ideas of Germanness and Russianness. Even though Anja seeks to rebuke German stereotypes of Russians as drunkards, for example, she also deploys such stereotypes strategically in her flirtation with an attractive German man whom she offers a Russian vodka-lemon. One critic speculated that a similar duplicity characterizes the writing of Gorelik, who "in her fiction . . . aims to undermine German clichés about Russians, yet also manages to exploit them as a selling point for her books."[12] Indeed, the novel pits noisy Russians against subdued Germans, obtrusive Russian mothers against distanced German mothers, and Russian interest in high culture against German ignorance of canonical authors. One effect of this dichotomous construction is that antisemitism appears to be a Russian problem alone. Anja's father, who is initially against immigration to Germany, changes his mind when he is the victim of an antisemitic attack in a Russian train. After the immigration, no mention is made of antisemitism, as if it fell squarely onto the Russian and not the German side. Another effect of the novel's either/or logic is the reification and commodification of cultural difference. Throughout the book Anja transforms her Russianness into tangible and consumable things, such as a vodka-lemon drink or a potato salad. Significantly, the book ends with a recipe for the Russian potato salad Anja just prepared for Jan to show him her love and her wish to continue the relationship. The reproduction of the recipe on one of the last pages of the book extends Anja's conciliatory gesture to the readers of the novel, inviting them to consume the story of the Russian-born author in the same way that Jan enjoys the meal made by his Russian-born girlfriend. The recipe functions as a paratext that sets the stage for the reception of the literary text.

But beyond this tendency toward stereotyping and commodification, what does *Meine weißen Nächte* accomplish, what new modes of belonging and participation does it create? The novel's cultural work becomes more obvious, I argue, when we read it alongside Gorelik's essays, many of which are collected in a volume entitled *"Sie können aber gut Deutsch!"* ("But your German is so good!"). The collection offers a critique of the integration paradigm that still dominates contemporary German debates about migration. Although it is often forgotten in these debates, Gorelik reminds us that Germany has long been an ethnically mixed society, an *Einwanderungsland* with a high degree of cultural, religious, and economic diversity—a fact we should celebrate as a source of strength and vitality. To support this argument, in her essays Gorelik deploys a rhetoric of arrival by which she claims Germany as the country to which she and other migrants naturally and rightfully belong. In so many ways, she expresses her sense of being here, of partaking (she repeatedly uses the word *Teilhabe*): Munich is her home, Germany her country; the migrants do not come here, they simply live here; and so on.[13] In fact, Gorelik rejects the term *migrant* altogether because its connotations of constant wandering do not fit someone who has arrived and intends to stay put: "Schließt dieser Begriff nicht schon von vorneherein aus, dass ich auch bleiben könnte, bleiben möchte, *angekommen bin*? Ich bin gewandert, das stimmt. Ich bin nach Deutschland ausgewandert, um hierzubleiben. Jetzt wandere ich nicht mehr herum, ich finde es hier schön."[14] (Doesn't this term automatically rule out the fact that I could also stay, that I want to stay, that I *have arrived*? I roamed, that's true. I emigrated to Germany in order to stay here. I'm no longer roaming around, I think it's nice here.) *Meine weißen Nächte* is a literary staging of this position and, as such, is politically productive. The nonchalant tone of the novel and its overall message—"I am here"—are politically expedient at a time when migrant or postmigrant writers find themselves easily categorized and marginalized. With her literary works, and especially with the emphatic scenes of arrival in her literary debut, Gorelik contributed to the emergence of a sizable, diverse, and confident group of self-identified Jews in Germany. (Although Jewishness is not the focus of *Meine weißen Nächte*, where it appears to be simply a more extreme form of Russianness, the Jewish perspective becomes more central in some of Gorelik's subsequent works.)

Furthermore, *Meine weißen Nächte* contains moments of literary self-reflection that complicate its project of arrival through language, demonstrating that this project is still incomplete and that the book's publication is part and parcel of it. Perhaps the most important of these moments is the reappearance of the book's title within the novel in a scene that links *Meine weißen Nächte* to young Anja's first literary endeavor. A turning point in Anja's German school career occurs when a supportive elementary teacher encourages her to write a story about her hometown, Saint Petersburg, and found a writers' club. Three German classmates immediately join the club and become her best friends, and the newly minted "Shriftstela" (229; "awther," meaning "author"; the German word is misspelled) Anja is no longer afraid of school. The fact that Anja's first story bears the same title as Gorelik's first novel—*Meine weißen Nächte*—suggests that the novel, too, is a means rather than an end of arrival. Its publication helped Gorelik claim a place in contemporary German literature, just as the original story helped Anja gain social standing in her class. The title also has additional associations that remind us of the tension between commodification and subversion in Gorelik's representation of Russianness. On the one hand, the book title invokes Saint Petersburg's famous "white nights" (i.e., the nearly round-the-clock daylight during the summer months) and the city's reputation as an attractive tourist destination, as Gorelik, who in 2008 published a travel memoir of Saint Petersburg that can also serve as a travel guide, must have been well aware. On the other hand, the title contains an intertextual allusion to Russian author

Fyodor Dostoevsky that potentially complicates the allegorical reading of Anja's love relationships. Among other things, the young woman in Dostoevsky's novella *White Nights* decides to return to her unreliable fiancé rather than stay with the young man (the narrator) who is truly devoted to her, a decision that calls into question Anja's own amorous choices.

Even more important, Gorelik's *Meine weißen Nächte* offers yet another account of its own origins, one that suggests a different motif of writing than the empowerment the teacher has in mind when he invites young Anja to write about her hometown. In the book, one of young Anja's first steps toward linguistic proficiency is the *shame* she feels when she realizes, for the very first time, that she just made a grammatical mistake in German (173). That shame seems to have stayed with her. Toward the beginning of the book, we learn that as much as she likes to flaunt her Russianness, she avoids the subject of the refugee shelter, even in conversations with her best friend: "Das Wohnheim führt zu unangenehmen Fragen. Es setzt mich ab, macht mich von einer russischen Exotin zu einem Fremdkörper, weil doch Wohnheim—und dann auch noch ein Asylantenwohnheim—na ja, schon komisch ist." (18; The residential home leads to uncomfortable questions. It sets me apart, changes me from an exotic Russian woman into a foreign body, because a residential home—and a residential home for asylum-seekers at that—is, after all, really quite strange.) The novel itself, then, can be construed as a response to such unpleasant questions, a reluctantly given account of Anja's first eighteen months in Germany, perhaps an attempt to overcome shame. In *Meine weißen Nächte*, the story of a migrant's empowerment through language and writing is not a triumphant one—the reader is unlikely to forget Anja's first experiences of linguistic uncertainty and shame—but it is nonetheless assertive. This kind of literary proclamation, the novel's emphatic "I am here," has been an important element in the remaking of German Jewish identity in the wake of the post-Soviet migration.

Arriving in Citizenship: Dmitrij Kapitelman's *Das Lächeln meines unsichtbaren Vaters*

Dmitrij Kapitelman's 2016 *Das Lächeln meines unsichtbaren Vaters* is another programmatic work that describes the successful arrival of a *Kontingentflüchtling* in Germany. In contrast to Gorelik, however, Kapitelman defines arrival in terms of citizenship rather than linguistic proficiency and expressivity. *Das Lächeln meines unsichtbaren Vaters* tells the story of a son who invites his father on a journey to Israel because he wants him to become more outspokenly Jewish. In Israel, the father, a secular Jew who never felt at home anywhere—neither in the Ukraine, where he suffered antisemitism, nor in Germany, where he is constantly reminded of the Holocaust—engages in ritual actions such as wearing a kippah and praying at the wailing wall. But in the end, it is the son (and the narrator of the book) who undergoes the more profound transformation. While the father goes back into hiding as soon as they return to Germany, the son, who initially feels "nirgendwo zu Hause" (nowhere at home), decides to apply for a German passport under a Jewish name.[15]

Das Lächeln meines unsichtbaren Vaters bears out Sander Gilman's observation that in works by post-Soviet Jewish migrants, the characters are becoming Jewish by becoming German.[16] During his trip to Israel, the narrator's sense of Jewish identity and his desire for German citizenship develop simultaneously, or at least in close succession. There are several reasons why the trip is so transformative. Toward the beginning of the journey, the narrator feels a discomfort with Israeli nationalism—in fact, with any form of nationalism—in a way that strikes him as typically German (93). But then he gradually begins to feel at home in Israel, especially while walking over the Carmel Market in Tel Aviv, where the vibrant multiculturalism compares favorably to the apartment complex in Leipzig-Grünau where he grew up in constant fear of neo-Nazis (115–18). A turning point occurs when the narrator visits the Diaspora Museum in Tel Aviv and learns that under Israel's Law of Return, he is considered Jewish and entitled to Israeli citizenship even though his mother is not Jewish. The sentence he hears from a museum employee—"Sie können sofort Bürger dieses Landes werden" (136; You can become a citizen of this country right away)—is repeated like a refrain over several pages and, among other things, induces the narrator to undergo a rapid Bar Mitzvah on the street. He experiences an ecstasy that silences his usual skepticism: "Das Herz dagegen ruft zu großen Freudenfesten auf, verfasst Pamphlete, in denen es von Erlösung, Geborgenheit und einer warmen Heimat schwärmt. Ich werde endlich ankommen, dazugehören. Kein in Klammern Migrationshintergrund, keine Skepsis, kein Inneres Gericht. Jude in Israel. Punkt." (142; The heart, by contrast, calls for great celebrations, writes pamphlets in which it raves about redemption, security, and a warm homeland. I will finally arrive, finally belong there. No "migration history" in parentheses, no skepticism, no Inner Court. Jew in Israel. Period.) That ecstasy is short lived, though. The "Überdosis Identität"

(157; identity overdose) is followed by an "Identitätskater" (157; identity hangover), and after a trip through the West Bank reminds the narrator of the complexities of Israeli politics, he returns to Germany for good.

I call the book an arrival story in part because the different phases of the narrator's transformation are tied to specific sites, such as the Carmel Market or the Diaspora Museum, which together form a distinct spatial trajectory: the narrator goes to Israel in order to truly arrive in Germany. It is in Israel that he transforms from a young man who carries a Ukrainian passport and feels like a "Falschjude" (14; fake Jew) into a self-conscious German Jew. It is there that he announces: "Papa, ich werde einen deutschen Pass beantragen. Einen deutschen Pass unter unserem jüdischem Namen." (270; Papa, I'm going to apply for a German passport. A German passport under our Jewish name.) Back in Germany, the narrator intends to replace Romashkan, the name of his Moldavian mother that had been given to him at birth out of fear of antisemitic repercussions, by Kapitelman, the recognizably Jewish name of his father. Interestingly, on the level of the narrative proper, that change never happens—the last thing we hear about it is that it will probably take a very long time (282). But on the level of the book, the change has evidently happened, for the narrator early on introduces himself to the reader as "Dimitrij Kapitelman" (12), which is also the author name printed on the book cover. As in Stein's *Die Leinwand* and Gorelik's *Meine weißen Nächte*, the interplay between text and paratext gives *Das Lächeln meines unsichtbaren Vaters* a performative dimension: the publication process itself expresses and performs the narrator's emergent Jewish identity.[17]

Two aspects of Kapitelman's arrival story are particularly noteworthy. First, it goes hand in hand with a reconceptualization of politics, especially the German policy toward Jewish quota refugees. Initially the narrator holds a cynical view of that policy as driven by political calculation and the logic of the market: "'Kontingentflüchtlinge'—mit dieser Artikelbezeichnung machte der ethnopolitische Unternehmer Deutschland eine neue Warengruppe auf. Mein Vater ergatterte sein Existenzschnäppchen, die BRD bekam Rabatte auf ihre Vergangenheit." (20; "Quota refugees"—with this item description, the ethnopolitical entrepreneur Germany opened up a new category of products. My father snagged a bargain on his existence, the Federal Republic of Germany got a discount on its past.) Yet over the course of the book, the notion of politics as a continuation of capitalism by other means gives way to a concern with political rights and responsibilities, which ultimately motivate the narrator's desire for German citizenship. Pondering the present situation of refugees in Germany, he deems his own refusal to become German "dekadent" (282; decadent) and concludes the book with an emphatic appeal—to himself and to his father—to assume political responsibility in the country. Second, Kapitelman's definition of arrival in terms of citizenship contrasts with Gorelik's model of linguistic proficiency and expressivity. It is telling that the only time Kapitelman's narrator thinks of immigration in terms of language, he does so with a view toward the capacity for citizenship. This happens when his father haltingly reads a letter from his landlord and the narrator comments: "Und wenn es noch eines Beweises bedurft hätte, dass mein Vater niemals in diesem Land angekommen ist, dann hat er ihn mit seiner Haspelei erbracht" (62; And if even more proof that my father never arrived in this country were required, he did it with his sputtering). The father's linguistic difficulties surface when he has to navigate the law and deal with authorities, not when he uses language for purposes of self-reflection and self-expression, as Anja Buchmann does. In other words, the two most programmatic arrival stories written in recent decades by post-Soviet Jewish migrants—Gorelik's *Meine weißen Nächte* and Kapitelman's *Das Lächeln meines unsichtbaren Vaters*—reinstate two distinctly gendered models of national belonging: the fatherland and the mother tongue.

Arriving in Memory: Jan Himmelfarb's *Sterndeutung*

Jan Himmelfarb is similar in age and background to Gorelik and Kapitelman, and he, too, wrote his first novel—*Sterndeutung* (2015)—about the immigration of a family of *Kontingentflüchtlinge* to Germany. In this case, however, the book's protagonist and first-person narrator, Arthur Segal, is roughly a generation older than the author. The choice of an older protagonist allows Himmelfarb to do something similar to Julya Rabinowich in *Spaltkopf*—namely, to write an arrival story that is interrupted by invocations of a traumatic past. The first chapter of *Sterndeutung* is set in 1992 on the eve of Arthur's fifty-first birthday and about a year after his arrival in Germany, where he is now writing up his family's history in Russia and Ukraine while contemplating his daughter's academic future. The second chapter zooms in on the year 1941, when Arthur was born on a train as his mother and grandmother fled from the Ukrainian city of Kharkiv to Stalingrad. The novel continues to shuttle back and forth between the early 1990s and the early 1940s—that is, between Arthur's life in postreunification

Germany and the events that happened in Eastern Europe fifty years earlier. This earlier strand of the narrative interlaces Arthur's "memories" of the first years of his life, which he largely spent in Tashkent in Uzbekistan, with "visions" of the deportations, shootings, and gassings of those Jews who, unlike his own family, had not been able to escape Nazi persecution.

I put *memories* and *visions* in quotation marks because the status and sources of these images are far from clear. The central stylistic device of *Sterndeutung* is the construction of a narrator who is capable of testifying to the Holocaust even though he was too young and too far away to personally witness it. This capacity is partly explained through intertextual allusions to Günter Grass's *Die Blechtrommel* (*The Tin Drum*), whose protagonist, Oskar Matzerath, was also fully conscious at birth. In addition, Arthur's peculiar memory references several influential conceptions of Holocaust memory, especially Primo Levi's notion of testimony and Marianne Hirsch's concept of postmemory. According to Primo Levi, all Holocaust testimony arises from silences that are preserved in the very structure of testimonial speech and writing. Even those who survived genocidal terror are not the "true witnesses"—the true witnesses are the *Muselmänner*, which was camp jargon for those who had grown so weak in body and spirit that they were doomed to perish. In Holocaust testimony, the words of the survivor, who can speak but does not know the full truth, are conjoined with the silence of the *Muselmann*, who knows the full truth but can no longer speak.[18] And as explained earlier, Marianne Hirsch observed that the children of survivors often connect so deeply to the events of the Holocaust, of which they can have only indirect knowledge, that they experience this connection as a form of memory—or, more precisely, as a postmemory. The mix of mediation and immediacy that is the hallmark of postmemory also characterizes Arthur's testimony in *Sterndeutung*: although it is clear that he is reconstructing the events of the early 1940s with the help of films, books, archival materials, and conversations with his mother, the text nevertheless presents many of these reconstructions as his own memories. The book's narrator, then, is a complex literary construct that combines and concretizes much-discussed ideas about survivorship and postmemory. The fact that Himmelfarb structures his book around such a narrator is another sign of the self-reflexivity of recent German Jewish writing and the metamemorial shift analyzed in part 2 of this book.

Beyond these metamemorial reflections, *Sterndeutung* is an arrival story as defined prior—that is, a story that relates a twofold beginning. The book describes the passage from the narrator's initial arrival in Germany to the moment he settles down more permanently. Not long after Arthur comes to Germany in 1991 with his wife, mother, and daughter, he begins to enjoy economic success and social integration. It helps that he is able to work in his profession as a translator from Russian to German and also trades in used cars (his attempts to stay honest in this notoriously sleazy business are quite comical). But the family's real force of integration is Arthur's daughter, Anna. Gifted and ambitious, Anna manages to secure a scholarship at a private elite university, where she majors in economics, meets her non-Jewish boyfriend, graduates with flying colors, and lands a high-paying first job in Frankfurt. All the while, she avoids thinking too much about the fact that the main donor of her university had been in the SS as a young man. While Arthur narrates Anna's successes with a sense of irony, his own desire to settle down, albeit in a different kind of place, comes across as both sensible and realistic. Like the literary debuts of Gorelik and Kapitelman, Himmelfarb's *Sterndeutung* ends on a scene of arrival: in the last chapter of the book—suggestively entitled "Wohin?" (Whereto?)—Arthur briefly returns to the refugee shelter in which his family lived during their first three months in Germany. There he contemplates whether and where he might want to strike roots, and he ultimately chooses writing and nearness to others in lieu of more permanent places.

More clearly than in Gorelik and Kapitelman, the ultimate arrival of Himmelfarb's narrator remains uncertain both because it happens only in his mind and because it involves places that signify mobility. While viewing the new duplex houses, which were converted from the former refugee shelter, Arthur realizes that unlike his wife, he has no desire to purchase a house and put down roots. Rather, he opts for the book, which Heinrich Heine famously called the portable home of the Jews, hoping to ensure continuity through the memoir he is writing: "Was ich hinterlassen will, sind nicht unterkellerte Häuser. . . . Was ich hinterlassen will: vielleicht jemanden, der Blätter nicht wegwirft, nur weil im Schrank wenig Platz ist. Vielleicht jemanden, der die Blätter liest."[19] (What I want to leave behind are not houses with basements. . . . What I want to leave behind: maybe someone who doesn't throw away sheets of paper just because there's only a little room left in the cupboard. Maybe someone who reads the sheets.) In the last scene of the book, Arthur is riding a train. The railway is both an emblem of modern mobility—and, in this book, the means by which some Jews were able to escape from the advancing German troops—and a central element of Holocaust iconography.[20] Ever since the screening of Claude Lanzmann's famous film *Shoah*, an important intertext throughout *Sterndeutung*, a single image of a track section suffices to refer to industrial genocide. This association between the railway and the Holocaust is reinforced when Arthur witnesses a disturbing xenophobic incident in the small North German town he visits: several men in jump boots occupy a train car, access the public address system, and bawl through the loudspeaker that Germans and foreigners are to be segregated and the latter transported in boxcars. After reassuring himself that he is in no real danger, Arthurs conjures in his mind what is perhaps the closest thing to a home he knows: "Es gibt einen Ort, der liegt ganz woanders als östlich oder westlich, der ist bei den Nächsten und wo sie sich versammeln" (394; There is a place that lies somewhere other than to the east or west, which is with thy neighbors and is where they gather). Arthur has in mind here the friends and relatives who will soon gather for another one of his birthday parties. The simple thought of this gathering allows him to settle comfortably into the train compartment and resume writing his memoir. His is still an arrival story, if a tempered one.

This arrival story ends in the possibility of remembrance, which is cast in distinctly spatial terms. *Sterndeutung* as a whole breaks with the idea of a linear movement, not unlike Rabinowich's *Spaltkopf*. But instead of the back-and-forth movement of *Spaltkopf*, where the narrator's eventual arrival in Austria is preceded by her physical return to Russia, *Sterndeutung* is structured around two opposing movements that are connected only in Arthur's consciousness. It is his mind that brings together the streams of people moving westward and eastward at two different junctures in history. Whereas in 1991 Arthur and other Russian Jewish *Kontingentflüchtlinge* migrate to Germany, in 1941 some Jews flee to the eastern parts of the Soviet Union while others are deported to the killing centers in eastern Europe. Throughout the novel Arthur conjures vivid images—for example, of the trains that transferred German Jews from Berlin to Riga or Polish Jews from the Warsaw ghetto to the Treblinka death camp. At one point he offers another compelling spatial image for the workings of his memory: we usually face our memories as if standing in front of a V, he writes. The vertex of that V is the first experience we remember, and from then on, our memory is growing, right up to the present moment. In his own case, however, the V is toppled over and expands into the past. Arriving in Germany, then, means to be able to fill out the toppled V—the first four years of Arthur's life that coincided with the destruction of European Jewry:

> Ganz hinten, am Scheitelpunkt, sitzt im Ursprung unserer Erinnerung ein Erlebnis. Dahinter nichts mehr von uns selbst, nur Fremderzähltes, das wir gutgläubig für bare Münze nehmen und uns aneignen—über den Ursprung des V hinausgeschossene Schenkel. So sollte es sein: ein liegendes V, das sich uns öffnet. Das meine ist auf die falsche Seite gekippt. Meine ersten vier Jahre sind länger als Kindheit, Jugend, Mannesalter. (388–89)
>
> Way in the back, at the apex, one experience sits at the origin of our memories. Behind it, nothing more from ourselves, only strangers' tales that we innocently take at face value and claim for ourselves—legs shooting out from the origin of the V. So it should be: a V lying down that opens for us. Mine is tilted to the wrong side. My first four years are longer than childhood, youth, adulthood.

I began this chapter by citing Stuart Hall's suggestion that migration is a form of arrival, but an uncertain one and therefore an opportunity for newness. The literary debuts of Gorelik, Kapitelman, and Himmelfarb are structured around emphatic scenes of arrival that signify such a new possibility: of linguistic mastery, active citizenship, and historical remembrance. This sense of possibility might explain why so many post-Soviet Jewish authors are writing detailed *stories* of arrival at a moment when the general public has tended to take their arrival for granted. While these stories end in a sense of empowerment—the narrators seem to proclaim emphatically, "I have arrived!"—they are also full of delays, bifurcations, and question marks. Each text is split into two narrative strands: the migration of the child and the experiences of the university student in *Meine weißen Nächte*, the story of the father and that of the son in *Das Lächeln meines unsichtbaren Vaters*, and the family's persecution in wartime Russia and its successes in postreunification Germany in *Sterndeutung*. Retarding moments caused by linguistic uncertainties, political doubts, and lost memories emphasize the protracted nature of the arrival process. In fact, the narrators tend to describe two arrivals in Germany: their initial arrival in the refugee shelter and their "true" arrival in a literal or metaphorical place of their own—a duality that calls into question the finality of each and every arrival. These manifold splittings complicate the linear model of migration associated with the political metaphor of arrival.

Of course, not all debut novels by post-Soviet authors neatly fit the genre of the arrival story as defined here. Olga Grjasnowa's *Der Russe ist einer, der Birken liebt* and Sasha Marianna Salzmann's *Außer sich*, for example, draw on their authors' experiences as quota refugees in Germany yet ultimately lead to other places. Mascha Kogan, the first-person narrator of *Der Russe ist einer, der Birken liebt*, is on a job assignment in Israel when she visits the West Bank and is overcome by memories of her recently deceased German boyfriend and the interethnic violence she witnessed in Azerbaijan many years earlier. Grjasnowa's novel ends inconclusively, giving no indication when and where Mascha might settle down. *Außer sich*, which is written from the perspective of the gender-fluid Ali, who migrated from Russia to Germany as a child, oscillates between different types of movements: the migration of Ali's family, their brief return to Russia, and Ali's journey to Turkey in search of her/his twin brother, Anton. With its nonlinear narrative and unconventional protagonist, Salzmann's novel subverts any clear sense of belonging—whether to a nation, a language, or a gender.[21] Even the status of the novel's characters remains in question. Is Anton really Ali's twin brother or a figment of her/his imagination or the person Ali becomes after gender transitioning? And yet, *Außer sich* still offers gestures of arrival. Toward the end of the first volume, it becomes clear that Ali has indeed returned to Germany and found her/his own voice while telling the story of Anton in Istanbul, which makes up large parts of the second volume. The titles of each volume's first chapter—"Nach Hause" (Homeward) and "Zu Hause" (At home)—are evocative signals of an arrival process, however unfinished, lending further evidence to the power of the genre. As argued here, the arrival story is uniquely suited to claim a place in a new country or culture and at the same interrogate existing notions of national and cultural belonging—and, as such, it is the quintessential founding gesture of a new German Jewish literature.

CONCLUSION

IN HIS NEW BOOK *GEGENWARTSBEWÄLTIGUNG* (Coming to terms with the present), Max Czollek sums up the story told in many Jewish museums across Germany and Austria: a premodern period of segregation and persecution was followed by a century of Jewish emancipation, which was brutally interrupted by the Holocaust but continued when Jews began to return to Germany and Austria after the war. According to Czollek, this narrative is problematic not only because it promises a rather facile redemption but also because it promotes an idea of integration that views the Jewish minority mainly in relation to the non-Jewish majority. In postreunification Germany, in particular, the official talk about the blossoming of Jewish life conjures the image of a country that has atoned for its crimes and once again boasts a vibrant culture—namely, an essentially German culture that is enriched by the cultural expressions of Jews and other minorities. Inner-Jewish perspectives and debates matter very little for this narrative, as do cultural affiliations and alliances that circumvent the majority culture altogether. In an effort to counter this narrative, Czollek insists that Jews were never truly integrated in Germany and that theirs has been the history of a parallel society. He suggests that such nonintegration can generate new models of belonging and communality if we take seriously the idea that "one's belonging to a society does not result from cultural or religious assimilation but from recognition."[1]

In *Making German Jewish Literature Anew*, I have charted the emergence of a new German Jewish literature while trying to avoid both the redemption narrative and the integrationist paradigm. Inspired by multiple meanings of the verb *to found*—to posit a beginning, to mark a site, to delineate a concept— I have proposed the concept of a *founding gesture* to map out the shifting terrain of contemporary German Jewish literature. A founding gesture is an act of differentiation or boundary setting that may give way to a new awareness of intersections and similarities. I have shown how writers embrace their Jewish identity while interrogating, deconstructing, and/or expanding the label "Jewish author"; how they turn their attention to the foundations of memory during a time of profound changes in Holocaust remembrance; and how they stake out claims to new places while telling their stories of flight and migration. These three founding gestures—*performing authorship*, *remaking memory*, and *claiming places*—do not, of course, exhaust the literary strategies of contemporary German Jewish writers. Yet they are recurrent, significant, and transformative—and they have something in common. They all ask about the possibility of belonging: How can a Jewish author belong to German literature? How can a Jewish individual belong in a German-language country or memory community? Part of my claim has been that in exploring these questions, the authors *de-integrate* the (imagined) unity of German culture and project new forms of togetherness. Their creation of a recognizably Jewish literature is a step toward the model of social belonging Czollek calls for—a model based on recognition rather than assimilation.

I have also suggested that the new German Jewish literature constitutes the kind of entity envisioned by Dan Miron—that is, a multifarious complex held together by relationships of contiguity. This literature is composed of works by second- and third-generation authors from diverse cultural backgrounds, not all of whom have been discussed or even mentioned in this book; other writers worthy of consideration include Adriana Altaras, Alina Bronsky, Mirna Funk, Kat Kaufmann, Lana Lux, and Oliver Polak. In what follows, I briefly consider a phenomenon that has attracted much attention in recent years—namely, the growing community of Jewish Israelis who spend part or all of their time in Berlin and who often self-consciously live and write between several languages and cultures. As Y. Michal Bodemann observed, the transnational existence of these Israeli expatriates does not necessarily entail their integration in Germany but rather affords an opportunity to reinvent Israeliness: "For many Israelis, Berlin has become a laboratory where a democratic and humane Zionism, and indeed Israelism, can be re-imagined by returning to the history of the Zionist movement in the first decades of the 20th century in Berlin and by recreating Hebrew in a different environment."[2] Interestingly—and perhaps a reason for political hope—this reimagination also sparks encounters and alliances with other people from the Middle East, including Arabs. Thus, the Hebrew-language poet, journalist, and activist Mati Shemoelof praises Berlin as a cosmopolitan city in which multiple barriers can be crossed and cultural, national, and religious differences renegotiated. For Shemoelof, who was born and raised in Haifa and has been living in Berlin since 2013, interacting with diverse people from the Middle East in Germany's capital has been an opportunity to explore his own identity as a Mizrahi Jew (i.e., a Jew of West Asian or North African origins). He recently cofounded a literary project subtitled *Jews and Arabs Writing in Berlin* and intended "to promote a cultural dialogue between writers and artists from the Middle East, Asia, and North Africa."[3] Shemoelof also occasionally experiments with multilingualism, as in his poem "Ish bin juden dichtar" (I am Jew poet), which alternates between Hebrew and transliterated German lines. The poem utilizes the homophony of the German personal pronoun *ich* (I) and the Hebrew noun *ish* (man) to create a new hybrid language and novel connections between German and Hebrew.[4]

In 2016, Tomer Gardi, an Israeli author who had lived in Berlin for several years, landed a surprise hit on the German literary scene with his experimental novel *Broken German*. In his book, Gardi expands the concept of linguistic belonging in yet another way—namely, by valorizing the nonstandard German spoken by migrants from all over the world as a source of creativity and self-expression. *Broken German* begins with an act of exclusion on linguistic grounds, as a group of skinheads harasses thirteen-year-old immigrant Radili Aduan and his friends for speaking improper German, and it goes on to tell several loosely connected stories of migrant life in Germany. The novel not only describes but also performs the German of migrants who are learning the language orally, without the help of a grammar book. The text is replete with errors in spelling and grammar, and the narrator often searches for the right German word or makes up new words. If the languages of narrator and characters are marked as broken German, paratexts such as interviews, prize-award discussions, and the publisher's promotion materials suggest this is also the language spoken by the author.[5] This fact initially caused significant confusion and consternation: when Gardi read an excerpt from *Broken German* at the 2016 Bachmann prize competition in Klagenfurt, most jury members refused to engage seriously with the text. Upon its publication a few weeks later, however, the book garnered enthusiastic reviews in major German newspapers, which praised the wit, ingenuity, and vitality of its writing style. Gardi seems indeed to have achieved the goal he set himself in an interview: "Everyone should be allowed to write in German"—that is, he has expanded the category of authors who legitimately belong to German literature.[6]

The experimentation with multilingualism and nonstandard German in Gardi and other Israeli writers could lead us to stipulate a fourth founding gesture in contemporary German Jewish literature—*diversifying language* or *generating new voices*. For the moment, however, I simply wish to point out that the three founding gestures analyzed in *Making German Jewish Literature Anew* are also present in *Broken German*, affording me an opportunity to sum up my main arguments.

To begin with part 3, which is focused on *claiming places*: there is a palpable tension in contemporary German Jewish literature between a thematic concern with *dis*placement and formal strategies of *em*placement. I have drawn on Barbara Mann's concept of diasporic place-making to analyze the ways that literary characters turn spaces into places and strike new roots in the diaspora. Mann's concept owes much to the dynamic understanding of place in contemporary anthropology and human geography, according to which places crystallize temporarily out of movements that never cease to reverberate in them. In *Broken German*, this is what happens as a diverse cast of characters inhabits transitory places by investing them with personal meaning, including a welcoming attitude toward migrants. Stops on migration routes become sites of international and multilingual encounters: in the "wunderschöne Kosmopolis" (beautiful cosmopolis) of the Atatürk airport in Istanbul, an Iranian man reminds the narrator of his own father.[7] In a Berlin hotel room, the narrator and his mother imaginatively connect with other migrants as they dress in their clothes, look at their photo album, and speculate about their fates. In one of many metaliterary allusions, a pub named "Zum roter Faden" (At the common thread) suggests that the text itself becomes a place of international encounters. Most importantly, the Call Shop in which Radili Aduan and his friends regularly meet, eat, drink, and make puns with German idioms brings together people from different cultural and linguistic backgrounds in a "Gebrochenesdeutschsprachigesraum" (23; Broken-German-language-room).[8] The constant repetition of the verb *to sit* in the depiction of this room creates the impression of migrants taking possession of and dwelling communally in a shared space. Furthermore, the twofold mention of the different languages that are streaming (23, 35; "strömen") into and through this room evokes an idea of multilingual conversations gradually filling—and thereby first constituting—this room.

The founding gesture identified in part 2 of this book, *remaking memory*, refers to the shifts in Holocaust memory in the wake of its globalization, remediation, and politicization at the turn of the millennium. I focus on the metamemorial turn in literature—that is, the ways that literary texts reflect on the foundations of memory, its paths of transmission, and its potential multidirectionality. Of particular interest are authors such as Doron Rabinovici and Katja Petrowskaja, who explore formal conditions of multidirectional memory rather than actual connections between historical atrocities. In *Broken German*, Tomer Gardi offers similarly incisive metamemorial reflections on memory and migration. The text repeatedly refers to a traumatic memory from the Rumanian town where the narrator's mother grew up: a Christian neighbor of hers once wished—or threatened—to put his arms deep in the blood of Jews. The narrator is haunted by the scene without knowing its details, which he initially makes up in his imagination. His storytelling recalls Marianne Hirsch's concept of postmemory, according to which the children of survivors creatively fill in memory gaps as they reconstruct traumatic experiences that overshadow their lives but remain inaccessible. Subsequently, however, we are given a more mundane explanation for the gaps in the narrator's knowledge: he had simply forgotten the details of his mother's story. In the space that opens up between postmemorial inventiveness and everyday forgetfulness, metamemorial reflections on the effects of linguistic dispersion on collective memory set in. The narrator literalizes the German verb for translation to describe the transmission of memories from mother to son as a physical movement, a "carrying over" (39; "Trägt ihm über"). And the cryptic and fragmentary chapter "*," which is all about the transfer of objects and memories to subsequent generations, refers to the Babylonian confusion of languages and debunks the idea of a stable mother tongue: "Meine Muttersprache ist nicht die Muttersprache meiner Mutter. Die Muttersprache meiner Mutter ist nicht die Muttersprache ihrer Mutter. Die Muttersprache ihre Mutter ist nicht die Muttersprache und so weiter." (91; My mother tongue is not my mother's mother tongue. My mother's mother tongue is not her mother's mother tongue. Her mother's mother tongue is not the mother tongue and so on.) It is the passage through different languages—rather than the passage of time or the structural inaccessibility of traumatic events—that leads to the inevitable distortion of memories.

Broken German, which features a subplot about the adventures of Israeli Jewish writer Abschalom Raucherzone in Germany, has the clearest bearing on the founding gesture identified in part 1 of this book: *performing authorship*. As I have shown, contemporary writers often position themselves *as* Jewish authors while interrogating, deconstructing, and/or expanding the very category of *Jewish author*. One example is that of the prose collections in which second-generation writers create a distinct Jewish author persona while exposing and disrupting the publishing mechanisms that first classify them as Jewish. Paratexts often play a key role in the process of authorial self-fashioning and self-staging. In Benjamin Stein's *Die Leinwand*, for example, the visual representation in the dust copy of the author as an observant Jew is oddly undermined by the emphasis on highly malleable, even fabricated, Jewish identities in the text itself. I have suggested that the simultaneous claiming and contesting of authorial labels is a form of de-integration as understood by Max Czollek—that is, an intervention in the German memory theater and a subversion of the prescribed roles of Jewish authors therein.

Tomer Gardi's novel reflects on Jewish authorship by means of the story of Abschalom Raucherzone and its extended references to Franz Kafka's "Ein Bericht für eine Akademie" (A Report to an Academy).[9] This short prose text famously traces the narrator's transformation from an African monkey into first a domesticated animal and then an almost-human civilized European. Often read as a parody of Jewish assimilation, Kafka's "Ein Bericht" can also be understood as a comment on the precarious situation of minority authors. The narrator presents his report to a scientific academy—that is, an institution that represents the very society that captures monkeys to display them in zoos or use them in scientific research. His report thus brings to a head the double bind of the minority writer who is forced to explain herself to the very culture that denigrates her. In *Broken German*, Gardi puts even more emphasis on this predicament as he dramatizes the fraught relationship between Abschalom Raucherzone (over long stretches the text's first-person narrator) and his audience and writing task. Abschalom has been invited to give the keynote at the reopening of Germany's state-sponsored cultural association, the Goethe Institute, which has been renamed Kafka Institute. While delivering his report, he vigilantly registers the sounds and lights in the hall and the moods and movements in the audience. He ponders the dilemmas of writing "nach Bestellung" (59; per order), seeks a way out when first asked to write the report, and eventually escapes from the lecture hall when he (now temporarily named Radili Aduan) is unexpectedly accused of antisemitism.[10] Whereas Kafka depicts a generic process of assimilation, Gardi zooms in on the faltering performance of a Jewish author in front of a philosemitic German audience. His literary representation of this performance, which ends with Abschalom's/Radili's stumbling over an oven and a bleaching agent while fleeing from his persecutors, is a rather grotesque actualization of Kafka's parable.

What do we make of Gardi's references to Franz Kafka, arguably the most famous German Jewish author of the twentieth century? Is *Broken German* an attempt to reconnect to pre-Holocaust traditions of German Jewish writing? As noted previously, authors such as Maxim Biller and Barbara Honigmann also draw on Kafka, in particular his concept of a *minor literature*, to recreate a German Jewish literature for the contemporary moment: Biller alludes to Kafka's concept in the closing story of his *Deutschbuch*, and Honigmann construes a tradition of a "truly minor literature" of female German Jewish authors in which she situates her own writing. The question of continuity in German Jewish writing of the twentieth and twenty-first centuries opens up exciting perspectives for future research. Scholars have already begun to explore such continuities, whether in literary genres such as satire and parody or in a thematic focus on migration, refugees, and human rights.[11] Stuart Taberner, for example, argues that a "Jewish worldliness" characterizes both pre-1933 German Jewish literature and recent writings by post-Soviet German Jewish authors. Thus, the Jewish perspective of Grjasnowa's 2020 novel *Der verlorene Sohn* (The lost son) manifests itself not so much in a thematic concern with Jews and Judaism but in an ethical and political commitment to migrants wherever they hail from. This commitment builds on a European Jewish tradition that includes Hannah Arendt's writings on stateless people, among others.[12]

In *Making German Jewish Literature Anew*, I have focused on the creative acts or founding gestures that have accompanied the rise of a new Jewish literature in contemporary Germany and Austria. Can such acts also bridge over the historical caesuras of the Holocaust, on the one hand, and German reunification, on the other hand, and connect contemporary texts to earlier traditions of German Jewish writing? Perhaps they can—but perhaps we do need to let go of the idea of continuity, as Dan Miron suggests for modern Jewish literature at large, and turn our attention to the more random forms of proximity, overlapping, and intersection associated with contiguity. The references to Kafka in *Broken German* show how intertextual references, typically a prime way of creating a literary continuum or tradition, can involve a great measure of rupture. Gardi transposes Kafka's parable into the present by putting the ape's phrases into the mouth of Abschalom, who gives a lecture at the opening of the renamed German cultural institute. Yet it is difficult to determine where, exactly, that lecture begins and where it ends, in part because Gardi uses the narrative technique of metalepsis—that is, a crossing of the boundaries between narrative levels.

Metalepsis often happens when an extradiegetic narrator intrudes upon the world he or she narrates or when the frame narrative collapses into the embedded tale.[13] In *Broken German*, the reverse process occurs as characters begin to act and speak on an extradiegetic level and as new frame narratives develop—for example, when the protagonist Radili is revealed to be the author of the story about him or when the text gradually morphs into the lecture delivered by Abschalom. These metaleptic transgressions help generate a new, amorphous, and discontinuous version of "Ein Bericht" that ends up taking up more than half of Gardi's text. Kafka's parable, then, neither provides an extradiegetic frame for the migrant stories of *Broken German* nor gives a deeper meaning to these stories as a literary allusion might do. Instead, its bold recreation from *within* Gardi's novel indicates that tradition, too, can and must be made anew.

NOTES

Introduction

1. "Es gibt eine Reihe von Schubladen, in die ich nach Belieben hineingelegt und aus denen ich wieder herausgeholt werden kann. So wurde ich zum Beispiel in einer Rezension als ein 'in Österreich lebender Russe' bezeichnet, was nachvollziehbar ist, auch wenn es nicht ganz der Wahrheit entspricht. Außerdem war ich 'russischer Schriftsteller,' ein 'in Deutschland lebender Israeli,' ein 'jüdisch-deutscher Schriftsteller russischer Abstammung,' ein 'österreichischer Russe,' ein 'deutscher Jude' und sogar ein 'hebräischer Autor,' obwohl ich in dieser Sprache gerade einmal mit Mühe und Not ein paar Höflichkeitsfloskeln formulieren kann." Vladimir Vertlib, *Spiegel im fremden Wort: Die Erfindung des Lebens als Literatur*. Dresdner Chamisso-Poetikvorlesungen 2006. 3rd rev. ed. (Dresden: Thelem, 2012), 141–42.

2. Throughout this book, *German* refers to the language of writing while *Jewish* indicates that the author identifies as Jewish or at least publicly responds to such an identification. For the theme of rebirth/reemergence/renaissance, see the titles of Sander L. Gilman and Karen Remmler, eds., *Reemerging Jewish Culture in Germany: Life and Literature since 1989* (New York: New York University Press, 1994); Hillary Hope Herzog, Todd Herzog, and Benjamin Lapp, eds., *Rebirth of a Culture: Jewish Identity and Jewish Writing in Germany Today* (New York: Berghahn Books, 2008); and Jakob Hessing, "Aufbrüche: Zur deutsch-jüdischen Literatur seit 1989," in *Handbuch der deutsch-jüdischen Literatur*, ed. Hans Otto Horch (Berlin: De Gruyter, 2016), 244–69. In her article "Writing by Germany's Jewish Minority," Erin McGlothlin states: "Since the late 1980s, and especially continuing after German unification in 1990, there has been a veritable *renaissance* in German-Jewish literature by writers born after the Holocaust" (in *Contemporary German Fiction: Writing in the Berlin Republic*, ed. Stuart Taberner [Cambridge: Cambridge University Press, 2007], 230–46, here 230, my emphasis). In the introduction to their coedited *Contemporary Jewish Writing in Europe: A Guide* (Bloomington: Indiana University Press, 2008), Vivian Liska and Thomas Nolden write that "the *revitalization* of Jewish literature" (xv, my emphasis) was not confined to Germany but could be observed throughout Europe.

3. "in dem noch eine ganze Weile eine originäre, selbstbestimmte jüdische Literatur entstehen wird." Maxim Biller, "Goodbye, Columbus: Randlage oder: Über die Voraussetzungen jüdischer Literatur," in *Deutschbuch* (Munich: dtv, 2001), 89–93, here 93. Originally published in *Frankfurter Rundschau* 52, March 2, 1995.

4. "Daß man als Jude in Deutschland nicht leben und schreiben sollte, ist logischerweise gleich der erste und triftigste Grund dafür, warum man ausgerechnet als Jude in Deutschland besonders bewußt jüdisch lebt und schreibt." Biller, 90.

5. I should note that the category of *generation* is not an organizing principle of this book. While the distinction among the survivors of the Holocaust, their children, and their grandchildren—and the corresponding notions of first-, second-, and third-generation German Jewish literature—is often useful, it also tends to draw rather rigid boundaries

between the generations and neglect stylistic and thematic overlaps among writers of different generations. For a critical discussion of the concept of *generation* (particularly of *second generation*), see Erin McGlothlin, *Second-Generation Holocaust Literature: Legacies of Survival and Perpetration* (Rochester, NY: Camden House, 2006), esp. 17–18.

6. Dan Diner, "Negative Symbiosis: Germans and Jews after Auschwitz," in *The Holocaust: Theoretical Readings*, ed. Neil Levi and Michael Rothberg (New Brunswick, NJ: Rutgers University Press, 2003), 423–430, here 423. For the German original, see "Negative Symbiose: Deutsche und Juden nach Auschwitz," *Babylon* 1 (1986): 9–20, here 9.

7. On these crises, see Katja Garloff, *Words from Abroad: Trauma and Displacement in Postwar German Jewish Writers* (Detroit, MI: Wayne State University Press, 2005). On the tensions between the West German public sphere and another group of post-Holocaust German Jewish writers, including Grete Weil, Edgar Hilsenrath, and Wolfgang Hildesheimer, see Stephan Braese, *Die andere Erinnerung: Jüdische Autoren in der westdeutschen Nachkriegsliteratur* (Berlin: Philo, 2001).

8. Cited in Sander L. Gilman and Jack Zipes, "Introduction: Jewish Writing in German through the Ages," in *Yale Companion to Jewish Writing and Thought in German Culture, 1096–1996*, ed. Sander L. Gilman and Jack Zipes (New Haven, CT: Yale University Press, 1997), xvii–xxxiv, here xxvi.

9. See the introductions to the following edited volumes and special issues: Godela Weiss-Sussex and Maria Roca Lizarazu, eds., *Rethinking "Minor Literatures"— Contemporary Jewish Women's Writing in Germany and Austria*, special collection of *Modern Languages Open* 1 (2020), https://www.modernlanguagesopen.org/collections/special/rethinking-minor-literatures-contemporary-jewish-women-s-writing-in-germany-and-austria/; Doerte Bischoff and Anja Tippner, eds., *Figurations of Mobile Identities in Contemporary European Jewish Literature, Yearbook for European Jewish Literature Studies, Yearbook for European Jewish Literature Studies* 5 (2018); and Katja Garloff and Agnes C. Mueller, eds., *German Jewish Literature after 1990* (Rochester, NY: Camden House, 2018), 60–79. See also Luisa Banki and Caspar Battegay, "Sieben Thesen zur deutschsprachigen jüdischen Gegenwartsliteratur," in *Zwischen Literarizität und Programmatik: Jüdische Literaturen der Gegenwart*, ed. Luisa Banki et al., special issue, *Jalta: Positionen zur jüdischen Gegenwart* (2019), 41–47; Stuart Taberner, "The Possibilities and Pitfalls of a Jewish Cosmopolitanism: Reading Natan Sznaider through Russian-Jewish Writer Olga Grjasnowa's German-Language Novel *Der Russe ist einer der Birken liebt* (All Russians Love Birch Trees)," *European Review of History / Revue européenne d'histoire* 23, no. 5–6 (2016): 912–30; and Andreas B. Kilcher, "Exterritorialitäten: Zur kulturellen Selbstreflexion der aktuellen deutsch-jüdischen Literatur," in *Deutsch-jüdische Literatur der neunziger Jahre: Die Generation nach der Shoah*, ed. Sander L. Gilman and Hartmut Steinecke (Berlin: Erich Schmidt, 2002), 131–46.

10. In this book I use *Russian Jewish* to refer to Jews from the (former) Soviet Union, whether they came from Russia, Ukraine, Georgia, or other Soviet republics—*Russian* refers here to a language rather than a geographical origin. Because of discrepancies between the statistics of the German administration and those of the Jewish communities, the numbers cited fluctuate between 170,000 and 300,000. See Yfaat Weiss and Lena Gorelik, "The Russian-Jewish Immigration," in *A History of Jews in Germany since 1945: Politics, Culture, and Society*, ed. Michael Brenner, trans. Kenneth Kronenberg (Bloomington: Indiana University Press, 2018), 394. Other scholarly works on the quota refugees include the following: Masha Belenky and Jonathan Skolnik, "Russian Jews in Today's Germany: End

of the Journey?," *European Judaism: A Journal for the New Europe* 31, no. 2 (Autumn 1998): 30–44; Judith Kessler, "Homo Sovieticus in Disneyland: The Jewish Communities in Germany Today," and Y. Michael Bodemann with Olena Bagno, "In the Ethnic Twilight: The Paths of Russian Jews in Germany," both in *The New German Jewry and the European Context: The Return of the European Diaspora*, ed. Y. Michal Bodemann (New York: Palgrave Macmillan, 2008), 131–43 and 158–76; Karen Körber, ed., *Russisch-jüdische Gegenwart in Deutschland: Interdisziplinäre Perspektiven auf eine Diaspora im Wandel* (Göttingen, Germany: Vandenhoeck & Ruprecht, 2015); and Joseph Cronin, "Community Responses to the Immigration of Russian-Speaking Jews to Germany, 1990–2006," in *Rebuilding Jewish Life in Germany*, ed. Jay Howard Geller and Michael Meng (New Brunswick, NJ: Rutgers University Press, 2020), 191–205.

11. Sveta Roberman, *Sweet Burdens: Welfare and Communality among Russian Jews in Germany* (Albany: State University of New York Press, 2015), 139.

12. "Deutsches Judentum 2.0"; see Dmitrij Belkin, "Mögliche Heimat: Deutsches Judentum zwei," in *Ausgerechnet Deutschland! Jüdisch-russische Einwanderung in die Bundesrepublik*, ed. Dmitrij Belkin and Raphael Gross (Berlin: Nicolai, 2010), 25–29. On the affinities between the Russian Jewish immigrants and German culture, see also Dan Diner, "Deutsch-jüdisch-russische Paradoxien oder Versuch eines Kommentars aus der Sicht eines Historikers," in *Ausgerechnet Deutschland!*, 18–20. For a different evaluation, see Zvi Y. Gitelman, "Wie konnten sie nur? Jüdische Immigranten aus der Sowjetunion in Deutschland," in *Ausgerechnet Deutschland!*, 21–24.

13. Benjamin Schreier, *The Impossible Jew: Identity and the Reconstruction of Jewish American Literary History* (New York: New York University Press, 2015), 12.

14. Schreier, 56.

15. Dan Miron, *From Continuity to Contiguity: Toward a New Jewish Literary Thinking* (Stanford, CA: Stanford University Press, 2010).

16. See Leopold Zunz, "Die jüdische Literatur" (1845), cited in Andreas B. Kilcher, "Die Sprachen der Literatur: Zur Erfindung der 'jüdischen Literatur' im 19. Jahrhundert," *Naharaim* 4, no. 2 (2011): 274–86, here 278.

17. "Die Diaspora transformiert die Bibliothek des Judentums vom geschlossenen, hebräischen Buch zum offenen, vielsprachigen und vernetzten Intertext der 'jüdischen Literatur.'" Kilcher, 284.

18. See Lital Levy and Allison Schachter, "Jewish Literature / World Literature: Between the Local and the Transnational," *PMLA* 130, no. 1 (2015): 92–109, and "A Non-Universal Global: On Jewish Writing and World Literature," *Prooftexts* 36, no. 1–2 (2017): 1–26. The editors of a volume on nineteenth-century Jewish literature similarly claim that modern Jewish literature is a transnational phenomenon because many works were quickly translated and consumed by Jewish (and non-Jewish) readers in other countries. See Jonathan M. Hess, Maurice Samuels, and Nadia Valman, eds., *Nineteenth-Century Jewish Literature: A Reader* (Stanford, CA: Stanford University Press, 2013), 5.

19. See Sheila E. Jelen, Michael P. Kramer, and L. Scott Lerner, "Introduction: Intersection and Boundaries in Modern Jewish Literary Study," in *Modern Jewish Literatures: Intersections and Boundaries*, ed. Sheila E. Jelen, Michael P. Kramer, and L. Scott Lerner (Philadelphia: University of Pennsylvania Press, 2011), 1–23. The editors describe their volume as an examination of "sets of relations, adopting the perspective, broadly conceived, of modern Jewish writing moving back and forth between and through categories, of

intersections and boundaries as mutually inclusive by way of continual movement across borders, of separations and syntheses" (1–2).

20. Jules Chametzky et al., eds., *Jewish American Literature: A Norton Anthology* (New York: W. W. Norton, 2001), 3.

21. See Michael P. Kramer, "Race, Literary History, and the 'Jewish' Question," *Prooftexts* 21, no. 3 (Fall 2001): 287–321; the responses to his essay by Bryan Cheyette, Morris Dickstein, Anne Golomb Hoffman, Hannah Naveh, and Gershon Shaked: 322–34; and Kramer's reply to the responses: "My Critics and *Mai Nafka Mina*: Further Reflections on Jewish Literary Historiography," 335–49.

22. Kramer, 342.

23. Miron, *From Continuity to Contiguity*, 405, my emphasis.

24. See Leslie Morris, *The Translated Jew: German Jewish Culture outside the Margins* (Evanston, IL: Northwestern University Press, 2018), esp. 65–112.

25. See Max Czollek, *Desintegriert euch!* (Munich: Carl Hanser, 2018). Czollek draws on Y. Michal Bodemann, *Gedächtnistheater: Die jüdische Gemeinschaft und ihre deutsche Erfindung* (Hamburg, Germany: Rotbuch, 1996). For a succinct summary of the cultural-political program of *desintegration*, see also Max Czollek et al., "Radical Diversity und Desintegration: Bausteine eines künstlerisch-politischen Projekts," *Jalta: Positionen zur jüdischen Gegenwart* 2 (2017): 71–76.

26. Max Czollek in an interview with Philipp Fritz, "'Wir wollen Berlin judaisieren': Max Czollek über genervte 'Judenschriftsteller' und die Veranstaltung am Maxim Gorki Theater," *Jüdische Allgemeine*, October 30, 2017, https://www.juedische-allgemeine.de/article/view/id/29977.

27. See Maria Roca Lizarazu, "'Integration ist definitiv nicht unser Anliegen, eher schon Desintegration': Postmigrant Renegotiations of Identity and Belonging in Contemporary Germany," *Humanities* 9, no. 2 (2020): 42, https://doi.org/10.3390/h9020042; Silvia Battegay, "Sprache der Stummen: Katja Petrowskajas *Vielleicht Esther* als literarische Praxis der Desintegration," in Bischoff and Tippner, *Figurations of Mobile Identities in Contemporary European Jewish Literature*, 51–66. Roca Lizarazu draws on the concepts of "disidentification," "non-authoritative narrative," and "ec-static self" to read Sasha Marianna Salzmann's novel *Außer sich* (2017; *Beside Myself*) as a radically decentered text that interrogates fixed notions of identity and belonging. Battegay argues that the fragmentation of the family's past in Katja Petrowskaja's *Vielleicht Esther* is a form of de-integration since it defies the (German) reader's desire for a coherent (Jewish) family history.

28. Aleida Assmann, "The Holocaust—a Global Memory? Extensions and Limits of a New Memory Community," in *Memory in a Global Age: Discourses, Practices and Trajectories*, ed. Aleida Assmann and Sebastian Conrad (New York: Palgrave Macmillan, 2010), 97–116, here 98.

29. Assmann, 114.

30. Daniel Levy and Natan Sznaider, *The Holocaust and Memory in the Global Age*, trans. Assenka Oksiloff (Philadelphia: Temple University Press, 2006), 4.

31. Michael Rothberg, *Multidirectional Memory: Remembering the Holocaust in the Age of Decolonization* (Stanford, CA: Stanford University Press, 2009).

32. Michael Rothberg, "From Gaza to Warsaw: Mapping Multidirectional Memory," *Criticism* 53, no. 4 (Fall 2011): 523–48, here 525.

33. Lucy Bond, Stef Craps, and Pieter Vermeulen, "Introduction: Memory on the Move," in *Memory Unbound: Tracing the Dynamics of Memory Studies*, ed. Lucy Bond, Stef Craps, and Pieter Vermeulen (New York: Berghahn Books, 2017), 1–26, here 6.

34. See Helen Finch, "Revenge, Restitution, *Ressentiment*: Edgar Hilsenrath's and Ruth Klüger's Late Writings as Holocaust Metatestimony," in Garloff and Mueller, *German Jewish Literature after 1990*, 60–79.

35. See Maria Roca Lizarazu, *Renegotiating Postmemory: The Holocaust in Contemporary German-Language Jewish Literature* (Rochester, NY: Camden House, 2020), 5.

36. See Barbara E. Mann, *Space and Place in Jewish Studies* (New Brunswick, NJ: Rutgers University Press, 2012).

37. See Daniel Boyarin and Jonathan Boyarin, "Diaspora: Generation and the Ground of Jewish Identity," *Critical Inquiry* 19 (1993): 693–725; Jonathan Boyarin and Daniel Boyarin, *Powers of Diaspora: Two Essays on the Relevance of Jewish Culture* (Minneapolis: University of Minnesota Press, 2002).

38. See James Clifford, *Routes: Travel and Translation in the Late Twentieth Century* (Cambridge, MA: Harvard University Press, 1997).

39. See Yi-Fu Tuan, *Space and Place: The Perspective of Experience* (Minneapolis: University of Minnesota Press, 1977), and Doreen Massey, *Space, Place, and Gender* (Minneapolis: University of Minnesota Press, 1994).

40. See Mann, *Space and Place in Jewish Studies*, esp. 98–115 and 137–47. Mann also cites Caryn Aviv and David Shneer, who believe that the polarity between Israel and the diaspora no longer adequately describes the situation of most contemporary Jews. Yet Aviv and Shneer are similarly focused on place-making—i.e., on the ways Jews are creating homes in a global world. See Caryn S. Aviv and David Shneer, *New Jews: The End of the Jewish Diaspora* (New York: New York University Press, 2005). On the practice of the *eruv*, see also Morris, *The Translated Jew*, 43–53. Morris notes the attraction of the *eruv* for contemporary artists while observing that this practice is mostly absent from contemporary Germany.

1. Authorial Self-Fashioning in Second-Generation Writers

1. See Thomas Nolden, *Junge jüdische Literatur: Konzentrisches Schreiben in der Gegenwart* (Würzburg, Germany: Königshausen & Neumann, 1995). On the themes of revival/reemergence/rebirth, see also note 2 in my introduction. For another important scholarly work on this generation of writers, see Sander L. Gilman, *Jews in Today's German Culture* (Bloomington: Indiana University Press, 1995).

2. See Sander L. Gilman, "Introduction: Ethnicity-Ethnicities-Literature-Literatures," *PMLA* 113, no. 1 (January 1998): 19–27.

3. "Dokumentationen einer bislang weitgehend unsichtbar gebliebenen jungen jüdischen Lebenswelt," cited in Nolden, *Junge jüdische Literatur*, 86. On Seligmann's initial attempts to find a publisher for his book, see also his *Mit beschränkter Hoffnung: Juden, Deutsche, Israelis*, rev. paperback ed. (Munich: Knaur, 1993), 152–54.

4. See Nolden, *Junge jüdische Literatur*, 86.

5. See David A. Hollinger, *Postethnic America: Beyond Multiculturalism*, 10th anniversary ed. (New York: Basic Books, 2006).

6. See Florian Sedlmeier, "Rereading Literary Form: Paratexts, Transpositions, and Postethnic Literature around 2000," *Journal of Literary Theory* 6, no. 1 (2012): 213–34, here 213. See also Florian Sedlmeier, *The Postethnic Literary: Reading Paratexts and Transpositions around 2000* (Berlin: De Gruyter, 2014).

7. See Doron Rabinovici, *Credo und Credit: Einmischungen* (Frankfurt: Suhrkamp, 2001) and Robert Schindel, *Mein liebster Feind: Essays, Reden, Miniaturen* (Frankfurt: Suhrkamp, 2004). See also the essays by other contemporary Jewish writers in *Altes Land, neues Land: Verfolgung, Exil, biographisches Schreiben*, ed. Walter Hinderer et al., special issue, *Zirkular* 56 (1999), especially the essay by Gila Lustiger (who lives in Paris), "Einige Überlegungen zur Lage der jüdischen Autoren in Deutschland," 50–53.

8. Maxim Biller, *Deutschbuch* (Munich: dtv, 2001), 91. All references to *Deutschbuch* are from this edition and hereafter will be cited parenthetically in the text.

9. See Miron, *From Continuity to Contiguity*.

10. Esther Dischereit, *Übungen jüdisch zu sein: Aufsätze* (Frankfurt: Suhrkamp, 1998), 36–52. All references to *Übungen jüdisch zu sein* are from this edition and hereafter will be cited parenthetically in the text.

11. See Barbara Honigmann, "Eine 'ganz kleine Literatur' des Anvertrauens: Glückel von Hameln, Rahel von Varnhagen, Anne Frank," in *Das Gesicht wiederfinden: Über Schreiben, Schriftsteller und Judentum* (Munich: Carl Hanser, 2006), 7–29. The lecture was originally given in 2000.

12. Honigmann, *Das Gesicht wiederfinden*, 26–27.

13. Barbara Honigmann, *Damals, dann und danach* (Munich: Carl Hanser, 1999), 53–54. All references to *Damals, dann und danach* are from this edition and hereafter will be cited parenthetically in the text.

14. On Strasbourg's Jewish community and Honigmann's conception of diasporic writing, see also Christina Guenther, "Exile and the Construction of Identity in Barbara Honigmann's Trilogy of Diaspora," *Comparative Literature Studies* 40, no. 2 (2003): 215–31.

15. For an interesting comparison of the two forms of "extraterritorialities" embodied by Biller and Honigmann, see Andreas B. Kilcher, "Exterritorialitäten: Zur kulturellen Selbstreflexion der aktuellen deutsch-jüdischen Literatur," in *Deutsch-jüdische Literatur der neunziger Jahre: Die Generation nach der Shoah*, ed. Sander L. Gilman and Hartmut Steinecke (Berlin: Erich Schmidt, 2002), 131–46. Kilcher distinguishes between German Jewish authors who write from a self-chosen geographical distance and construe "ein sublimiertes Kultur- und Literatur-Deutschland . . . , das dem historischen und realen entgegensteht" (134) and those who write a Jewish literature from within Germany or Austria and engage in a more radical critique of German language and aesthetics. While this is a useful distinction, my own analysis shows that Biller, too, imagines himself at some geographical distance from Germany.

16. Barbara Honigmann, "On My Great-Grandfather, My Grandfather, My Father, and Me," trans. Meghan W. Barnes, *World Literature Today* 69, no. 3 (1995): 512–16, here 513–14.

17. Annette Seidel-Arpaci draws attention to this spatialization in her "'Writing in Jewish' as an Act of Prostitution? Esther Dischereit's (Self-)Positioning as a Female Jewish Writer in Germany," in *Esther Dischereit*, ed. Katharina Hall (Cardiff: University of Wales Press, 2007), 116–25, here 122. For Dischereit's conception of Jewish writing as a space, see also her essay "Vom Verschwinden der Worte," in which she uses the prostitution metaphor again and adds that her writing makes it possible for the murderers "an den Schauplatz ihrer Tat zurückzukehren" (*Übungen jüdisch zu sein*, 47).

18. Esther Dischereit, "Gelebte Zeit und aufgeschriebene Zeit," in *Mit Eichmann an der Börse: In jüdischen und anderen Angelegenheiten* (Berlin: Ullstein, 2001), 144–65, here 153.

19. Honigmann, "On My Great-Grandfather," 513–14. See similarly in Honigmann's "Selbstporträt als Jüdin": "Als Jude bin ich aus Deutschland weggegangen, aber in meiner

Arbeit, in einer sehr starken Bindung an die deutsche Sprache, kehre ich immer wieder zurück" (*Damals, dann und danach*, 18; I left Germany as a Jew, but in my work, in a very strong connection to the German language, I return over and over again). Elsewhere I discuss how Honigmann works through this duality—her simultaneous departure from and return to the German Jewish cultural tradition—by means of the trope of the "German-Jewish love affair." See Katja Garloff, "Interreligious Love in Contemporary German Film and Literature," in *Judaism, Christianity, and Islam: Collaboration and Conflict in the Age of Diaspora*, ed. Sander Gilman (Hong Kong: Hong Kong University Press, 2014), 153–64, here 158–63.

20. The nuances of Kafka's concept are easily lost in Gilles Deleuze and Félix Guattari's famous interpretation of the concept in terms of radical deterritorialization and subversion of the majority culture in *Kafka: Toward a Minor Literature*, trans. Dana Polan (Minneapolis: University of Minnesota Press, 1986). When Kafka speaks of "minor literatures," he has in mind Czech literature in Prague and Yiddish literature in Poland, neither of which was composed in the language of the cultural elite. He compares such literatures to a nation's diary and emphasizes their separateness from other literatures. For an in-depth critique of Deleuze and Guattari's approach to Kafka, see Stanley Corngold, *Lambent Traces: Franz Kafka* (Princeton, NJ: Princeton University Press, 2004), 142–57.

21. Franz Kafka, Letter to Max Brod, June 1921, in Franz Kafka, *Briefe 1902–1924*, ed. Max Brod (New York: Schocken Books, 1958), 338.

22. Biller, Dischereit, and Honigmann also reflect on the conditions of Jewish authorship within their literary texts proper. For example, Biller's fictional works often feature commercial writers, including Biller himself, as narrators and/or protagonists. See Chase Jefferson, "Shoah Business: Maxim Biller and the Problem of Contemporary German-Jewish Literature," *German Quarterly* 74, no. 2 (2001): 111–31.

23. Brad Prager suggested this reading in a position paper given in a 2014 GSA conference seminar on "German Jewish Literature after 1945: Working through and beyond the Holocaust." On Hilsenrath's *Berlin . . . Endstation*, see also Finch, "Revenge, Restitution, Ressentiment," 66–71.

24. On this meaning of the prefix *post-* (in a different context), see Schreier, *The Impossible Jew*, 10: "The *post* of postrace is not like the *post* of post-structuralism; it is more like the *post* of postcolonial, that is, a term designating not a chronological but a conceptual frame." On the term *post-Jewish*, see also Staci Boris, *The New Authentics: Artists of the Post-Jewish Generation* (Chicago: Spertus, 2007), 18–23.

2. Playing with Paratext

1. Ijoma Mangold, "Religion ist kein Wunschkonzert," *Die Zeit*, April 8, 2010, 47.

2. On the representation of religion in *Die Leinwand*, see also Agnes C. Mueller, "Religion and the Holocaust: Imre Kertész, Benjamin Stein, and *Kaddish for a Friend*," in Garloff and Mueller, *German Jewish Literature after 1990*, 202–20, esp. 213–18. Mueller argues that the book invites us to rethink the notion of authenticity, including religious authenticity. For a more critical reading of Stein's representation of Orthodox Judaism, see Roca Lizarazu, *Renegotiating Postmemory*, 52–58.

3. Some texts that are not materially appended to the book, such as interviews, letters, and author-endorsed book reviews, also fall into this category. See Gérard Genette,

Paratexts: Thresholds of Interpretation, trans. Jane E. Lewin (New York: Cambridge University Press, 1997).

4. Barbara Honigmann, *Ein Kapitel aus meinem Leben* (Munich: Carl Hanser, 2004). Here and elsewhere, quotes from paratexts are taken from the first German edition of the book.

5. Edgar Hilsenrath, *Gesammelte Werke in elf Bänden* (Cologne, Germany: Dittrich, 2003).

6. See Florian Sedlmeier, "Rereading Literary Form," 213.

7. Maxim Biller, *Wenn ich einmal reich und tot bin: Erzählungen* (Cologne, Germany: Kiepenheuer & Witsch, 1990).

8. Benjamin Stein, *Turmsegler* (blog), https://turmsegler.net.

9. Benjamin Stein, *Die Leinwand* (Munich: C. H. Beck, 2010), W, 82. All references to *Die Leinwand* are from this edition and hereafter will be cited parenthetically in the text. The letters W (for Wechsler) and Z (for Zichroni) refer to the two different parts of the book. In English, Benjamin Stein, *The Canvas*, trans. Brian Zumhagen (Rochester, NY: Open Letter Books, 2012), here W, 66. References to this translation will hereafter be cited parenthetically in the text after the reference to the German edition.

10. In his literary blog *Turmsegler*, Stein explicitly rejects the reduction of the literary work to the presumed identity of its author. After the publication of the *Zeit* article, which sparked new queries about his Jewish background, he clarified that his parents are not Jewish in the halachic definition and that he himself converted twice, first to Reform and then to Orthodox Judaism. The gist of this entry is a critique of the public voyeurism that forces the author to disclose such information. See "Der Autor als Seelenstripper," *Turmsegler*, June 3, 2010, http://turmsegler.net/20100603/der-autor-als-seelenstripper/.

11. For a comprehensive reconstruction of Wilkomirski's fraud, see Stefan Maechler, *The Wilkomirski Affair: A Study in Biographical Truth*, trans. John E. Woods (New York: Schocken Books, 2001). Maechler had been commissioned by Schocken to conduct an investigation into Wilkomirski's life and publish his findings. For a detailed and perceptive comparison between Wilkomirski and Stein, see also Roca Lizarazu, *Renegotiating Postmemory*, 30–52. She sums up that "Stein's text counters . . . the representational naivety of *Bruchstücke* with a hyperawareness of its own mediality and an ethics of self- and metareflexivity" (36).

12. Zichroni asks himself rhetorically, "Was . . . ist eine Wahrheit, die tötet, wert gegenüber einer Wahrheit, die jemanden leben lässt?" (Z, 179/146; What . . . is the value of a truth that kills, compared to a truth that allows a person to live?). Wechsler, who is tormented by feelings of guilt about his role in the campaign, seems to agree that the public exposure of Minsky was an act of violence: "Meine Schuld hat einen Namen: Minsky. Das muss ich immer gewusst haben. Ich habe ihm eine lückenlos belegbare Identität geschenkt. Seine Erinnerungen aber habe ich ihm geraubt . . . ich habe noch immer Angst vor Entdeckung und einer Strafe, die ich mir nicht einmal auszumalen wage." (W, 189–90/156; My guilt has a name: Minsky. I must have always known that. I gave him an identity that has no holes in it. But I robbed him of his memories . . . I'm still afraid of being discovered and enduring a punishment that I don't even dare to imagine.)

13. Amy Hungerford, "Memorizing Memory," *Yale Journal of Criticism* 14, no. 1 (2001): 67–92, here 69.

14. Hungerford, 88.

15. Marianne Hirsch, *The Generation of Postmemory: Writing and Visual Culture after the Holocaust* (New York: Columbia University Press, 2012), 36. For a reading of *Die Leinwand* in terms of witnessing, postmemory, and fictionalization, see also Silke Horstkotte, "'Ich bin, woran ich mich erinnere': Benjamin Steins *Die Leinwand* und der Fall Wilkomirski," in *Der Nationalsozialismus und die Shoah in der deutschsprachigen Gegenwartsliteratur*, ed. Torben Fischer, Philipp Hammermeister, and Sven Kramer (New York: Rodopi, 2014), 115–32.

16. See Philippe Lejeune, *On Autobiography*, trans. Katherine Leary (Minneapolis: University of Minnesota Press, 1989), esp. 3–31.

17. See Binjamin Wilkomirski, *Bruchstücke: Aus einer Kindheit 1939–1948* (Frankfurt: Jüdischer Verlag im Suhrkamp Verlag, 1995), 44, 102–3, 106. In English, *Fragments: Memories of a Wartime Childhood*, trans. Carol Brown Janeway (New York: Schocken Books, 1996), 46, 109–10, 113.

18. Wilkomirski, *Bruchstücke*, 143; *Fragments*, 154. The published English translation is slightly different than the German original. A more precise translation of the third sentence would be: "But this date is not consistent with either my life story or my memories."

19. Hirsch, *The Generation of Postmemory*, 41.

3. Memory and Mobility

1. See Doron Rabinovici, *Eichmann's Jews: The Jewish Administration of Holocaust Vienna, 1938–1945*, trans. Nick Somers (Cambridge: Polity, 2011), and the German original: *Instanzen der Ohnmacht: Wien 1938–1945: Der Weg zum Judenrat* (Frankfurt: Jüdischer Verlag im Suhrkamp Verlag, 2000).

2. The essay appeared in two parts in two consecutive issues. I am quoting here from part 1: Doron Rabinovici, "Wie es war und wie es gewesen sein wird: Geschichtsschreibung und Literatur zur Shoah," *Wespennest: Zeitschrift für brauchbare Texte und Bilder* 128 (September 2002): 20–24, here 2. For part 2, see "Wie es war und wie es gewesen sein wird (2. Teil): Geschichtsschreibung und Literatur zur Shoah," *Wespennest* 129 (December 2002): 24–28.

3. Rabinovici is far from alone in his view that the memory of the past opens up perspectives for the future. On the future orientation of memory in a broad range of contemporary literary works, see Amir Eshel, *Futurity: Contemporary Literature and the Quest for the Past* (Chicago: University of Chicago Press, 2012). On Rabinovici's essay, and on the relation between literature and historiography in his work more generally, see also Dirk Niefanger, "'Wie es gewesen sein wird': Opfer und Täter bei Doron Rabinovici," in *Literatur und Holocaust*, ed. Gerd Bayer and Rudolf Freiburg (Würzburg: Königshausen & Neumann, 2009), 193–209.

4. See Assmann, "The Holocaust—a Global Memory?," 11. For the definitions of these concepts, see Pierre Nora, "Between Memory and History: *Les Lieux de Mémoire*," *Representations* 26 (Spring 1989): 7–24 and Astrid Erll, "Travelling Memory," *Parallax* 17, no. 4 (2011): 4–18.

5. See Levy and Sznaider, *The Holocaust and Memory in the Global Age*, which I briefly discuss in the introduction to this book. For the collaboration between Rabinovici and Sznaider, see their coedited and coauthored books: Doron Rabinovici, Ulrich Speck, and Natan Sznaider, eds., *Neuer Antisemitismus? Eine globale Debatte* (Frankfurt: Suhrkamp, 2004); Christian Heilbronn, Doron Rabinovici, and Natan Sznaider, eds., *Neuer Antisemitismus? Fortsetzung einer globalen Debatte* (Berlin: Suhrkamp, 2019); and Doron

Rabinovici and Natan Sznaider, *Herzl Relo@ded: Kein Märchen* (Berlin: Jüdischer Verlag im Suhrkamp Verlag, 2016).

6. Doron Rabinovici, "Wie es war und wie es gewesen sein wird: Eine Fortschreibung von Geschichte und Literatur nach der Shoah," accessed February 27, 2021, http://www.rabinovici.at/texte_wieeswar.html. This online version differs somewhat from the version published earlier in *Wespennest*, in which Rabinovici explicitly cites the book by Levy and Sznaider.

7. In his book *Multidirectional Memory*, Rothberg makes this case primarily for France, where the re-remembrance of the Holocaust in the wake of the 1961 Eichmann trial coincided with the decolonization debates sparked by the Algerian War of Independence. He reiterates this argument in a poignant fashion in "Multidirectional Memory and the Universalization of the Holocaust," in *Remembering the Holocaust: A Debate*, by Jeffrey C. Alexander, with commentaries by Martin Jay et al. (New York: Oxford University Press, 2009), 123–34.

8. This chapter, which explores theoretical questions about memory and mobility, to some extent brackets the difference between German and Austrian Jewish literature, which nevertheless bears mentioning. As Vivian Liska argues, at least three characteristics set contemporary Austrian Jewish writers apart: (1) they have to contend with the *Opferlüge* and the relative silence about the Holocaust in postwar Austria; (2) they express their Jewish identity more indeterminately and assume a less antagonistic attitude toward their non-Jewish audiences; and (3) they consciously connect to the multiethnic and multireligious heritage of the Habsburg Empire. See Vivian Liska, "Secret Affinities: Contemporary Jewish Writing in Austria," in *Contemporary Jewish Writing in Europe: A Guide*, ed. Vivian Liska and Thomas Nolden (Bloomington: Indiana University Press, 2008), 1–22. On the particularities of Austrian Jewish literature, see also Andrea Reiter, *Contemporary Jewish Writing: Austria after Waldheim* (New York: Routledge, 2013) and Matthias Beilein, *86 und die Folgen: Robert Schindel, Robert Menasse und Doron Rabinovici im literarischen Feld Österreichs* (Berlin: Erich Schmidt, 2008). Both authors emphasize the impact of the Waldheim affair (i.e., Kurt Waldheim's 1986 presidential campaign and the ensuing debates about his past membership in the German Wehrmacht) on the cultural and political self-awareness of Austrian Jewish writers. Reiter's study focuses on the appropriation of places and the performance of Jewish identity in contemporary literature while Beilein draws on the methodology of Pierre Bourdieu to analyze the positioning of Robert Menasse, Doron Rabinovici, and Robert Schindel in the Austrian literary field.

9. Doron Rabinovici, *Suche nach M.: Roman in zwölf Episoden* (Frankfurt: Suhrkamp, 1997), 28. All references to *Suche nach M.* are from this edition and hereafter will be cited parenthetically in the text. In English, Doron Rabinovici, *The Search for M*, trans. Francis M. Sharp (Riverside, CA: Ariadne, 2000), 15. References to this translation will hereafter be cited parenthetically in the text after the reference to the German edition.

10. Later Siebert remembers very similar lines from his first interview with Mullemann: "Zuweilen scheint mir, als wäre Mullemann nichts als ein Schmerzpaket, ein Erinnerungsbündel aus verschiedenen, zufällig verwobenen Mullrollen, Verletzungen und Wunden" (228/158–59; It seems to me, at times, as if Mullemann is nothing more than a packet of pains, a bundle of memories from different, accidentally interwoven rolls of gauze, injuries and wounds).

11. See also the use of this metaphor of bandages, communities, and their dissolution. Some older people are afraid of Mullemann's revelations: "wenn all das nun aufgerollt werden sollte, würde Schrecklichstes geschehen, würde sich bei solch einer Abwicklung der Gesamtverband der Gemeinschaft auflösen." (182/125; if all that should be brought into

the open there would be terrible consequences. If these things began to unwind, the very bindings holding the community together would dissolve.)

12. See Doerte Bischoff, "Herkunft und Schuld: Identitätsverhandlungen in Doron Rabinovici's *Suche nach M*," in *Herkünfte: Historisch, ästhetisch, kulturell*, ed. Barbara Thums et al. (Heidelberg, Germany: Winter, 2004), 249–79, here 277–78.

13. Doron Rabinovici, *Ohnehin: Roman* (Frankfurt: Suhrkamp, 2004), 66. All references to *Ohnehin* are from this edition and hereafter will be cited parenthetically in the text.

14. One example can be found in part 2 of Rabinovici's "Wie es war und wie es gewesen sein wird," 26: "Das Vergessen hat einen durchaus notwendigen, auch ordnenden Sinn, um den Blick auf das Wesentliche zu richten. Es ist Grundvoraussetzung des Erinnerns. Jede Reminiszenz bedeutet eine Auswahl und eine Ausblendung dessen, was nicht ins Zentrum rückt." On the relationship between memory and forgetting, see also Friedrich Nietzsche, "On the Utility and Liability of History for Life," in *Unfashionable Observations*, trans. Richard T. Gray (Stanford, CA: Stanford University Press, 1995), 83–167, and Paul Ricoeur, *Memory, History, Forgetting*, trans. Kathleen Blamey and David Pellauer (Chicago: University of Chicago Press, 2004).

15. Birgit Neumann, "The Literary Representation of Memory," in *A Companion to Cultural Memory Studies*, ed. Astrid Erll and Ansgar Nünning in collaboration with Sarah B. Young (New York: De Gruyter, 2010), 333–43, here 337.

16. See Aleida Assmann, *Das neue Unbehagen an der Erinnerungskultur: Eine Intervention* (Munich: C. H. Beck, 2013), 68–69.

17. Walser's *Friedenspreisrede* and the reactions and responses to it are reprinted in Frank Schirrmacher, *Die Walser-Bubis-Debatte: Eine Dokumentation* (Frankfurt: Suhrkamp, 1999). See also Doerte Bischoff, "'Einmal muß Schluß sein'? Über Abrechnungen, Entschuldungen und kommunikative Erinnerung anläßlich einer Lektüre von Doron Rabinovici," in *Erinnern des Holocaust? Eine neue Generation sucht Antworten*, ed. Jens Birkmeyer and Cornelia Blasberg (Bielefeld, Germany: Aisthesis, 2006), 187–219.

18. See Rosa Pérez Zancas, "Die Vergangenheit bleibt ohnehin unscharf: Doron Rabinovicis *Ohnehin* (2004) und Ulla Hahns *Unscharfe Bilder* (2003)," in *WortKulturen, TonWelten: Festschrift für Alfonsina Janés zum 70. Geburtstag*, ed. Marisa Siguan, M. Loreta Vilar, and Rosa Pérez Zancas (Marburg, Germany: Tectum, 2014), 269–88, here 274. On the proliferation of and tension between different historical narratives in *Ohnehin*, see also Carl Niekerk, "The Postmodern Moment and the Return of History in Doron Rabinovici's *Ohnehin* (2004)," *Germanistik in Ireland* 6, special issue: *After Postmodernism / Nach der Postmoderne* (2011): 55–69.

19. See Sebastian Wogenstein, "Negative Symbiosis? Israel, Germany, and Austria in Contemporary Germanophone Literature," *Prooftexts* 33, no. 1 (2013): 105–32; Kirstin Gwyer, "Beyond Lateness? 'Postmemory' and the Late(st) German-Language Family Novel," *New German Critique* 42, no. 2 (2015): 137–53; Doerte Bischoff, "Das Erbe der Väter: Schoah-Erinnerung, Zeugenschaft und die Grenzen des Generationenkonzepts in Doron Rabinovicis 'Andernorts,'" in *"Horchet, ihr Söhne, der Moral des Vaters, und höret zu, um Weisheit zu erkennen" (Sprüche 4,1): Die Zehnte Joseph Carlebach-Konferenz: Väter und Vaterfiguren in jüdischer Geschichte, Religion und Kultur*, ed. Miriam Gillis-Carlebach, George Yaakov Kohler, and Ingrid Lohmann (Munich: Dölling and Galitz, 2016), 131–53. For another approach, one that resembles mine more closely in its emphasis on the geographic displacement of memory, see Christina Guenther, "Changing Places in Doron Rabinovici's *Andernorts*," *Seminar* 49, no. 4 (2013): 385–99.

20. Doron Rabinovici, *Andernorts: Roman* (Berlin: Suhrkamp, 2010), 51. All references to *Andernorts* are from this edition and hereafter will be cited parenthetically in the text. In English, Doron Rabinovici, *Elsewhere*, trans. Tess Lewis (London: Haus, 2014), 37. References to this translation will hereafter be cited parenthetically in the text after the reference to the German edition.

21. Bond, Craps, and Vermeulen, "Introduction: Memory on the Move," 6.

22. The narrator of *Andernorts* repeatedly mentions that Ethan Rosen composes his essays in a state of heightened affect. Ethan writes, for example, newspaper articles to discharge nervous energy (11/2).

23. See Roca Lizarazu, *Renegotiating Postmemory*, 95–129.

4. Memory and Similarity

1. Katja Petrowskaja, *Vielleicht Esther: Geschichten* (Berlin: Suhrkamp, 2014), 17. All references to *Vielleicht Esther* are from this edition and hereafter will be cited parenthetically in the text. In English, Katja Petrowskaja, *Maybe Esther: A Family Story*, trans. Shelley Frisch (New York: Harper Perennial, 2019), 11. References to this translation will hereafter be cited parenthetically in the text after the reference to the German edition.

2. In a personal conversation, Katja Petrowskaja explained to me that she rejects the genre designation "family memoir" for her work and also is not happy with the subtitle of the English translation, "A Family Story."

3. See Karen Körber, "Zäsur, Wandel oder Neubeginn? Russische Juden in Deutschland zwischen Recht, Repräsentation und Realität," in *Russisch-jüdische Gegenwart in Deutschland: Interdisziplinäre Perspektiven auf eine Diaspora im Wandel*, ed. Karen Körber (Göttingen, Germany: Vandenhoeck & Ruprecht, 2015), 13–36, here 28.

4. See Vladimir Vertlib's *Das besondere Gedächtnis der Rosa Masur: Roman* (Vienna: Deuticke, 2001), Lena Gorelik's *Meine weißen Nächte: Roman* (Munich: Schirmer-Graf, 2004), and Lena Muchina's *Lenas Tagebuch: Leningrad 1941-42*, trans. Lena Gorelik and Gero Fedtke (Berlin: Ullstein, 2013).

5. For a reading of Grjasnowa's novel as an example of multidirectional memory, see Elizabeth Loentz, "Beyond Negative Symbiosis: The Displacement of Holocaust Trauma and Memory in Alina Bronsky's *Scherbenpark* and Olga Grjasnowa's *Der Russe is einer, der Birken liebt*," in Garloff and Mueller, *German Jewish Literature after 1990*, 102–22. For an alternative reading that focuses on the centrality of Holocaust memory in the novel, see Jonathan Skolnik, "Memory without Borders? Migrant Identity and the Legacy of the Holocaust in Olga Grjasnowa's *Der Russe is einer, der Birken liebt*," in Garloff and Mueller, *German Jewish Literature after 1990*, 123–45.

6. Anil Bhatti and Dorothee Kimmich, introduction to *Similarity: A Paradigm for Culture Theory*, ed. Anil Bhatti and Dorothee Kimmich, with the assistance of Sara Bangert (New Delhi, India: Tulika Books, 2018), 1–22, here 9, emphasis in original.

7. See, for example, Klaus Hödl, "'Jewish History' beyond Binary Conceptions: Jewish Performing Musicians in Vienna around 1900," *Journal of Modern Jewish Studies* 16, no. 3 (2017): 377–94, https://doi.org/10.1080/14725886.2017.1345189.

8. For Celan's translation of the poem, see Jewgenij Jewtuschenko, "Babij Jar," in *Gesammelte Werke in fünf Bänden*, vol. 5, *Übertragungen II*, by Paul Celan, ed. Beda Allemann and Stefan Reichert with the assistance of Rolf Bücher (Frankfurt: Suhrkamp, 1986), 281–87,

here 281. The next line in the poem (which, however, is not cited in *Vielleicht Esther*) indicates a relationship of contiguity that places the speaker in the midst of the Jewish people: "Wir ziehn aus Ägyptenland aus, ich zieh mit."

9. Jewtuschenko, 285. Cited in Petrowskaja, *Vielleicht Esther*, 190. The English translation does not use enjambments: "I am each old man here shot dead, / I am every child here shot dead" (*Maybe Esther*, 169).

10. See Jan T. Gross, *Neighbors: The Destruction of the Jewish Community in Jedwabne, Poland* (Princeton, NJ: Princeton University Press, 2001). The book is cited in *Vielleicht Esther*, 110.

11. Dora Osborne, "Encountering the Archive in Katja Petrowskaja's *Vielleicht Ester*," *Seminar* 52, no. 3 (2016), 255–72, here 256. Osborne's main argument is that the documents the narrator uses to reconstruct her family history are fragmentary and the archives incomplete, with biases and power structures of their own.

12. Walter Benjamin defines the "mimetic faculty" as the human ability to recognize and produce similarity—for example, through dance and other bodily movements. See Walter Benjamin, "On the Mimetic Faculty," trans. Edmund Jephcott, in *Selected Writings*, vol. 2, *1927–1934*, ed. Michael W. Jennings, Howard Eiland, and Gary Smith (Cambridge, MA: Belknap Press of Harvard University Press, 1999), 720–22.

13. For a similar series of sections of the same image, see the photographs of Ozjel and his school in *Vielleicht Esther* (95/83, 97/84, 98/85).

14. Bond, Craps, and Vermeulen, "Introduction: Memory on the Move," 15.

15. See especially José van Dijck, *The Culture of Connectivity: A Critical History of Social Media* (Oxford: Oxford University Press, 2013) and "Connective Memory: How Facebook Takes Charge of Your Past," in *Memory Unbound: Tracing the Dynamics of Memory Studies*, ed. Lucy Bond, Stef Craps, and Pieter Vermeulen (New York: Berghahn Books, 2017), 151–72.

16. The word is later revealed to be the name of a train company but initially gives rise to speculations and storytelling on the narrator's part.

17. Roman Jakobson, "Linguistics and Poetics," in *Language in Literature*, by Roman Jakobson, ed. Krystyna Pomorska and Stephen Rudy (Cambridge, MA: Belknap Press of Harvard University Press, 1987), 62–94, here 71, emphasis in original.

18. On Petrowskaja's poetics of multilingualism, see especially Andree Michaelis-König's "Multilingualism and Jewishness in Katja Petrowskaja's *Vielleicht Esther*," in Garloff and Mueller, *German Jewish Literature after 1990*, 146–66. See also Anna Rutka, "'Wünschelrute' Deutsch: Über Sprachkritik und Sprachreflexion als Modi der Erinnerungshandlungen in Katja Petrowskajas 'Vielleicht Esther' (2014)," *Colloquia Germanica Stetinensia* 25 (2016): 85–99, and Gabriele Eckart, "The Functions of Multilingual Language Use in Katja Petrowskaja's *Vielleicht Esther*," *Glossen* 40 (June 2015), http://blogs.dickinson.edu/glossen/archive/most-recent-issue-glossen-402015/gabriele-eckart-glossen40-2015/.

19. "Ich habe versucht, in diesem Buch nichts zu *erdichten*. Ich habe sehr viel mit Dokumenten gearbeitet und verschiedenen Aussagen. Man versucht, wenn man nicht sicher ist, alle Versionen reinzunehmen. Und auch diese vage *Vermutung*. Das ist vielleicht die einzige Möglichkeit, irgendwie in Richtung Wahrheit zu gehen, dass man Fakten kennt, Grundlagen, Nacherzählungen und auch weitergeht mit *Vermutungen*." Cited in Holger Heimann, "Katja Petrowskaja: Familiensaga im Kontext des Zweiten Weltkriegs," Deutschlandfunk, May 12, 2014, https://www.deutschlandfunk.de/katja-petrowskaja-familiensaga-im-kontext-des-zweiten.700.de.html?dram:article_id=285117, my emphasis.

20. See Petrowskaja, *Vielleicht Esther*, 9/3. It later turns out that the story about the French musical was not completely invented, since years ago an advertisement for *Les Misérables* had upset travelers at the Berlin train station in a way similar to the *Bombardier* advertisement. The most self-reflexive story in *Maybe Esther*—that of the ficus, or fig tree, that had to be removed from a van to make room for the narrator's father during the family's flight from Kyiv—further illustrates both the importance of storytelling and the difficulty of clearly distinguishing between *Vermutung* and *Erdichtung*. The narrator concedes that she may have invented the story of the ficus in order to fill the gaps in her knowledge, and she engages in a series of puns that blur the lines between reality and fantasy: "Ich war auf den Fikus fixiert, ich war fikussiert. . . . Gab es den Fikus, oder ist er eine Fiktion? Wurde die Fiktion aus dem Fikus geboren—oder umgekehrt?" (Petrowskaja, 219/194-95; I was fixated on that ficus, I was ficusated. . . . Did the ficus exist, or was it a fiction? Was the fiction born from the ficus, or the other way around?).

21. For an incisive reading of *Vielleicht Esther* in these terms, see Maria Roca Lizarazu, "The Family Tree, the Web, and the Palimpsest: Figures of Postmemory in Katja Petrowskaja's *Vielleicht Esther* (2014)," *Modern Language Review* 113, no. 1 (January 2018): 168-89. According to Roca Lizarazu, *Vielleicht Esther* features three different modes of relating to the dead—genealogy, affiliation, and palimpsestic memory—the first two of which remain indebted to biological models of contagion, as is the concept of postmemory at large.

22. Bhatti and Kimmich, introduction to *Similarity*, 9, emphasis in original.

5. Returning

1. Barbara Honigmann, "Selbstporträt als Jüdin," in *Damals, dann und danach*, 11-18, here 18.
2. Honigmann, *Damals, dann und danach*, 15.
3. On the heterogeneous character of Strasbourg's Jewish community and Honigmann's conception of diasporic writing, see also Guenther, "Exile and the Construction of Identity."
4. See Honigmann, "Von meinem Urgrossvater, meinem Grossvater, meinem Vater und von mir," in *Damals, dann und danach*, 39-55, esp. 51.
5. Barbara Honigmann, "'Wenn mir die Leute vorwerfen, daß ich zuviel von mir spreche, so werfe ich ihnen vor, daß sie überhaupt nicht über sich selbst nachdenken': Zürcher Poetikvorlesung (I): Über autobiographisches Schreiben," in *Das Gesicht wiederfinden*, 31-60, here 39, emphasis in original.
6. See Yfaat Weiss, "Im Schreiben das Leben verändern—Barbara Honigmann als Chronistin des jüdischen Lebens in Deutschland," in *Kurz hinter der Wahrheit und dicht neben der Lüge: Zum Werk Barbara Honigmanns*, ed. Amir Eshel and Yfaat Weiss (Munich: Wilhelm Fink, 2013), 17-28. Weiss draws special attention to Honigmann's GDR background and the prejudices and antisemitism encountered by former Jewish refugees, especially those who had spent their exile in Western Europe.
7. Barbara Honigmann, *Eine Liebe aus nichts* (Berlin: Rowohlt, 1991), 31. All references to *Eine Liebe aus nichts* are from this edition and hereafter will be cited parenthetically in the text. In English, Barbara Honigmann, *A Love Made Out of Nothing* and *Zohara's Journey: Two Novels*, trans. John Barrett (Boston, MA: David R. Godine, 2003), 22. References to this translation will hereafter be cited parenthetically in the text after the reference to the German edition.

8. See Jeffrey Herf, *Divided Memory: The Nazi Past in the Two Germanys* (Cambridge, MA: Harvard University Press, 1997).
9. See Lejeune, *On Autobiography*, esp. 3–31.
10. See Barbara Honigmann, *Eine Liebe aus nichts* (Reinbek bei Hamburg: Rowohlt Taschenbuch, 1993), paperback ed., my emphasis.
11. Honigmann, *Damals, dann und danach*, 14.
12. Honigmann, *Damals, dann und danach*, 59.
13. On the multiple meanings of "return" in Honigmann's book, see also Godela Weiss-Sussex, "Between Distance and Belonging: Space, Time, and Multilingualism in *Das überirdische Licht*," forthcoming in *Barbara Honigmann*, ed. Robert Gillett and Godela Weiss-Sussex (New York: Peter Lang, 2022).
14. As Emily Jeremiah observes, the potential "pathos of this statement" is cut short right away, as a friend "informs her that it no longer exists." Emily Jeremiah, *Nomadic Ethics in Contemporary Women's Writing in German: Strange Subjects* (Rochester, NY: Camden House, 2012), 178.
15. Barbara Honigmann, *Das überirdische Licht: Rückkehr nach New York* (Munich: Carl Hanser, 2008), 64.
16. See Barbara Honigmann, *Roman von einem Kinde: Sechs Erzählungen* (Darmstadt, Germany: Luchterhand, 1986), 90.
17. Honigmann, *Roman von einem Kinde*, 96.
18. Honigmann, *Damals, dann und danach*, 28.
19. Honigmann, *Damals, dann und danach*, 29.
20. Honigmann, *Damals, dann und danach*, 37.
21. Honigmann, *Damals, dann und danach*, 34. In another story in *Damals, dann und danach*, titled "Der Untergang von Wien" (89–120), the Jewish cemetery provides a similar opportunity to reconnect with the past, which is realized not in funeral rituals but through the narrator's movement and storytelling. The text opens with a description of the Viennese Jewish cemetery in which mother was buried. We learn once again that the mother is uninterested in remembering the past; that she refuses for example to revisit the Viennese places that mattered to her as a child. In the end it is her daughter who attempts to get a sense of the Viennese past by visiting the cemetery and other significant places (101).
22. See Mikhail M. Bakhtin, "Forms of Time and Chronotope in the Novel," in *The Dialogic Imagination: Four Essays*, ed. Michael Holquist, trans. Caryl Emerson and Michael Holquist (Austin: University of Texas Press, 1981), 84–258, esp. 243–45.
23. Cited in Mann, *Space and Place*, 5. The original quote is in Tuan, *Space and Place*, 6.
24. Barbara Honigmann, *Chronik meiner Straße* (Munich: Carl Hanser, 2015), 5. All references to *Chronik meiner Straße* are from this edition and hereafter will be cited parenthetically in the text.
25. See, e.g. Honigmann, *Chronik meiner Straße*, 9: "Wiwifak."
26. See Miriam Lipis, "A Hybrid Place of Belonging: Constructing and Siting the Sukkah," *Jewish Topographies: Visions of Space, Traditions of Place*, ed. Julia Brauch, Anna Lipphardt, and Alexandra Nocke (Burlington, VT: Ashgate 2008), 27–41. See also Sonja Dickow, "Unbehaustes Wohnen: Zum Chronotopos der Laubhütte in Michal Govrins *Hevzekim* (2002) und Barbara Honigmann's *Chronik meiner Straße* (2015), in Bischoff and Tippner, *Figurations of Mobile Identities*, 156–71.
27. Kilcher, "Exterritorialitäten."

6. Transitioning

1. Vladimir Vertlib, *Zwischenstationen: Roman* (Vienna: Deuticke, 1999), 30. All references to *Zwischenstationen* are from this edition and hereafter will be cited parenthetically in the text.
2. See Julya Rabinowich, "Mir war es wichtig, schnell Deutsch zu lernen," conversation with Katja Lückert, Deutschlandfunk, August 23, 2016, https://www.deutschlandfunk.de/julya-rabinowich-mir-war-es-wichtig-schnell-deutsch-zu.691.de.html?dram:article_id=363896. Julya Rabinowich, "Zurück in die Zukunft," *Der Standard*, August 1, 2015, https://derstandard.at/2000020078821/Zurueck-in-die-Zukunft.
3. Leslie A. Adelson, *The Turkish Turn in Contemporary German Literature: Toward a New Critical Grammar of Migration* (New York: Palgrave Macmillan, 2005), 4.
4. Vladimir Vertlib, "Die Erfindung des Lebens als Literatur: Emigration und autobiographisches Schreiben," in *Spiegel im fremden Wort*, 9–42, here 39–40, my emphasis.
5. See Clifford, *Routes: Travel and Translation*.
6. Vladimir Vertlib, *Abschiebung: Erzählung* (Salzburg, Austria: Otto Müller, 1995), 7. All references to *Abschiebung* are from this edition and hereafter will be cited parenthetically in the text.
7. "Gegen-Orte zum Autochthonen . . . ephemere Transiträume, in denen sich eine Vielheit territorialer Signifikationen überlagern oder nur flüchtig kreuzen." Katrin Molnár, "'Die bessere Welt war immer anderswo.' Literarische Heimatkonstruktionen bei Jakob Hessing, Chaim Noll, Wladimir Kaminer und Vladimir Vertlib im Kontext von Alija, jüdischer Diaspora und säkularer Migration," in *Von der nationalen zur internationalen Literatur: Transkulturelle deutschsprachige Literatur und Kultur im Zeitalter globaler Migration*, ed. Helmut Schmitz (New York: Rodopi, 2009), 311–36, here 325.
8. See, for example, the chapter "Ostia," which is titled after one of the way stations in which Russian migrants reside on an interim basis. Even if their sojourn is only temporary, the migrants are taking possession of the place. One Russian Jewish family found a cheap room, and many others followed until the place was "in russischer Hand" (139).
9. Massey, *Space, Place, and Gender*, 120.
10. Massey, *Space, Place, and Gender*, 154.
11. Brigid Haines, "Poetics of the 'Gruppenbild': The Fictions of Vladimir Vertlib," *German Life and Letters* 62, no. 2 (2009): 233–44, here 236.
12. Julya Rabinowich, *Spaltkopf: Roman* (Vienna: Deuticke, 2011), 58. All references to *Spaltkopf* are from this edition and hereafter will be cited parenthetically in the text. In English, Julya Rabinowich, *Splithead*, trans. Tess Lewis (London: Portobello Books, 2011), 56. References to this translation will hereafter be cited parenthetically in the text after the reference to the German edition.
13. On the experimental style of *Spaltkopf*, see also Weertje Willms, "Zum Zusammenhang von Identität und literarischer Form in Texten russisch-deutscher Autorinnen der Gegenwart am Beispiel von Julya Rabinowich und Lena Gorelik," in *Migration et identité*, ed. Thomas Klinkert (Freiburg, Germany: Rombach, 2014), 169–94.
14. See Julya Rabinowich, "Es muss verändert werden," in *Ankommen: Gespräche mit Dimitré Dinev, Anna Kim, Radek Knapp, Julya Rabinowich, Michael Stavarič*, by Brigitte Schwens-Harrant (Vienna: Styria, 2014), 55–85, here 58.
15. Julya Rabinowich, *Dazwischen: Ich* (Munich: Carl Hanser, 2016), 62. All references to *Dazwischen: Ich* are from this edition and hereafter will be cited parenthetically in the

text. The novel is based on Rabinowich's theater play *Tagfinsternis*, which premiered in 2014. While the play focuses on the problems of the adults, the novel adopts the perspective of Madina. On *Tagfinsternis*, see Julia Danielczyk, "'Die Zeichen auf meiner Haut sind bindend' (Oder) Menschen sind keine Dunkelziffern: Über Julya Rabinowichs Theatertexte *Tagfinsternis* und *Fluchtarien*," in *Flucht, Migration, Theater: Dokumente und Positionen*, ed. Birgit Peter and Gabriele C. Pfeiffer (Göttingen, Germany: Vandenhoeck & Ruprecht, 2017), 221–27.

16. On Vertlib's work as a volunteer during the refugee crisis, see Vladimir Vertlib, "Auslass der Flüchtlinge," *Das Jüdische Echo* (blog), February 7, 2017, http://juedischesecho.at/auslass-der-fluechtlinge-von-vladimir-vertlib/. Some sentences of this report are repeated verbatim in *Viktor hilft*. For a compelling reading of *Viktor hilft* as an—albeit limited—critique of Western humanitarianism, see Stuart Taberner, "Narrative and Empathy: The 2015 'Refugee Crisis' in Vladimir Vertlib's *Viktor hilft* and Olga Grjasnowa's *Gott ist nicht schüchtern*," *German Life and Letters* 74, no. 2 (2021): 247–62.

17. Vladimir Vertlib, *Viktor hilft: Roman* (Vienna: Deuticke, 2018). All references to *Viktor hilft* are from this edition and hereafter will be cited parenthetically in the text.

18. Bala Venkat Mani pointed out this nationalist tendency to erase histories of migration in his paper "Reading with Refugees: Hyperlinked Literary Histories," MLA Convention, Seattle, January 2020.

7. Arriving

1. Stuart Hall, "Minimal Selves," in *Identity: The Real Me*, ed. Lisa Appigananesi and Homi K. Bhabha (London: Institute of Contemporary Arts, 1987), 44–46, here 44. For a longer description of Hall's intellectual and political development, see also "The Formation of a Diasporic Intellectual: An Interview with Stuart Hall by Kuan-Hsing Chen," in *Stuart Hall: Critical Dialogues in Cultural Studies*, ed. David Morley and Kuan-Hsing Chen (New York: Routledge, 1996), 486–503.

2. Hall, "Minimal Selves," 45.

3. See Franziska Becker, "Ankommen," in *Das neue Deutschland: Von Migration und Vielfalt*, ed. Özkan Ezli and Gisela Staupe (Paderborn, Germany: Konstanz University Press, 2014), 63–66. See also the fuller account of the arrival process of Russian Jewish *Kontingentflüchtlinge* in Franziska Becker, *Ankommen in Deutschland: Einwanderungspolitik als biographische Erfahrung im Migrationsprozeß russischer Juden* (Berlin: Reimer, 2001).

4. Dmitrij Belkin, "Babel 21: Ein Diaspora-Update," in *#Babel 21: Migration und jüdische Gemeinschaft*, ed. Dmitrij Belkin (Berlin: Hentrich & Hentrich, 2017), 10–13.

5. See Czollek, *Desintegriert euch!*, 139–40, 144–45. Czollek emphasizes that today's German Jewish community is the product of "social engineering"—that is, the government's decision to promote the post-Soviet Jewish migration and recreate a sizable Jewish community in Germany. See Czollek, 186.

6. On the ludic character of the narrator's gesture and his performance of an Austrian identity, see Haines, "Poetics of the 'Gruppenbild,'" 236–37.

7. One example of how *arrival* signifies such an inner transformation, however open ended, is the GDR literary genre of *Ankunftsliteratur*. *Ankunftsliteratur* is composed of a number of short novels written between 1960 and 1965 that depict the encounter of an individual with the new socialist order. The focus of the genre is on subjective dispositions

and individual processes of adaptation. See Matthias Aumüller, "Ankunftsliteratur: Explikation eines literaturhistorischen Begriffs," in *Wirkendes Wort* 61, no. 2 (2011): 293–311.

8. See Pierre Bourdieu, *The Rules of Art: Genesis and Structure of the Literary Field*, trans. Susan Emanuel (Stanford: Stanford University Press, 1996).

9. "Migrantenliteratur ist die Literatur von außen, und sie wird in meinen Augen definiert als die Literatur der ursprünglichen Mängel, nachträglich angereichert mit Kompensationen. Keine Literatur per se." Julya Rabinowich, "Wir haben das Ministerium der Liebe," *Der Standard*, October 29, 2010, https://www.derstandard.at/story/1288160305059/integrationsdebatte-julya-rabinowich-wir-haben-das-ministerium-der-liebe.

10. Adrian Wanner, *Out of Russia: Fictions of a New Translingual Diaspora* (Evanston, IL: Northwestern University Press, 2011), 72.

11. See Gorelik, *Meine weißen Nächte*, 261–62. All references to *Meine weißen Nächte* are from this edition and hereafter will be cited parenthetically in the text.

12. Wanner, *Out of Russia*, 73. For another incisive critical reading of the novel, see Anke S. Biendarra, "Cultural Dichotomies and Lived Transnationalism in Recent Russian-German Narratives," in *Transnationalism in Contemporary German-Language Literature*, ed. Elisabeth Herrmann, Carrie Smith-Prei, and Stuart Taberner (Rochester, NY: Camden House, 2015), 209–27, esp. 212–15. For a more appreciative reading of Gorelik's narrative style, see Willms, "Zum Zusammenhang von Identität und literarischer Form." According to Willms, the choice of the genre of *Unterhaltungsliteratur*, the lack of literary experimentation, and the use of humor all reflect the narrator's confidence in herself and her Russian Jewish German identity.

13. See Lena Gorelik, *"Sie können aber gut Deutsch!" Warum ich nicht mehr dankbar sein will, dass ich hier leben darf, und Toleranz nicht weiterhilft* (Munich: Pantheon, 2012), 11, 23, 66.

14. Gorelik, *"Sie können aber gut Deutsch!,"* 33, my emphasis.

15. Dmitrij Kapitelman, *Das Lächeln meines unsichtbaren Vaters* (Munich: Carl Hanser, 2016), 13. All references to *Das Lächeln meines unsichtbaren Vaters* are from this edition and hereafter will be cited parenthetically in the text. One of the few scholars who have written about *Das Lächeln meines unsichtbaren Vaters* is Agnes C. Mueller, who focuses on the book's representation of the father and the significance of the state of Israel in German (Jewish) Holocaust remembrance. See Mueller, "Germans, Migration, and Holocaust Memory in Contemporary Literature," in *The Holocaust Across Borders: Trauma, Atrocity, and Representation in Literature and Culture*, ed. Hilene S. Flanzbaum (Lanham, MD: Lexington Books, 2021), 71–87, esp. 76–79.

16. Sander L. Gilman, "Becoming a Jew by Becoming a German: The Newest Jewish Writing from the 'East,'" *Shofar: An Interdisciplinary Journal of Jewish Studies* 25, no. 1 (2006): 16–32.

17. This ongoing process of identity formation also contributes to the difficulty of identifying the book's genre. *Das Lächeln meines unsichtbaren Vaters* lacks fiction signals such as the genre designation "Roman." The eventual homonymy of protagonist, narrator, and author suggests an autobiographical reading, as does the fact that the birth name of the book's narrator—Dimitrij Romashkan (12, 65)—is the name under which the real-life author published his first journalistic pieces. Other biographical data ascribed to the narrator in the jacket copy also agree with the facts of the author's life: Kapitelman was born in Kyiv to a Jewish father and a non-Jewish mother and has lived in Germany since he was eight years

old. Nevertheless, most reviewers have focused on the literary character of the work, and at least one reviewer has read it as a novel.

18. See Primo Levi, *The Drowned and the Saved*, trans. Raymond Rosenthal (New York: Vintage International, 1989), 83–84. See also Giorgio Agamben's interpretation of this structure in *Remnants of Auschwitz: The Witness and the Archive*, trans. Daniel Heller-Roazen (New York: Zone Books, 1999), 41–86.

19. Jan Himmelfarb, *Sterndeutung: Roman* (Munich: C. H. Beck, 2015), 388. All references to *Sterndeutung* are from this edition and hereafter will be cited parenthetically in the text.

20. On the significance of the railway in the German Jewish context, see also Todd Samuel Presner, *Mobile Modernity: Germans, Jews, Trains* (New York: Columbia University Press, 2007).

21. See Maria Roca Lizarazu, "Ec-static Existences: The Poetics and Politics of Non-Belonging in Sasha Marianna Salzmann's *Außer sich* (2017)," *Modern Languages Open* 1, no. 9 (2020): 1–19, https://doi.org/10.3828/mlo.v0i0.284.

Conclusion

1. "Zugehörigkeit zur Gesellschaft entsteht nicht durch kulturelle oder religiöse Anpassung, sondern durch Anerkennung." Max Czollek, *Gegenwartsbewältigung* (Munich: Carl Hanser, 2020), 172.

2. Y. Michal Bodemann, "Ideologische Arbeit: Thesen zum jüdischen und nicht-jüdischen Gedächtnistheater in Deutschland," in *Desintegration: Ein Kongress zeitgenössischer jüdischer Positionen*, ed. Max Czollek and Sasha Marianna Salzmann (Bielefeld, Germany: Kerber, 2017), 33–49, here 46. On Jewish Israelis in Berlin, see especially the work of Dani Kranz (to whom Bodemann refers), e.g.: Dani Kranz, "Forget Israel—The Future Is in Berlin! Local Jews, Russian Immigrants, and Israeli Jews in Berlin and Across Germany," *Shofar: An Interdisciplinary Journal of Jewish Studies* 34, no. 4 (2016): 5–28, and Hadas Cohen and Dani Kranz, "Israeli Jews in the New Berlin: From Shoah Memories to Middle Eastern Encounters," in *Cultural Topographies of the New Berlin*, ed. Karin Bauer and Jennifer Ruth Hosek (London: Berghahn, 2017), 322–46.

3. See the personal website of Mati Shemoelof at https://mati-s.com/bio.

4. See Mati Shemoelof, "Drei Gedichte," *Jalta: Positionen zur jüdischen Gegenwart* 7 (2020): 50–53, and Jan Kühne, "Vom Misrachipoet zum *Juden Dichter*: Mati Shemoelof setzt über," *Jalta: Positionen zur jüdischen Gegenwart* 7 (2020): 54–58. On Hebrew-German connections in Shemoelof, see also Rachel Seelig with Amir Eshel, editors' introduction to *The German-Hebrew Dialogue: Studies of Encounter and Exchange*, ed. Amir Eshel and Rachel Seelig (Berlin: De Gruyter, 2017), 1–15, here 7–8.

5. See Sandra Vlasta, "'Was ist ihre Arbeit hier, in Prosa der deutschsprachigen Sprach?' Mehrsprachige Räume der Begegnung und Empathie in Tomer Gardis Roman *broken german*," in *Affektivität und Mehrsprachigkeit: Dynamiken der deutschsprachigen Gegenwartsliteratur*, ed. Marion Acker, Anne Fleig, and Matthias Lüthjohann (Tübingen, Germany: Narr Francke Attempto, 2019), 143–57.

6. Tomer Gardi, "Jeder sollte auf Deutsch schreiben dürfen," interview in *Die Welt*, August 18, 2018, https://www.welt.de/kultur/literarischewelt/article157738156/Jeder-sollte-auf-Deutsch-schreiben-duerfen.html.

7. Tomer Gardi, *Broken German: Roman* (Graz, Austria: Droschl, 2016), 48. All references to *Broken German* are from this edition and hereafter will be cited parenthetically in the text.

8. See also Vlasta, "'Was ist ihre Arbeit hier,'" 154–55. Vlasta uses a different terminology, arguing that in *Broken German*, "Nicht-Orte" (Marc Augé) becomes "Räume" (Michel de Certeau); the latter are constituted by the activities and interactions of the people therein.

9. See Franz Kafka, "Ein Bericht für eine Akademie," in Kafka, *Kritische Ausgabe: Drucke zu Lebzeiten*, edited by Wolf Kittler, Hans-Gerd Koch, and Gerhard Neumann (Frankfurt: Fischer, 1994), 299–313. In English, "A Report to an Academy," in *Kafka's Selected Stories: New Translations, Backgrounds, and Criticism*, translated and edited by Stanley Corngold (New York: W. W. Norton, 2007), 76–84.

10. The anecdotes he tells about an alleged scam literary-prize award and his visit to the Berlin Jewish Museum (where he wonders whether a Jew who enters the museum becomes part of the exhibition) further draw attention to the mechanisms of the culture industry.

11. The 2021 German Studies Association Conference featured a double panel on continuities and contiguities in twentieth- and twenty-first-century German Jewish writing. Participants included panelists Agnes Mueller, Jonathan Skolnik, Rebekah Slodounik, Corey Twitchell, and Sebastian Wogenstein as well as commentators Elizabeth Loentz and Erin McGlothlin. The panelists explored literary genres and themes such as satire, exile, and human rights and traced connections between individual authors such as Franz Werfel and Olga Grjasnowa, Anna Seghers and Deborah Feldmann, Hugo Bettauer and Edgar Hilsenrath, and Peter Weiss and Mirna Funk. See also Jonathan Skolnik, "'Jewish' Writing and the Place of Refuge: Olga Grjasnowa's *Gott ist nicht schüchtern*," *Yearbook for European Jewish Literature* 8 (2021): 148–57.

12. See Stuart Taberner, "Worldliness, Jewish Purpose and the Non-Jewish Jewish Narrator in Olga Grjasnowa's *Der verlorene Sohn* (2020)," *Seminar* (forthcoming).

13. On the narratological concept of metalepsis, see Gérard Genette, *Narrative Discourse: An Essay in Method*, trans. Jane E. Lewin (Ithaca, NY: Cornell University Press, 1980), 234–37.

WORKS CITED

Adelson, Leslie A. *The Turkish Turn in Contemporary German Literature: Toward a New Critical Grammar of Migration*. New York: Palgrave Macmillan, 2005.
Agamben, Giorgio. *Remnants of Auschwitz: The Witness and the Archive*. Translated by Daniel Heller-Roazen. New York: Zone Books, 1999.
Assmann, Aleida. *Das neue Unbehagen an der Erinnerungskultur: Eine Intervention*. Munich: C. H. Beck, 2013.
———. "The Holocaust—a Global Memory? Extensions and Limits of a New Memory Community." In *Memory in a Global Age: Discourses, Practices and Trajectories*, edited by Aleida Assmann and Sebastian Conrad, 97–116. New York: Palgrave Macmillan, 2010.
Aumüller, Matthias. "Ankunftsliteratur: Explikation eines literarhistorischen Begriffs." *Wirkendes Wort* 61, no. 2 (2011): 293–311.
Aviv, Caryn S., and David Shneer. *New Jews: The End of the Jewish Diaspora*. New York: New York University Press, 2005.
Bakhtin, Mikhail M. "Forms of Time and Chronotope in the Novel." In *The Dialogic Imagination: Four Essays*, edited by Michael Holquist, translated by Caryl Emerson and Michael Holquist, 84–258. Austin: University of Texas Press, 1981.
Banki, Luisa, and Caspar Battegay. "Sieben Thesen zur deutschsprachigen jüdischen Gegenwartsliteratur." In *Zwischen Literarizität und Programmatik: Jüdische Literaturen der Gegenwart*, edited by Luisa Banki, Yevgeniy Breyger, Micha Brumlik, Marina Chernivsky, Max Czollek, Hannah Peaceman, Anna Schapiro, and Leah Wohl von Haselberg, special issue, *Jalta: Positionen zur jüdischen Gegenwart* (2019): 41–47.
Battegay, Sylvia. "Sprache der Stummen: Katja Petrowskajas *Vielleicht Esther* als literarische Praxis der Desintegration." In *Figurations of Mobile Identities in Contemporary European Jewish Literature*, edited by Doerte Bischoff and Anja Tippner. *Yearbook for European Jewish Literature Studies* 5 (2018): 51–66.
Becker, Franziska. "Ankommen." In *Das neue Deutschland: Von Migration und Vielfalt*, edited by Özkan Ezli and Gisela Staupe, 63–66. Paderborn, Germany: Konstanz University Press, 2014.
———. *Ankommen in Deutschland: Einwanderungspolitik als biographische Erfahrung im Migrationsprozeß russischer Juden*. Berlin: Reimer, 2001.
Beilein, Matthias. *86 und die Folgen: Robert Schindel, Robert Menasse und Doron Rabinovici im literarischen Feld Österreichs*. Berlin: Erich Schmidt, 2008.
Belenky, Masha, and Jonathan Skolnik. "Russian Jews in Today's Germany: End of the Journey?" *European Judaism* 31, no. 2 (Autumn 1998): 30–44.
Belkin, Dmitrij. "Babel 21: Ein Diaspora-Update." In *#Babel 21: Migration und jüdische Gemeinschaft*, edited by Dmitrij Belkin, 10–13. Berlin: Hentrich & Hentrich, 2017.
———. "Mögliche Heimat: Deutsches Judentum zwei." In *Ausgerechnet Deutschland! Jüdisch-russische Einwanderung in die Bundesrepublik*, edited by Raphael Gross and Dmitrij Belkin, 25–29. Berlin: Nicolai, 2010.

Benjamin, Walter. "On the Mimetic Faculty." Translated by Edmund Jephcott. In *1927–1934*, edited by Michael W. Jennings, Howard Eiland, and Gary Smith, 720–22. Vol. 2 of *Selected Writings*. Cambridge, MA: Belknap Press of Harvard University Press, 1999.

Bhatti, Anil, and Dorothee Kimmich. Introduction to *Similarity: A Paradigm for Culture Theory*, edited by Anil Bhatti and Dorothee Kimmich with the assistance of Sarah Bangert, 1–22. New Delhi, India: Tulika Books, 2018.

Biendarra, Anke S. "Cultural Dichotomies and Lived Transnationalism in Recent Russian-German Narratives." In *Transnationalism in Contemporary German-Language Literature*, edited by Elisabeth Herrmann, Carrie Smith-Prei, and Stuart Taberner, 209–27. Rochester, NY: Camden House, 2015.

Biller, Maxim. *Deutschbuch*. Munich: dtv, 2001.

——. *Wenn ich einmal reich und tot bin: Erzählungen*. Cologne, Germany: Kiepenheuer & Witsch, 1990.

Bischoff, Doerte. "Das Erbe der Väter: Schoah-Erinnerung, Zeugenschaft und die Grenzen des Generationenkonzepts in Doron Rabinovicis 'Andernorts.'" In *"Horchet, ihr Söhne, der Moral des Vaters, und höret zu, um Weisheit zu erkennen" (Sprüche 4,1): Die zehnte Joseph Carlebach-Konferenz : Väter und Vaterfiguren in jüdischer Geschichte, Religion und Kultur*, edited by Miriam Gillis-Carlebach, George Yaakov Kohler, and Ingrid Lohmann, 131–53. Munich: Dölling & Galitz, 2016.

——. "'Einmal muß Schluß sein'? Über Abrechnungen, Entschuldungen und kommunikative Erinnerung anläßlich einer Lektüre von Doron Rabinovici." In *Erinnern des Holocaust? Eine neue Generation sucht Antworten*, edited by Jens Birkmeyer and Cornelia Blasberg, 187–219. Bielefeld, Germany: Aisthesis, 2006.

——. "Herkunft und Schuld: Identitätsverhandlungen in Doron Rabinovici's *Suche nach M.*" In *Herkünfte: Historisch, ästhetisch, kulturell*, edited by Barbara Thums, Volker Mergenthaler, Nicola Kaminski, and Doerte Bischoff, 249–79. Heidelberg, Germany: Winter, 2004.

Bischoff, Doerte, and Anja Tippner, eds. *Figurations of Mobile Identities in Contemporary European Jewish Literature*. Yearbook for European Jewish Literature Studies 5 (2018).

Bodemann, Y. Michal. *Gedächtnistheater: Die jüdische Gemeinschaft und ihre deutsche Erfindung*. Hamburg, Germany: Rotbuch, 1996.

——. "Ideologische Arbeit: Thesen zum jüdischen und nicht-jüdischen Gedächtnistheater in Deutschland." In *Desintegration: Ein Kongress zeitgenössischer jüdischer Positionen*, edited by Max Czollek and Sasha Marianna Salzmann, 33–49. Bielefeld, Germany: Kerber, 2017.

Bodemann, Y. Michal, and Olena Bagno. "In the Ethnic Twilight: The Paths of Russian Jews in Germany." In *The New German Jewry and the European Context: The Return of the European Jewish Diaspora*, edited by Y. Michal Bodemann, 158–76. New York: Palgrave Macmillan, 2008.

Bond, Lucy, Stef Craps, and Pieter Vermeulen. "Introduction: Memory on the Move." In *Memory Unbound: Tracing the Dynamics of Memory Studies*, edited by Lucy Bond, Stef Craps, and Pieter Vermeulen, 1–26. New York: Berghahn Books, 2017.

Boris, Staci. *The New Authentics: Artists of the Post-Jewish Generation*. Chicago: Spertus, 2007.

Borowski, Tadeusz. *Bei uns in Auschwitz: Erzählungen*. Translated by Vera Cerny. München: Piper, 1999.

Bourdieu, Pierre. *The Rules of Art: Genesis and Structure of the Literary Field*. Translated by Susan Emanuel. Stanford: Stanford University Press, 1996.

Boyarin, Daniel, and Jonathan Boyarin. "Diaspora: Generation and the Ground of Jewish Identity." *Critical Inquiry* 19, no. 4 (Summer 1993): 693–725.
Boyarin, Jonathan, and Daniel Boyarin. *Powers of Diaspora: Two Essays on the Relevance of Jewish Culture*. Minneapolis: University of Minnesota Press, 2002.
Braese, Stephan. *Die andere Erinnerung: Jüdische Autoren in der westdeutschen Nachkriegsliteratur*. Berlin: Philo, 2001.
Chametzky, Jules, John Felstiner, Hilene Flanzbaum, and Kathryn Hellerstein, eds. *Jewish American Literature: A Norton Anthology*. New York: W. W. Norton, 2001.
Clifford, James. *Routes: Travel and Translation in the Late Twentieth Century*. Cambridge, MA: Harvard University Press, 1997.
Cohen, Hadas, and Dani Kranz. "Israeli Jews in the New Berlin: From Shoah Memories to Middle Eastern Encounters." In *Cultural Topographies of the New Berlin*, edited by Karin Bauer and Jennifer Ruth Hosek, 322–46. London: Berghahn Books, 2017.
Corngold, Stanley. *Lambent Traces: Franz Kafka*. Princeton, NJ: Princeton University Press, 2004.
Cronin, Joseph. "Community Responses to the Immigration of Russian-Speaking Jews to Germany, 1990–2006." In *Rebuilding Jewish Life in Germany*, edited by Jay Howard Geller and Michael Meng, 191–205. New Brunswick, NJ: Rutgers University Press, 2020.
Czollek, Max. *Desintegriert euch!* Munich: Carl Hanser, 2018.
———. *Gegenwartsbewältigung*. Munich: Carl Hanser, 2020.
———. "'Wir wollen Berlin judaisieren': Max Czollek über genervte 'Judenschriftsteller' und die Veranstaltung am Maxim Gorki Theater." Interview by Philipp Fritz. *Jüdische Allgemeine*, October 30, 2017. https://www.juedische-allgemeine.de/kultur/wir-wollen-berlin-judaisieren/.
Czollek, Max, Corinne Kaszner, Leah Carola Czollek, and Gudrun Perko. "Radical Diversity und Desintegration: Bausteine eines künstlerisch-politischen Projekts." *Jalta: Positionen zur jüdischen Gegenwart* 2 (2017): 71–76.
Danielczyk, Julia. "'Die Zeichen auf meiner Haut sind bindend' (oder) Menschen sind keine Dunkelziffern: Über Julya Rabinowichs Theatertexte *Tagfinsternis* und *Fluchtarien*." In *Flucht, Migration, Theater: Dokumente und Positionen*, edited by Birgit Peter and Gabriele C. Pfeiffer, 221–27. Göttingen, Germany: Vandenhoeck & Ruprecht, 2017.
Deleuze, Gilles, and Félix Guattari. *Kafka: Toward a Minor Literature*. Translated by Dana Polan. Minneapolis: University of Minnesota Press, 1986.
Dickow, Sonja. "Unbehaustes Wohnen: Zum Chronotopos der Laubhütte in Michal Govrins *Hevzekim* (2002) und Barbara Honigmanns *Chronik meiner Straße* (2015)." In *Figurations of Mobile Identities in Contemporary European Jewish Literature*, edited by Doerte Bischoff and Anja Tippner. *Yearbook for European Jewish Literature Studies* 5 (2018): 156–71.
Dijck, José van. "Connective Memory: How Facebook Takes Charge of Your Past." In *Memory Unbound: Tracing the Dynamics of Memory Studies*, edited by Lucy Bond, Stef Craps, and Pieter Vermeulen, 151–72. New York: Berghahn Books, 2017.
———. *The Culture of Connectivity: A Critical History of Social Media*. Oxford: Oxford University Press, 2013.
Diner, Dan. "Deutsch-jüdisch-russische Paradoxien oder Versuch eines Kommentars aus der Sicht eines Historikers." In *Ausgerechnet Deutschland! Jüdisch-russische Einwanderung in die Bundesrepublik*, edited by Raphael Gross and Dmitrij Belkin, 18–20. Berlin: Nicolai, 2010.

———. "Negative Symbiose: Deutsche und Juden nach Auschwitz." *Babylon* 1 (1986): 9–20.
———. "Negative Symbiosis: Germans and Jews after Auschwitz." In *The Holocaust: Theoretical Readings*, edited by Neil Levi and Michael Rothberg, 423–30. New Brunswick, NJ: Rutgers University Press, 2003.
Dischereit, Esther. "Gelebte Zeit und aufgeschriebene Zeit." In *Mit Eichmann an der Börse: In jüdischen und anderen Angelegenheiten*, 144–65. Berlin: Ullstein, 2001.
———. *Übungen jüdisch zu sein: Aufsätze*. Frankfurt: Suhrkamp, 1998.
Eckart, Gabriele. "The Functions of Multilingual Language Use in Katja Petrowskaja's *Vielleicht Esther*." *Glossen* 40 (June 2015). http://blogs.dickinson.edu/glossen/archive/most-recent-issue-glossen-402015/gabriele-eckart-glossen40-2015/.
Erll, Astrid. "Travelling Memory." *Parallax* 17, no. 4 (2011): 4–18.
Eshel, Amir. *Futurity: Contemporary Literature and the Quest for the Past*. Chicago: University of Chicago Press, 2012.
Finch, Helen. "Revenge, Restitution, *Ressentiment*: Edgar Hilsenrath's and Ruth Klüger's Late Writings as Holocaust Metatestimony." In *German Jewish Literature after 1990*, edited by Katja Garloff and Agnes C. Mueller, 60–79. Rochester, NY: Camden House, 2018.
Gardi, Tomer. *Broken German: Roman*. Graz, Austria: Droschl, 2016.
———. "Jeder sollte auf Deutsch schreiben dürfen. "Interview in *Die Welt*, August 18, 2018. https://www.welt.de/kultur/literarischewelt/article157738156/Jeder-sollte-auf-Deutsch-schreiben-duerfen.html.
Garloff, Katja. "Interreligious Love in Contemporary German Film and Literature." In *Judaism, Christianity, and Islam: Collaboration and Conflict in the Age of Diaspora*, edited by Sander L. Gilman, 153–64. Hong Kong: Hong Kong University Press, 2014.
———. *Words from Abroad: Trauma and Displacement in Postwar German Jewish Writers*. Detroit, MI: Wayne State University Press, 2005.
Garloff, Katja, and Agnes C. Mueller, eds. *German Jewish Literature after 1990*. Rochester, NY: Camden House, 2018.
Genette, Gérard. *Narrative Discourse: An Essay in Method*. Translated by Jane E. Lewin. Ithaca, NY: Cornell University Press, 1980.
———. *Paratexts: Thresholds of Interpretation*. Translated by Jane E. Lewin. New York: Cambridge University Press, 1997.
Gilman, Sander L. "Becoming a Jew by Becoming a German: The Newest Jewish Writing from the 'East.'" *Shofar: An Interdisciplinary Journal of Jewish Studies* 25, no. 1 (2006): 16–32.
———. "Introduction: Ethnicity-Ethnicities-Literature-Literatures." *PMLA* 113, no. 1 (January 1998): 19–27.
———. *Jews in Today's German Culture*. Bloomington: Indiana University Press, 1995.
Gilman, Sander L., and Karen Remmler, eds. *Reemerging Jewish Culture in Germany: Life and Literature since 1989*. New York: New York University Press, 1994.
Gilman, Sander L., and Jack Zipes. "Introduction: Jewish Writing in German through the Ages." In *Yale Companion to Jewish Writing and Thought in German Culture, 1096–1996*, edited by Sander L. Gilman and Jack Zipes, xvii–xxxiv. New Haven, CT: Yale University Press, 1997.
Gitelman, Zvi Y. "Wie konnten sie nur? Jüdische Immigranten aus der Sowjetunion in Deutschland." In *Ausgerechnet Deutschland!: Jüdisch-russische Einwanderung in die Bundesrepublik*, edited by Dmitrij Belkin and Raphael Gross, 21–24. Berlin: Nicolai, 2010.

Gorelik, Lena. *Meine weißen Nächte: Roman*. Munich: Schirmer-Graf, 2004.
———. *"Sie können aber gut Deutsch!" Warum ich nicht mehr dankbar sein will, dass ich hier leben darf, und Toleranz nicht weiterhilft*. Munich: Pantheon, 2012.
Grass, Günter. *Die Blechtrommel*. Darmstadt: Luchterhand, 1959.
———. *The Tin Drum*. Translated by Ralph Manheim. New York: Pantheon, 1961.
Grjasnowa, Olga. *All Russians Love Birch Trees*. Translated by Eva Bacon. New York: Other Press, 2014.
———. *Der Russe ist einer, der Birken liebt: Roman*. Munich: Hanser, 2012.
Gross, Jan T. *Neighbors: The Destruction of the Jewish Community in Jedwabne, Poland*. Princeton, NJ: Princeton University Press, 2001.
Guenther, Christina. "Changing Places in Doron Rabinovici's *Andernorts*." *Seminar* 49, no. 4 (2013): 385–99.
———. "Exile and the Construction of Identity in Barbara Honigmann's Trilogy of Diaspora." *Comparative Literature Studies* 40, no. 2 (2003): 215–31.
Gwyer, Kirstin. "Beyond Lateness? 'Postmemory' and the Late(st) German-Language Family Novel." *New German Critique* 42, no. 2 (2015): 137–53.
Haines, Brigid. "Poetics of the 'Gruppenbild': The Fictions of Vladimir Vertlib." *German Life and Letters* 62, no. 2 (2009): 233–44.
Hall, Stuart. "The Formation of a Diasporic Intellectual: An Interview with Stuart Hall by Kuan-Hsing Chen." In *Stuart Hall: Critical Dialogues in Cultural Studies*, edited by David Morley and Kuan-Hsing Chen, 486–503. New York: Routledge, 1996.
———. "Minimal Selves." In *Identity: The Real Me*, edited by Lisa Appignanesi and Homi K. Bhabha, 44–46. London: Institute of Contemporary Arts, 1987.
Heilbronn, Christian, Doron Rabinovici, and Natan Sznaider, eds. *Neuer Antisemitismus? Fortsetzung einer globalen Debatte*. Berlin: Suhrkamp, 2019.
Heimann, Holger. "Katja Petrowskaja: Familiensaga im Kontext des Zweiten Weltkriegs." Deutschlandfunk, March 12, 2014. https://www.deutschlandfunk.de/katja-petrowskaja-familiensaga-im-kontext-des-zweiten.700.de.html?dram:article_id=285117.
Herf, Jeffrey. *Divided Memory: The Nazi Past in the Two Germanys*. Cambridge, MA: Harvard University Press, 1997.
Herzog, Hillary Hope, Todd Herzog, and Benjamin Lapp, eds. *Rebirth of a Culture: Jewish Identity and Jewish Writing in Germany and Austria Today*. New York: Berghahn Books, 2008.
Hess, Jonathan M., Maurice Samuels, and Nadia Valman, eds. *Nineteenth-Century Jewish Literature: A Reader*. Stanford, CA: Stanford University Press, 2013.
Hessing, Jakob. "Aufbrüche: Zur deutsch-jüdischen Literatur seit 1989." In *Handbuch der deutsch-jüdischen Literatur*, edited by Hans Otto Horch, 244–69. Berlin: De Gruyter, 2016.
Hilsenrath, Edgar. *Gesammelte Werke in elf Bänden*. Cologne, Germany: Dittrich, 2003.
Himmelfarb, Jan. *Sterndeutung: Roman*. Munich: C. H. Beck, 2015.
Hinderer, Walter, Claudia Holly, Heinz Lunzer, and Ursula Seeber, eds. *Altes Land, neues Land: Verfolgung, Exil, biografisches Schreiben*, special issue, *Zirkular* 56 (1999).
Hirsch, Marianne. *The Generation of Postmemory: Writing and Visual Culture after the Holocaust*. New York: Columbia University Press, 2012.
Hödl, Klaus. "'Jewish History' beyond Binary Conceptions: Jewish Performing Musicians in Vienna around 1900." *Journal of Modern Jewish Studies* 16, no. 3 (2017): 377–94. https://doi.org/10.1080/14725886.2017.1345189.

Hollinger, David A. *Postethnic America: Beyond Multiculturalism*. 10th anniversary ed. New York: Basic Books, 2006.
Honigmann, Barbara. *Chronik meiner Straße*. Munich: Carl Hanser, 2015.
———. *Damals, dann und danach*. Munich: Carl Hanser, 1999.
———. *Das Gesicht wiederfinden: Über Schreiben, Schriftsteller und Judentum*. Munich: Carl Hanser, 2006.
———. *Das überirdische Licht: Rückkehr nach New York*. Munich: Carl Hanser, 2008.
———. *Eine Liebe aus nichts*. Berlin: Rowohlt, 1991.
———. *Eine Liebe aus nichts*. Reinbek bei Hamburg: Rowohlt Taschenbuch, 1993. Paperback edition.
———. *Ein Kapitel aus meinem Leben*. Munich: Carl Hanser, 2004.
———. *A Love Made Out of Nothing* and *Zohara's Journey: Two Novels*. Translated by John Barrett. Boston, MA: David R. Godine, 2003.
———. "On My Great-Grandfather, My Grandfather, My Father, and Me." Translated by Meghan W. Barnes. *World Literature Today* 69, no. 3 (1995): 512–16.
———. *Roman von einem Kinde: Sechs Erzählungen*. Darmstadt, Germany: Luchterhand, 1986.
Horstkotte, Silke. "'Ich bin, woran ich mich erinnere': Benjamin Steins *Die Leinwand* und der Fall Wilkomirski." In *Der Nationalsozialismus und die Shoah in der deutschsprachigen Gegenwartsliteratur*, edited by Torben Fischer, Philipp Hammermeister, and Sven Kramer, 115–32. New York: Rodopi, 2014.
Hungerford, Amy. "Memorizing Memory." *Yale Journal of Criticism* 14, no. 1 (2001): 67–92.
Jakobson, Roman. "Linguistics and Poetics." In *Language in Literature*, by Roman Jakobson, edited by Krystyna Pomorska and Stephen Rudy, 62–94. Cambridge, MA: Belknap Press of Harvard University Press, 1987.
Jefferson, Chase. "Shoah Business: Maxim Biller and the Problem of Contemporary German-Jewish Literature." *German Quarterly* 74, no. 2 (2001): 111–31.
Jelen, Sheila E., Michael P. Kramer, and L. Scott Lerner. "Introduction: Intersection and Boundaries in Modern Jewish Literary Study." In *Modern Jewish Literatures: Intersections and Boundaries*, edited by Sheila E. Jelen, Michael P. Kramer, and L. Scott Lerner, 1–23. Philadelphia: University of Pennsylvania Press, 2011.
Jeremiah, Emily. *Nomadic Ethics in Contemporary Women's Writing in German: Strange Subjects*. Rochester, NY: Camden House, 2012.
Jewtuschenko, Jewgenij. "Babij Jar." In Paul Celan, *Gesammelte Werke in fünf Bänden*. Vol. 5, *Übertragungen II*, edited by Beda Allemann and Stefan Reichert with the assistance of Rolf Bücher, 281–87. Frankfurt: Suhrkamp, 1986.
Kafka, Franz. *Briefe 1902–1924*. Edited by Max Brod. New York: Schocken Books, 1958.
———. "Ein Bericht für eine Akademie." In Kafka, *Kritische Ausgabe: Drucke zu Lebzeiten*, edited by Wolf Kittler, Hans-Gerd Koch, and Gerhard Neumann, 299–313. Frankfurt: Fischer, 1994.
———. "A Report to an Academy," in *Kafka's Selected Stories: New Translations, Backgrounds, and Criticism*, translated and edited by Stanley Corngold, 76–84. New York: W. W. Norton, 2007.
Kaminer, Wladimir. *Russendisko*. Munich: Goldmann, 2000.
———. *Russian Disco: Tales of Everyday Lunacy on the Streets of Berlin*. Translated by Michael Hulse. London: Ebury, 2009.
Kapitelman, Dmitrij. *Das Lächeln meines unsichtbaren Vaters*. Munich: Carl Hanser, 2016.

Kessler, Judith. "Homo Sovieticus in Disneyland: The Jewish Communities in Germany Today." In *The New German Jewry and the European Context: The Return of the European Jewish Diaspora*, edited by Y. Michal Bodemann, 131–43. New York: Palgrave Macmillan, 2008.
Kilcher, Andreas B. "Die Sprachen der Literatur: Zur Erfindung der 'jüdischen Literatur' im 19. Jahrhundert." *Naharaim* 4, no. 2 (2011): 274–86.
———. "Exterritorialitäten: Zur kulturellen Selbstreflexion der aktuellen deutsch-jüdischen Literatur." In *Deutsch-jüdische Literatur der neunziger Jahre: Die Generation nach der Shoah*, edited by Sander L. Gilman and Hartmut Steinecke, 131–46. Berlin: Erich Schmidt, 2002.
Körber, Karen, ed. *Russisch-jüdische Gegenwart in Deutschland: Interdisziplinäre Perspektiven auf eine Diaspora im Wandel*. Göttingen, Germany: Vandenhoeck & Ruprecht, 2015.
———. "Zäsur, Wandel oder Neubeginn? Russische Juden in Deutschland zwischen Recht, Repräsentation und Realität." In *Russisch-jüdische Gegenwart in Deutschland: Interdisziplinäre Perspektiven auf eine Diaspora im Wandel*, edited by Karen Körber, 13–36. Göttingen, Germany: Vandenhoeck & Ruprecht, 2015.
Kramer, Michael P. "Race, Literary History, and the 'Jewish' Question." *Prooftexts* 21, no. 3 (Fall 2001): 287–321. With responses to his essay by Bryan Cheyette, Morris Dickstein, Anne Golomb Hoffman, Hannah Naveh, and Gershon Shaked, 322–34, and a reply by Kramer: "My Critics and *Mai Nafka Mina*: Further Reflections on Jewish Literary Historiography," 335–49.
Kranz, Dani. "Forget Israel—The Future Is in Berlin! Local Jews, Russian Immigrants, and Israeli Jews in Berlin and across Germany." *Shofar: An Interdisciplinary Journal of Jewish Studies* 34, no. 4 (2016): 5–28.
Kühne, Jan. "Vom Misrachipoet zum *Juden Dichtar*: Mati Shemoelof setzt über." *Jalta: Positionen zur jüdischen Gegenwart* 7 (2020): 54–58.
Lejeune, Philippe. *On Autobiography*. Translated by Katherine Leary. Minneapolis: University of Minnesota Press, 1989.
Levi, Primo. *The Drowned and the Saved*. Translated by Raymond Rosenthal. New York: Vintage International, 1989.
Levy, Daniel, and Natan Sznaider. *The Holocaust and Memory in the Global Age*. Translated by Assenka Oksiloff. Philadelphia, PA: Temple University Press, 2006.
Levy, Lital, and Allison Schachter. "Jewish Literature/World Literature: Between the Local and the Transnational." *PMLA* 130, no. 1 (2015): 92–109.
———. "A Non-Universal Global: On Jewish Writing and World Literature." *Prooftexts* 36, no. 1–2 (2017): 1–26.
Lipis, Miriam. "A Hybrid Place of Belonging: Constructing and Siting the Sukkah." In *Jewish Topographies: Visions of Space, Traditions of Place*, edited by Julia Brauch, Anna Lipphardt, and Alexandra Nocke, 27–41. Burlington, VT: Ashgate, 2008.
Liska, Vivian. "Secret Affinities: Contemporary Jewish Writing in Austria." In *Contemporary Jewish Writing in Europe: A Guide*, edited by Vivian Liska and Thomas Nolden, 1–22. Bloomington: Indiana University Press, 2008.
Liska, Vivian, and Thomas Nolden, eds. *Contemporary Jewish Writing in Europe: A Guide*. Bloomington: Indiana University Press, 2008.
Loentz, Elizabeth. "Beyond Negative Symbiosis: The Displacement of Holocaust Trauma and Memory in Alina Bronsky's *Scherbenpark* and Olga Grjasnowa's *Der Russe ist einer, der*

Birken liebt." In *German Jewish Literature after 1990*, edited by Katja Garloff and Agnes C. Mueller, 102–22. Rochester, NY: Camden House, 2018.

Lustiger, Gila. "Einige Überlegungen zur Lage der jüdischen Autoren in Deutschland." In *Altes Land, neues Land: Verfolgung, Exil, biographisches Schreiben*, special issue, *Zirkular* 56 (1999), edited by Walter Hinderer, Claudia Holly, Heinz Lunzer, and Ursula Seeber, 50–53.

Maechler, Stefan. *The Wilkomirski Affair: A Study in Biographical Truth*. Translated by John E. Woods. New York: Schocken Books, 2001.

Mangold, Ijoma. "Religion ist kein Wunschkonzert." *Die Zeit*, April 8, 2010.

Mani, Bala Venkat. "Reading with Refugees: Hyperlinked Literary Histories." Paper presented at the MLA Convention, Seattle, WA, January 2020.

Mann, Barbara E. *Space and Place in Jewish Studies*. New Brunswick, NJ: Rutgers University Press, 2012.

Maron, Monika. *Pawels Briefe: Eine Familiengeschichte*. Frankfurt: Fischer, 1999.

———. *Pawel's Letters*. Translated by Brigitte Goldstein. London: Harvill, 2002.

Massey, Doreen. *Space, Place, and Gender*. Minneapolis: University of Minnesota Press, 1994.

McGlothlin, Erin. *Second-Generation Holocaust Literature: Legacies of Survival and Perpetration*. Rochester, NY: Camden House, 2006.

———. "Writing by Germany's Jewish Minority." In *Contemporary German Fiction: Writing in the Berlin Republic*, edited by Stuart Taberner, 230–46. Cambridge: Cambridge University Press, 2007.

Mendelsohn, Daniel. *The Lost: A Search for Six of Six Million*. New York: HarperCollins, 2006.

Michaelis-König, Andree. "Multilingualism and Jewishness in Katja Petrowskaja's *Vielleicht Esther*." In *German Jewish Literature after 1990*, edited by Katja Garloff and Agnes C. Mueller, 146–66. Rochester, NY: Camden House, 2018.

Miron, Dan. *From Continuity to Contiguity: Toward a New Jewish Literary Thinking*. Stanford, CA: Stanford University Press, 2010.

Molnár, Katrin. "'Die bessere Welt war immer anderswo': Literarische Heimatkonstruktionen bei Jakob Hessing, Chaim Noll, Wladimir Kaminer und Vladimir Vertlib im Kontext von Alija, jüdischer Diaspora und säkularer Migration." In *Von der nationalen zur internationalen Literatur: Transkulturelle deutschsprachige Literatur und Kultur im Zeitalter globaler Migration*, edited by Helmut Schmitz, 311–36. New York: Rodopi, 2009.

Morris, Leslie. *The Translated Jew: German Jewish Culture outside the Margins*. Evanston, IL: Northwestern University Press, 2018.

Muchina, Lena. *Lenas Tagebuch: Leningrad 1941–42*. Translated by Lena Gorelik and Gero Fedtke. Berlin: Ullstein, 2013.

Mueller, Agnes C. "Germans, Migration, and Holocaust Memory in Contemporary Literature." In *The Holocaust Across Borders: Trauma, Atrocity, and Representation in Literature and Culture*, edited by Hilene S. Flanzbaum, 71–87. Lanham, MD: Lexington Books, 2021.

———. "Religion and the Holocaust: Imre Kertész, Benjamin Stein, and *Kaddish for a Friend*." In *German Jewish Literature after 1990*, edited by Katja Garloff and Agnes C. Mueller, 202–20. Rochester, NY: Camden House, 2018.

Neumann, Birgit. "The Literary Representation of Memory." In *A Companion to Cultural Memory Studies*, edited by Astrid Erll and Ansgar Nünning in collaboration with Sarah B. Young, 333–43. New York: De Gruyter, 2010.

Niefanger, Dirk. "'Wie es gewesen sein wird': Opfer und Täter bei Doron Rabinovici." In *Literatur und Holocaust*, ed. Gerd Bayer and Rudolf Freiburg, 193–209. Würzburg: Königshausen & Neumann, 2009.
Niekerk, Carl. "The Postmodern Moment and the Return of History in Doron Rabinovici's *Ohnehin* (2004)." *After Postmodernism / Nach der Postmoderne*, special issue, *Germanistik in Ireland* 6 (2011): 55–69.
Nietzsche, Friedrich. "On the Utility and Liability of History for Life." In *Unfashionable Observations*, translated by Richard T. Gray, 83–167. Stanford, CA: Stanford University Press, 1995.
Nolden, Thomas. *Junge jüdische Literatur: Konzentrisches Schreiben in der Gegenwart*. Würzburg, Germany: Königshausen & Neumann, 1995.
Nora, Pierre. "Between Memory and History: *Les Lieux de Mémoire*." *Representations* 26 (Spring 1989): 7–24.
Osborne, Dora. "Encountering the Archive in Katja Petrowskaja's *Vielleicht Esther*." *Seminar* 52, no. 3 (2016): 255–72.
Pérez Zancas, Rosa. "Die Vergangenheit bleibt ohnehin unscharf: Doron Rabinovicis *Ohnehin* (2004) und Ulla Hahns *Unscharfe Bilder* (2003)." In *WortKulturen, TonWelten: Festschrift für Alfonsina Janés zum 70. Geburtstag*, edited by Marisa Siguan, M. Loreta Vilar, and Rosa Pérez Zancas, 269–88. Marburg, Germany: Tectum, 2014.
Petrowskaja, Katja. *Maybe Esther: A Family Story*. Translated by Shelley Frisch. New York: Harper Perennial, 2019.
———. *Vielleicht Esther: Geschichten*. Berlin: Suhrkamp, 2014.
Presner, Todd Samuel. *Mobile Modernity: Germans, Jews, Trains*. New York: Columbia University Press, 2007.
Rabinovici, Doron. *Andernorts: Roman*. Berlin: Suhrkamp, 2010.
———. *Credo und Credit: Einmischungen*. Frankfurt: Suhrkamp, 2001.
———. *Eichmann's Jews: The Jewish Administration of Holocaust Vienna, 1938–1945*. Translated by Nick Somers. Cambridge, UK: Polity, 2011.
———. *Elsewhere*. Translated by Tess Lewis. London: Haus, 2014.
———. *Instanzen der Ohnmacht: Wien 1938–1945: Der Weg zum Judenrat*. Frankfurt: Jüdischer Verlag im Suhrkamp Verlag, 2000.
———. *Ohnehin: Roman*. Frankfurt: Suhrkamp, 2004.
———. *The Search for M*. Translated by Francis M. Sharp. Riverside, CA: Ariadne, 2000.
———. *Suche nach M.: Roman in zwölf Episoden*. Frankfurt: Suhrkamp, 1997.
———. "Wie es war und wie es gewesen sein wird: Eine Fortschreibung von Geschichte und Literatur nach der Shoah." http://www.rabinovici.at/texte_wieeswar.html.
———. "Wie es war und wie es gewesen sein wird: Geschichtsschreibung und Literatur zur Shoah." *Wespennest: Zeitschrift für brauchbare Texte und Bilder* 128 (September 2002): 20–24 and *Wespennest* 129 (December 2002): 24–28.
Rabinovici, Doron, Ulrich Speck, and Natan Sznaider, eds. *Neuer Antisemitismus? Eine globale Debatte*. Frankfurt: Suhrkamp, 2004.
Rabinovici, Doron, and Natan Sznaider. *Herzl Relo@ded: Kein Märchen*. Berlin: Jüdischer Verlag im Suhrkamp Verlag, 2016.
Rabinowich, Julya. *Dazwischen: Ich*. Munich: Carl Hanser, 2016.
———. *Die Erdfresserin: Roman*. Vienna: Deuticke, 2012.

———. "Es muss verändert werden." In *Ankommen: Gespräche mit Dimitré Dinev, Anna Kim, Radek Knapp, Julya Rabinowich, Michael Stavarič*, by Brigitte Schwens-Harrant, 55–85. Vienna: Styria, 2014.

———. "Mir war es wichtig, schnell Deutsch zu lernen." Deutschlandfunk, August 23, 2016. https://www.deutschlandfunk.de/julya-rabinowich-mir-war-es-wichtig-schnell-deutsch-zu.691.de.html?dram:article_id=363896.

———. *Spaltkopf: Roman*. Vienna: Deuticke, 2011.

———. *Splithead*. Translated by Tess Lewis. London: Portobello Books, 2011.

———. "Wir haben das Ministerium der Liebe." *Der Standard*, October 29, 2010. https://www.derstandard.at/story/1288160305059/integrationsdebatte-julya-rabinowich-wir-haben-das-ministerium-der-liebe.

———. "Zurück in die Zukunft." *Der Standard*, August 1, 2015. https://www.derstandard.at/story/2000020078821/zurueck-in-die-zukunft.

Reiter, Andrea. *Contemporary Jewish Writing: Austria after Waldheim*. New York: Routledge, 2013.

Ricoeur, Paul. *Memory, History, Forgetting*. Translated by Kathleen Blamey and David Pellauer. Chicago: University of Chicago Press, 2004.

Roberman, Sveta. *Sweet Burdens: Welfare and Communality among Russian Jews in Germany*. Albany: State University of New York Press, 2015.

Roca Lizarazu, Maria. "Ec-static Existences: The Poetics and Politics of Non-Belonging in Sasha Marianna Salzmann's *Außer sich* (2017)." *Modern Languages Open* 1, no. 9 (2020): 1–19. https://doi.org/10.3828/mlo.v0i0.284.

———. "The Family Tree, the Web, and the Palimpsest: Figures of Postmemory in Katja Petrowskaja's *Vielleicht Esther* (2014)." *Modern Language Review* 113, no. 1 (2018): 168–89.

———. "'Integration ist definitiv nicht unser Anliegen, eher schon Desintegration': Postmigrant Renegotiations of Identity and Belonging in Contemporary Germany." *Humanities* 9, no. 2 (2020): 42. https://doi.org/10.3390/h9020042.

———. *Renegotiating Postmemory: The Holocaust in Contemporary German-Language Jewish Literature*. Rochester, NY: Camden House, 2020.

Rothberg, Michael. "From Gaza to Warsaw: Mapping Multidirectional Memory." *Criticism* 53, no. 4 (2011): 523–48.

———. "Multidirectional Memory and the Universalization of the Holocaust." In *Remembering the Holocaust: A Debate*, by Jeffrey C. Alexander, with commentaries by Martin Jay, Bernhard Giesen, Michael Rothberg, Robert Manne, Nathan Glazer, and Elihu & Ruth Katz, 123–34. New York: Oxford University Press, 2009.

———. *Multidirectional Memory: Remembering the Holocaust in the Age of Decolonization*. Stanford, CA: Stanford University Press, 2009.

Rutka, Anna. "'Wünschelrute' Deutsch: Über Sprachkritik und Sprachreflexion als Modi der Erinnerungshandlungen in Katja Petrowskajas 'Vielleicht Esther' (2014)." *Colloquia Germanica Stetinensia* 25 (2016): 85–99.

Salzmann, Sasha Marianna. *Außer sich: Roman*. Berlin: Suhrkamp, 2017.

———. *Beside Myself*. Translated by Imogen Taylor. New York: Other Press, 2019.

Schindel, Robert. *Born-Where*. Translated by Michael Roloff. Riverside, CA: Ariadne Press, 1995.

———. *Gebürtig: Roman*. Frankfurt am Main: Suhrkamp, 1992.

———. *Mein liebster Feind: Essays, Reden, Miniaturen*. Frankfurt: Suhrkamp, 2004.

Schirrmacher, Frank. *Die Walser-Bubis-Debatte: Eine Dokumentation*. Frankfurt: Suhrkamp, 1999.
Schreier, Benjamin. *The Impossible Jew: Identity and the Reconstruction of Jewish American Literary History*. New York: New York University Press, 2015.
Sedlmeier, Florian. *The Postethnic Literary: Reading Paratexts and Transpositions around 2000*. Berlin: De Gruyter, 2014.
———. "Rereading Literary Form: Paratexts, Transpositions, and Postethnic Literature around 2000." *Journal of Literary Theory* 6, no. 1 (2012): 213–34.
Seelig, Rachel, with Amir Eshel. Editors' introduction to *The German-Hebrew Dialogue: Studies of Encounter and Exchange*, edited by Amir Eshel and Rachel Seelig, 1–15. Berlin: De Gruyter, 2017.
Seidel-Arpaci, Annette. "'Writing in Jewish' as an Act of Prostitution? Esther Dischereit's (Self-)Positioning as a Female Jewish Writer in Germany." In *Esther Dischereit*, edited by Katharina Hall, 116–25. Cardiff: University of Wales Press, 2007.
Seligmann, Rafael. *Mit beschränkter Hoffnung: Juden, Deutsche, Israelis*. Rev. paperback ed. Munich: Knaur, 1993.
Shemoelof, Mati. "Drei Gedichte." *Jalta: Positionen zur jüdischen Gegenwart* 7 (2020): 50–53.
Skolnik, Jonathan. "'Jewish' Writing and the Place of Refuge: Olga Grjasnowa's *Gott ist nicht schüchtern*." *Yearbook for European Jewish Literature* 8 (2021): 148–57.
———. "Memory without Borders? Migrant Identity and the Legacy of the Holocaust in Olga Grjasnowa's *Der Russe ist einer, der Birken liebt*." In *German Jewish Literature after 1990*, edited by Katja Garloff and Agnes C. Mueller, 123–45. Rochester, NY: Camden House, 2018.
Stein, Benjamin. *The Canvas*. Translated by Brian Zumhagen. Rochester, NY: Open Letter Books, 2012.
———. "Der Autor als Seelenstripper." *Turmsegler* (blog), June 3, 2010. https://turmsegler.net/20100603/der-autor-als-seelenstripper/.
———. *Die Leinwand*. Munich: C. H. Beck, 2010.
Taberner, Stuart. "Narrative and Empathy: The 2015 'Refugee Crisis' in Vladimir Vertlib's *Viktor hilft* and Olga Grjasnowa's *Gott ist nicht schüchtern*." *German Life and Letters* 74, no. 2 (2021): 247–62.
———. "The Possibilities and Pitfalls of a Jewish Cosmopolitanism: Reading Natan Sznaider through Russian-Jewish Writer Olga Grjasnowa's German-Language Novel *Der Russe ist einer, der Birken liebt* (All Russians Love Birch Trees)." *European Review of History / Revue européenne d'histoire* 23, no. 5–6 (2016): 912–30.
———. "Worldliness, Jewish Purpose and the Non-Jewish Jewish Narrator in Olga Grjasnowa's *Der verlorene Sohn* (2020)." *Seminar* (forthcoming).
Tuan, Yi-Fu. *Space and Place: The Perspective of Experience*. Minneapolis: University of Minnesota Press, 1977.
Vertlib, Vladimir. *Abschiebung: Erzählung*. Salzburg, Austria: Otto Müller, 1995.
———. "Auslass der Flüchtlinge." *Das Jüdische Echo* (blog), February 7, 2017. http://juedischesecho.at/auslass-der-fluechtlinge-von-vladimir-vertlib/.
———. *Das besondere Gedächtnis der Rosa Masur: Roman*. Vienna: Deuticke, 2001.
———. *Schimons Schweigen: Roman*. Vienna: Deuticke, 2012.
———. *Spiegel im fremden Wort: Die Erfindung des Lebens als Literatur*. Dresdner Chamisso-Poetikvorlesungen 2006. 3rd rev. ed. Dresden: Thelem, 2012.
———. *Viktor hilft: Roman*. Vienna: Deuticke, 2018.
———. *Zwischenstationen: Roman*. Vienna: Deuticke, 1999.

Vlasta, Sandra. "'Was ist ihre Arbeit hier, in Prosa der deutschsprachigen Sprach?' Mehrsprachige Räume der Begegnung und Empathie in Tomer Gardis Roman *broken german*." In *Affektivität und Mehrsprachigkeit: Dynamiken der deutschsprachigen Gegenwartsliteratur*, edited by Marion Acker, Anne Fleig, and Matthias Lüthjohann, 143–57. Tübingen, Germany: Narr Francke Attempto, 2019.

Wanner, Adrian. *Out of Russia: Fictions of a New Translingual Diaspora*. Evanston, IL: Northwestern University Press, 2011.

Weiss, Yfaat. "Im Schreiben das Leben verändern—Barbara Honigmann als Chronistin des jüdischen Lebens in Deutschland." In *Kurz hinter der Wahrheit und dicht neben der Lüge: Zum Werk Barbara Honigmanns*, edited by Amir Eshel and Yfaat Weiss, 17–28. Munich: Wilhelm Fink, 2013.

Weiss, Yfaat, and Lena Gorelik. "The Russian-Jewish Immigration." In *A History of Jews in Germany since 1945: Politics, Culture, and Society*, edited by Michael Brenner, translated by Kenneth Kronenberg, 379–416. Bloomington: Indiana University Press, 2018.

Weiss-Sussex, Godela. "Between Distance and Belonging: Space, Time, and Multilingualism in *Das überirdische Licht*." In *Barbara Honigmann*, ed. Robert Gillett and Godela Weiss-Sussex. New York: Peter Lang, 2022. Forthcoming.

Weiss-Sussex, Godela, and Maria Roca Lizarazu, eds. *Rethinking "Minor Literatures"— Contemporary Jewish Women's Writing in Germany and Austria*. Special collection of *Modern Languages Open* 1 (2020). https://www.modernlanguagesopen.org/collections/special/rethinking-minor-literatures-contemporary-jewish-women-s-writing-in-germany-and-austria/.

Wilkomirski, Binjamin. *Bruchstücke: Aus einer Kindheit 1939–1948*. Frankfurt: Jüdischer Verlag im Suhrkamp Verlag, 1995.

———. *Fragments: Memories of a Wartime Childhood*. Translated by Carol Brown Janeway. New York: Schocken Books, 1996.

Willms, Weertje. "Zum Zusammenhang von Identität und literarischer Form in Texten russisch-deutscher Autorinnen der Gegenwart am Beispiel von Julya Rabinowich und Lena Gorelik." In *Migration et identité*, edited by Thomas Klinkert, 169–94. Freiburg, Germany: Rombach, 2014.

Wogenstein, Sebastian. "Negative Symbiosis? Israel, Germany, and Austria in Contemporary Germanophone Literature." *Prooftexts* 33, no. 1 (2013): 105–32.

INDEX

Abschiebung [Deportation] (Vertlib, 1995), 118, 119–23, 124, 128, 138, 140
acculturation, 40
Adelson, Leslie, 118
Algerian War of Independence, 170n7
Altaras, Adriana, 154
Améry, Jean, 16, 31
Andernorts [*Elsewhere*] (Rabinocivi, 2010), 21, 56, 59; family novel evoked and parodied in, 73; transnational travel of memory in, 61, 72–77
anthropology, 18, 156
antisemitism, 1, 4, 6, 68, 141, 158; in Austria, 59; under Communist regimes, 14, 174n6; long history of, 83; in Poland, 134; in the Soviet Union, 5, 82, 117, 120, 129; in Ukraine, 145
Arabic language, 47, 133, 135
Aramaic language, 47
Arendt, Hannah, 13, 159
Aristotle, 59–60
Armenian genocide (1915), 79
arrival, 21–22, 131–32; citizenship and, 144–47, 151; etymology of, 139; language and integration into German society, 140–44, 151; memory and, 147–52; as political metaphor for migration processes, 137
assimilation, 153, 154, 158
Assmann, Aleida, 15, 68
Auf dem Boden der Fremde [On the soil of a foreign country] (Lander, 1972), 31
Auschwitz death camp, 31, 48, 74
Ausser sich [*Beside Myself*] (Salzmann, 2017), 152, 164n27
Austria, 2, 8, 72, 124, 159; Austrian Jewish writers, 25, 27–28; denial of Nazi complicity, 17, 71; Holocaust memory culture in, 68; repression of Nazi past, 20; right-wing populism in, 59; Russian Jewish emigration to, 117
authenticity, 80, 167n2
authorial positions, inscribing of, 34–37
authorship, 28, 42; ethnic, 40, 46; literary market classifications and, 42; performing of, 3, 10–14, 20, 154, 157–59
autofiction, 102–3, 105
Aviv, Caryn, 165n40
Azerbaijan, ethnic conflict in, 79, 152

"Babi Yar" (Yevtushenko, 1961), 82–84, 97
Babi Yar massacre, 80, 81–88, 95. *See also* Holocaust
Babylon: Beiträge zur jüdischen Gegenwart (journal, 1986–2010), 4
Bakhtin, Mikhail, 76
Becker, Franziska, 137
Beckermann, Ruth, 2, 25
Behrens, Katja, 2
Beilein, Matthias, 170n8
Bei uns in Auschwitz [*Here in Our Auschwitz*] (Borowski), 31
Belkin, Dmitrij, 6, 138
Bellow, Saul, 29
belonging, 112, 142, 152; confused aspects of, 1; gendered models of national belonging, 147; ironic gestures of, 138; nonintegration and, 153; political, 140; recognition versus assimilation, 154; restored sense of, 110; unconscious, 131
Benjamin, Walter, 88–89, 173n12
"Bericht für eine Akademie, Ein" [A Report to an Academy] (Kafka), 158, 160
Berlin ... Endstation [Berlin ... Final destination] (Hilsenrath, 2006), 41
Besondere Gedächtnis der Rosa Masur, Das [The peculiar memory of Rosa Masur] (Vertlib, 2001), 76, 117

193

Bettauer, Hugo, 180n11
Bhatti, Anil, 80
Bialystok pogrom (1906), 83
Biller, Maxim, 17, 27, 30–31, 42, 115, 159; authorial self-fashioning and, 28, 34–36; characterized as Jewish in indirect manner, 45; continuity versus contiguity, 33; on Germany's importance to Jewish literature, 2; on Holocaust remembrance, 8; Jewish authorship and, 20; as part of second generation, 14, 25. See also *Deutschbuch*; *Wenn ich einmal reich und tot bin*
biographies, 13
Bischoff, Doerte, 64
Bitburg military cemetery, 4
Blechtrommel, Die [The Tin Drum] (Grass), 148
Bodemann, Y. Michal, 13, 154
Bond, Lucy, 16
Borowski, Tadeusz, 31
boundaries, 10, 96, 118, 127, 161n5, 164n19; blurring of, 80, 83, 119, 136; empathy across, 16, 74, 132, 133, 135; Holocaust memories and, 62; of Jewish literature, 6; metalepsis and, 159; paratext and, 46
Bourdieu, Pierre, 140, 170n8
Boyarin, Daniel, 18
Boyarin, Jonathan, 18
Brasch, Thomas, 29
Broder, Henryk, 29
Broken German (Gardi), 155, 156, 157–60
Bronsky, Alina, 154
Bruchstücke [Fragments] (Wilkomirski, 1995), 15, 43–44, 49–51, 53, 55, 56
Brumlik, Micha, 4

Celan, Paul, 4, 83, 97
cemeteries, Jewish: claiming places and, 19; generational differences and, 109; Honigmann and, 102, 108–10, 115, 175n21; in Vertlib's *Letzter Wunsch*, 1
Chronik meiner Straße [Chronicle of my street] (Honigmann, 2015), 21, 111–16, 138
chronotopes, 111
citizenship, 144–47
claiming places. See *under* place
Clifford, James, 19, 119, 124
Cohen, Albert, 29

Cold War, end of, 15
communism, 14, 101, 103, 105
contiguity, 8, 28, 30, 32, 154, 159
continuity, 8, 33, 159
Craps, Stef, 16
Credo und Credit [Creed and credit] (Rabinovici, 2001), 27–28
Czech literature, 167n20
Czechoslovakia, 17
Czollek, Max, 12–13, 16, 138, 153, 158, 177n5

Damals, dann und danach [Back then, then and after] (Honigmann, 1999), 27, 29, 32–33, 34; on emigration to Strasbourg as form of return, 106; "Gräber in London" (Graves in London), 109–10; "Der Untergang von Wien," 175n21; "Von meinem Urgroßvater, meinem Großvater, meinem Vater und mir" ("On My Great-Grandfather, My Grandfather, My Father and Me"), 39–40
Dazwischen: Ich (Rabinowich, 2016), 132–34
decolonization (1960s), 61, 170n7
decontextualization, 59
de-integration, 13, 16, 138, 154, 158
Deleuze, Gilles, 32, 167n20
Desintegrationskongress (De-integration Congress, 2016), 12
Desintegriert euch! [De-integrate!] (Czollek, 2018), 13, 138
Deutschbuch [German book] (Biller, 2001), 27, 29, 30, 159; "Deutscher wider Willen" (German against my will), 34–35; "Kleine Autobiographie" (Small/minor autobiography), 40–41; "Schlappschwanz-Literatur" (limp-dick literature), 34; "So wird das nichts, Deutschland" ("It won't work like that, Germany"), 34
diaspora literature, 3, 6, 8
digital memory media, 81
Diner, Dan, 4
Dischereit, Esther, 2, 14, 26, 36, 42, 115; authorial self-fashioning and, 28; characterized as Jewish in indirect manner, 45; continuity versus contiguity, 33; on difficulty of writing about the Holocaust, 31–32; encounters with

audiences, 38; genealogy of female German Jewish authors, 39; Jewish authorship and, 20; as part of second generation, 25; prostitution metaphor and, 37, 166n17
Dischereit, Esther, works of: *Joemis Tisch: Eine jüdische Geschichte* [Joemi's table: A Jewish story] (1988), 26; *Mit Eichmann an der Börse* [With Eichmann on the stock market] (1998), 27; "Vom Verschwinden der Worte" [On the disappearance of words], 31. See also *Übungen jüdisch zu sein* [Exercises in being Jewish]
displacement, 59, 61, 127; dialectic with emplacement, 18, 21, 116, 119, 120, 156; of Holocaust memory, 64–65; in Honigmann's novels, 103, 104, 105, 111; literature of, 17; in Vertlib's novels, 119, 120, 123, 127
dissimilation, 29
Döblin, Alfred, 31
Dössekker, Bruno. *See* Wilkomirski, Binjamin
Dostoevsky, Fyodor, 144
Dreyfus, Alfred, 83

Eichborn press, 26
Eichmann, Adolf, trial of (1961), 170n7
Eichmann's Jews: The Jewish Administration of Holocaust Vienna (Rabinovici), 59
emancipation, Jewish, 32
empathy, transcultural, 136
English language, 9, 94, 135
Enlightenment, 7
Erdfresserin, Die [The earth eater] (Rabinowich, 2012), 118
Erll, Astrid, 60
eruv (Jewish religious practice of enclosure), 19, 165n40
Europe, Eastern, 18, 25, 148
exile, 25, 103, 111

family memoir, genre of, 78, 172n2
Fassbinder, Rainer Werner, 4
Feldmann, Deborah, 180n11
Felman, Shoshana, 50
France, 2, 28, 170n7. *See also* Strasbourg
Frank, Anne, 29, 32, 33, 39, 83

Freud, Sigmund, 129
Friedenspreis des deutschen Buchhandels (Peace Prize of the German Book Trade), 38
Friedmann, Alice, 101
From Continuity to Contiguity: Toward a New Jewish Literary Thinking (Miron, 2010), 7–8, 9
Funk, Mirna, 154, 180n11

Gardi, Tomer, 155, 157, 159
Gebürtig [Born-Where] (Schindler), 30
Gegenwartsbewältigung [Coming to terms with the present] (Czollek), 153
genealogies, 37, 39–42
generation, concept of, 8, 161–62n5
Generations of Postmemory, The (Hirsch), 51
Genette, Gérard, 44, 48
genocide, 2, 16, 60, 86, 95, 150; Armenian genocide (1915), 79; Holocaust comparisons with other historical traumas, 15, 61; traumatic legacy of, 25. *See also* Holocaust geography, 156
German Jewish literature: contiguity and, 28; founding gestures and, 20; as literature of displacement, 17; as literature of exiles and survivors, 3; prostitution metaphor and, 37, 38, 166n17; racially inflected notion of authorship and, 10–11; rebirth/renaissance of, 2, 26, 161n2; theorizing of, 6–10; as transnational phenomenon, 163n18
"German-Jewish symbiosis," myth of, 26
German Jewish writers: first-generation, 25–26; mobility in lives of, 18; post-Soviet, 9, 12; pre-Holocaust, 31; self-reflexivity and, 148; third-generation, 2, 154
German Jewish writers, second-generation, 2, 3, 8, 25, 154; Jewish authorial identity and, 157–58; postethnic literature and, 26–27
German language, 9, 94, 161n2, 166n15; deconstructed from within, 115; grammatical differences with Yiddish, 69; Holocaust legacy and, 3; integration of migrants into German society and, 140–44; Jewish identity and, 101; Jewish immigrants from former Soviet Union and, 5; writing in German as form of return, 39–40

German Studies Association Conference (2021), 180n11
Germany, East (GDR), 4, 27, 33, 48, 106; *Ankunftsliteratur* genre (1960–1965), 177n7; Honigmann's departure from, 18, 21, 34, 35; political resistance to Nazism glorified in, 105; postwar return of Jewish exiles to, 21, 103
Germany, reunified (post-1990), 2, 8, 25, 42, 153, 159; emigration triangle with United States and Israel, 120, 121, 123–24; Jewish community as product of "social engineering," 177n5; "normalized" German-Jewish relations, 17; Quota Refugee Act (*Kontingentflüchtlingsgesetz*), 18, 137
Germany, West (Federal Republic), 4, 27, 79, 146
Gesammelte Werke [Collected works] (Hilsenrath), 45
Gesicht wiederfinden, Das [Rediscovering the face] (Honigmann, 2006), 27, 29
gestures, founding, 3, 8; arrival stories as, 152; boundary setting and, 10; claiming places, 3, 17–20, 115, 123, 154, 156; defined, 153; diversification of language, 155–56; performing authorship, 3, 10–14, 20, 154, 157–59; remaking memory, 3, 14–17, 154, 156
Gilman, Sander, 26, 145
Glückel von Hameln, 29, 32, 39
Goethezeit (Age of Goethe), 116
"Goodbye, Columbus" (Biller), 29, 30
Gorelik, Lena, 18, 21, 79, 86, 137, 140; *"Sie können aber gut Deutsch!"* (2012), 142; travel memoir of Saint Petersburg, 143. See also *Meine weißen Nächte* [My white nights]
Grass, Günter, 148
"Grenze, Die" [The border] (Radzyner), 134, 136
Grjasnowa, Olga, 12, 79, 86, 152, 180n11; *Der Russe ist einer, der Birken liebt* [All Russians Love Birch Trees] (2012), 12, 79, 152; *Der verlorene Sohn* [The lost son] (2020), 159
Gross, Jan, 84
Guattari, Felix, 32, 167n20

Haider, Jörg, 71
Hall, Stuart, 137, 151
Haredi ("ultra-Orthodox") Jews, 46, 48
Haskalah, 9
Hebrew language, 6, 8, 47, 74, 94, 133; biliguality with German, 73; Hebrew letters on Jewish graves, 110; Honigmann and, 101; multilingual poems and, 155; revival of, 9
Heine, Heinrich, 31
Herrmann, Matthias, 31
Hilsenrath, Edgar, 16, 41, 45, 180n11; *Berlin . . . Endstation* [Berlin . . . Final destination] (2006), 41; *Gesammelte Werke* [Collected works], 45
Himmelfarb, Jan, 18, 21, 137, 139, 140, 147. See also *Sterndeutung* [Stargazing]
Hirsch, Marianne, 51, 56, 148, 157
Hollinger, David, 26, 42
Holocaust, 2, 21, 40, 41, 80, 145; Babi Yar massacre, 79, 81–88; changes in remembrance of, 14–15, 154; comparisons with other historical traumas, 15, 61, 65, 66, 70–72, 87; construction of Jewish identity and, 5; as floating signifier, 15; generations following, 161–62n5; German Jewish culture nearly eradicated by, 3; German-Jewish "negative symbiosis" and, 4; German versus Russian memory culture and, 79; globalized memory of, 60, 61, 65, 94, 156; Holocaust memory as universal concern, 64; Jewish emancipation interrupted by, 153; Jewish identity and, 43; *Muselmänner* (doomed concentration camp prisoners), 148; paratext in memoirs of, 51; railways in iconography of, 149–50; remaking of memory and, 3, 20; ritualized remembrance of, 21, 66; shift from memory to history, 79; silence surrounding, 14, 170n8; testimony of "true witnesses," 148; Ukrainians as collaborators and witnesses, 81, 82, 84; Wilkomirski's fake memoir of, 15, 43–44, 96. See also Babi Yar massacre; genocide
Holocaust and Memory in a Global Age, The (Levy and Sznaider, 2006), 15

Holocaust studies, 15, 96
Holocaust survivors, 50, 53, 56, 69, 73; children of, 62; dwindling number of, 56, 75–76; survivor's guilt, 104, 105; writers, 16
Honigmann, Barbara, 2, 8, 14, 42; authorial position of, 34–35; authorial self-fashioning and, 28; on autofiction, 102–3; characterized as Jewish in indirect manner, 45; continuity versus contiguity, 33–34; continuum of Jewish literature and, 32–33; dialectic of departure and return in, 103–8; invocation of other Jewish writers, 32–34; Jewish authorship and, 20; Jewish cemeteries in writings of, 102, 108–10, 175n21; Jewish identity and, 31, 101; move from GDR to France, 18, 21, 34, 35; as part of second generation, 25; on return to the German language, 101; trope of German-Jewish love affair, 39, 167n19; "truly minor literature" and, 32, 33, 39, 40, 159
Honigmann, Barbara, works of: *Chronik meiner Straße* [Chronicle of my street] (2015), 21, 111–16, 138; *Das Gesicht wiederfinden* [Rediscovering the face] (2006), 45; *Ein Kapitel aus meinem Leben* [A chapter from my life] (2004), 45; *Eine Liebe aus nichts* [A Love Made Out of Nothing] (1991), 45, 102, 103–6, 108, 110; *Roman von einem Kinde* [Novel of a child] (1986), 101, 108–9; *Das überirdische Licht* [The supernatural light] (2008), 107–8. See also *Damals, dann und danach* [Back then, then and after]
Honigmann, Georg, 101, 108
Hungerford, Amy, 50, 51, 55
hybridity, cultural, 73

identity, Jewish, 20, 26, 153; construction and deconstruction of, 10; construction versus representation of, 7; Jewish authorial identity, 12; questioning of centrality of Holocaust to, 25
Impossible Jew, The (Schreier), 7
influence, 8
International Holocaust Remembrance Alliance (IHRA), 15
Internet, 90, 91, 92, 93
intersections, 8, 10, 159
intertextuality, 8, 143, 148, 159
Israel, 2, 5, 17, 25, 54, 152; Diaspora Museum (Tel Aviv), 145, 146; emigration triangle with Germany and United States, 120, 121, 123–24; "Kischlak," 124; Law of Return, 145; Soviet Jews' emigration to, 117; state-sponsored youth trips to Auschwitz, 74
Italy, 124

Jakobson, Roman, 92, 94
Jalta: Positionen zu jüdischen Gegenwart (journal, 2017–), 4
Jelen, Sheila, 10
Jewish American Literature: A Norton Anthology (2001), 10
Jewishness, 31, 139, 143; declared versus ascribed Jewishness, 42; descent-based models of, 11; dominant German notions of, 14; as empty signifier, 6; Holocaust and, 44; as inner difference, 40; literary criticism and, 7; performance of, 6; recreated, 8
Jewish studies, 7, 18
Joëmis Tisch: Eine jüdische Geschichte [Joëmi's table: A Jewish story] (Dischereit, 1988), 26
Judaism, 6, 19, 30, 93; collective identity in genealogy, 18; distance from, 104; identification with, 27; Jewish immigrants from former USSR and, 5; memory and, 68; non-Orthodox conversion to, 1; Orthodox, 43–44; rediscovery of, 110; Reform, 115
Jüdischer Verlag (Jewish Publishing House), reopening of, 30

Kafka, Franz, 8, 31, 158–60; "Ein Bericht für eine Akademie" [A Report to an Academy], 158, 160; German Jewish literature described by, 41; "minor literature" concept, 32, 40, 167n20
Kaminer, Wladimir, 12, 141
Kapitel aus meinem Leben, Ein [A chapter from my life] (Honigmann, 2004), 45

Kapitelman, Dmitrij, 18, 21, 137, 139, 140, 144–47; biography of, 178n17; paratextual representation of, 146. See also *Lächeln meines unsichtbaren Vaters, Das* [The smile of my invisible father]
Karpeles, Gustav, 9
Kaufmann, Kat, 154
Kilcher, Andreas, 9, 115, 166n15
Kimmich, Dorothee, 80
Klüger, Ruth, 16
Körber, Karen, 79
Korczak, Janusz, 87
Korsakoff syndrome, 66, 68
Kramer, Michael, 10–11
Kugelmann, Cilly, 4
Kuznetsov, Anatoly, 82, 84–85, 86

Lächeln meines unsichtbaren Vaters, Das [The smile of my invisible father] (Kapitelman, 2016), 139, 144–47, 151, 178n15, 178n17
Lagerkvist, Amanda, 90
Lander, Jeannette, 29, 31
Lang, Fritz, 64
language, 11, 31, 143, 147; belonging and, 152; diversification of, 155–56; empowerment through, 144; experience and, 50, 53; hybrid, 155; mother-tongue, 157; othering through, 85; place-making and, 19; poetic function of, 92
Lanzmann, Claude, 150
Lasker-Schüler, Else, 31
Laub, Gabriel, 34
Leinwand, Die [The Canvas] (Stein, 2010), 14, 15, 20, 62, 116; authenticity and, 167n2; as commentary on the Wilkomirski affair, 43–44, 46, 49–56, 96; paratextual representation of author in, 44–49, 146, 158; self-reflexivity in, 41; testimonial authority in, 49–56; two parts/endings of, 53–55
Lejeune, Philippe, 51–52, 105
Lerner, Scott, 10
Letzter Wunsch [Last wish] (Vertlib), 1–2
Levi, Primo, 148
Levy, Daniel, 15, 61, 64
Levy, Lital, 9

Liebe aus nichts, Eine [A Love Made Out of Nothing] (Honigmann, 1991), 45, 102, 103–6, 108, 110
Liska, Vivian, 170n8
literary criticism, 7
"Little Odessa" (New York), 124
Loentz, Elizabeth, 180n11
Lost, The (Mendelsohn, 2006), 88
Lux, Lana, 154

M (film, dir. Lang, 1931), 64
Maechler, Stefan, 168n11
Mann, Barbara, 18–19, 112, 124, 156, 165n40; on diasporic place-making, 18; on places as social constructs, 126–27; on space-place distinction, 112
Maron, Monika, 88, 89
Massey, Doreen, 19, 126
Maxim Gorki Theater (Berlin), 13
McGlothlin, Erin, 180n11
Meine weißen Nächte [My white nights] (Gorelik, 2004), 138, 140–44, 146, 151
Mein liebster Feind [My dearest enemy] (Schindel, 2004), 28
memory, 12, 21; analog and digital media as aids to, 88–91; contestation of public memory, 17; cosmopolitan, 61; dialectic of remembering and forgetting, 65, 66; disruption of, 59; fabrication of, 67; familial and affiliative postmemory, 51, 56; future-oriented memory culture, 64; German and German Jewish memory culture, 79, 86; German "theater of memory," 13; institutionalization of, 94; languages and distortion of, 157; lapses/displacement of memory in, 61, 66–72, 76; movements of, 60–62; multidirectional, 61, 64, 79, 80; postmemory, 72, 148, 157; remaking of, 3, 14–17, 154, 156–57; repressed, 63; ritualization of remembrance, 60; Russian Jews' arrival in Germany and, 147–52; Russian memory culture, 76; transfer between victims and perpetrators, 62–65, 76; transnational travels of, 61, 72–77; traumatic, 129; travels of, 61, 72–77. See also metamemory
memory studies, paradigm shift in, 60

Menasse, Eva, 17, 76
Menasse, Robert, 2, 25, 29, 170n8
Mendelssohn, Daniel, 88
Mendelssohn, Moses, 7
metalepsis, 159–60
metamemory, 20, 68, 73, 148; metamemorial turn in literature, 156; reflexivity and, 17
migration, literature of, 119
mimesis ("mimetic faculty"), 88–89, 173n12
"Minimal Selves" (Hall), 137
Miron, Dan, 7–8, 9, 30, 154; contiguity concept, 30, 159; intrinsic and extrinsic definitions of Jewishness, 11
Mit Eichmann an der Börse [With Eichmann on the stock market] (Dischereit, 1998), 27
Morris, Leslie, 12
Mueller, Agnes C., 178n15, 180n11
Müll, die Stadt und der Tod, Der [Garbage, the city, and death] (Fassbinder play), 4
Multidirectional Memory (Rothberg, 2009), 15–16, 170n7
multilingualism, 78, 94–95, 155

Nachträglichkeit (deferred understanding), 129
nationalism, 8, 136, 145
nation-state, 9
Nazism, 13, 71, 148; Austrian complicity in, 17, 71; Nazi characters in novels, 65, 66, 72, 96; neo-Nazis, 145
Neighbors (Gross), 84
New York Goethe Institute, 30
Nietzsche, Friedrich, 68
Nolden, Thomas, 26, 46, 116
Noll, Chaim, 2, 31
Nora, Pierre, 60

Ohnehin [Anyway] (Rabinovici, 2004), 21, 59, 96, 116; *Andernorts* compared with, 72; lapses/displacement of memory in, 61, 66–72
Orthodox Jews, 20, 41
Osborne, Dora, 88, 173n11
Other/otherness/othering, 36, 41, 80, 85

parallelisms, 8
paratexts, 14, 20, 41, 146, 155; authorial self-fashioning and, 158; construction of author and, 44–49; defined, 44; fake Holocaust memoir and, 44, 51–53
particularity, 9
Pawel's Briefe [Pavel's Letters] (Maron, 2002), 88, 89
performing authorship. *See under* authorship
Petrowskaja, Katja, 2, 17, 18, 77; critical attention on, 78; on facts and conjectures, 96; German memory culture and, 21; immigration from Soviet Union to Germany, 79; Ingeborg Bachmann Prize awarded to, 81; on multidirectional memory, 157; poetics of multidirectionality, 80. *See also Vielleicht Esther*
philosemitism, 33, 158
photography, 89–90
place: claiming of, 3, 17–20, 115, 123, 154, 156; dialectic of displacement and emplacement, 18, 21, 116, 156; diasporic place-making, 18, 113–14, 115, 118, 136, 156, 165n40; movement and, 119; social relations networks and, 126–27; space distinguished from, 112; strategies of emplacement, 119, 120, 125, 156. *See also* displacement
Place and Space in Jewish Studies (Mann, 2012), 18
Polak, Oliver, 154
Polish language, 94
postethnic literature, 26–27
postethnic literary, the, 42
post-Jewish literature, 20, 42
post- prefix, 42, 167n24
public sphere, German, 4, 13
publishers, 26

quota refugees (*Kontingentflüchtlinge*), Russian Jewish, 5, 9, 12, 79, 117, 136; in arrival stories, 139; citizenship and, 144–47; German law concerning, 18, 137; Holocaust memory and, 147–51; language and integration into German society, 140–44; writers who left the Soviet Union as children, 137, 138

Rabinovici, Doron, 2, 17, 20–21, 27–28, 56, 115, 170n8; characterized as Jewish in indirect manner, 45; on memory and forgetting, 67; on multidirectional memory, 157; on new comparative perspectives on the Holocaust, 61; as part of second generation, 25; on relationships between Jews and non-Jewish Austrians, 62

Rabinovici, Doron, works of: *Eichmann's Jews: The Jewish Administration of Holocaust Vienna*, 59; "Wies es was und wie es gewesen sein wird," 59–60. See also *Andernorts* [*Elsewhere*]; *Ohnehin* [*Anyway*]; *Suche nach M.* [*The Search for M.*]

Rabinowich, Julya, 2, 17, 117–19; "migrant literature" label rejected by, 140; migration from Leningrad to Vienna, 21; psychotherapy training of, 128; refugee crisis in Europe and, 132–34

Rabinowich, Julya, works of: *Dazwischen: Ich* [*In-between: I*] (2016), 132–34; *Die Erdfresserin* [*The earth eater*] (2012), 118; *Tagfinsternis* (theater play, 2014), 177n15. See also *Spaltkopf* [*Splithead*]

racism, 59, 63

Radikale Jüdische Kulturtage (Radical Jewish Days of Culture), 12

Radzyner, Tamar, 134, 136

Reagan, Ronald, 4

recognition, belonging and, 154

references, webs of, 29–34

refugee crisis, in Europe, 132–36

Reiter, Andrea, 170n8

remaking memory. See under memory

Renegotiating Postmemory (Roca Lizarazu, 2020), 17

resentment, as source of moral knowledge, 16

Richler, Mordecai, 29, 30

Ricoeur, Paul, 68

Roberman, Sveta, 6

Roca Lizarazu, Maria, 17, 76, 164n27

Roma and Sinti people, 81

Roman von einem Kinde [Novel of a child] (Honigmann, 1986), 101, 108–9

Roth, Philip, 29, 30

Rothberg, Michael, 15–16, 61, 170n7

Rubinsteins Versteigerung [Auctioning off Rubinstein] (Seligmann, 1988), 26

Russe ist einer, der Birken liebt, Der [*All Russians Love Birch Trees*] (Grjasnowa, 2012), 12, 79, 152

Russendisko [*Russian Disco*] (Kaminer, 2002), 12

Russia, post-Soviet, 18

Russian Jews, 5–6, 123–28, 162n10. See also quota refugees (*Kontingentflüchtlinge*)

Russian language, 94, 162n10

Sachs, Nelly, 4, 29, 37, 38, 39

Salzmann, Sasha Marianna, 13, 152, 164n27. See also *Ausser sich* [*Beside Myself*]

Schachter, Allison, 9

Schimons Schweigen [Schimon's silence] (Vertlib, 2012), 118

Schindel, Robert, 2, 28, 29, 30, 115, 170n8; characterized as Jewish in indirect manner, 45; *Gebürtig* [*Born-Where*], 30; *Mein liebster Feind* [My dearest enemy] (2004), 28

Schindler's List (film, dir. Spielberg, 1993), 95

Scholem, Gershom, 108–9

Schreier, Benjamin, 7

Schrobsdorff, Angelika, 45

Sebald, W. G., 12

secularization, 7

Sedlmeier, Florian, 26–27, 40, 42

Seghers, Anna, 180n11

self-reflexivity, 20, 40, 41

Seligmann, Rafael, 2, 26; characterized as Jewish in indirect manner, 45; as part of second generation, 25; *Rubinsteins Versteigerung* [Auctioning off Rubinstein] (1988), 26

Shemoelof, Mati, 154–55

Shneer, David, 165n40

Shoah (film, dir. Lanzmann, 1985), 150

Shostakovich, Dmitri, 82

"*Sie können aber gut Deutsch!*" (Gorelik, 2012), 142

similarity, 21, 80, 81; Internet and, 93; poetics of, 94–97; spatial proximity and, 84; thinking in, 80, 84, 97; in Yevtushenko's "Babi Yar," 83

Singer, Isaac Bashevis, 46
Skolnik, Jonathan, 180n11
Slodounik, Rebekah, 180n11
Soviet Union, 14, 18, 128, 162n10; antisemitism in, 82, 117, 120; disintegration of, 5, 117; German invasion of, 81; holiday of victory over fascism, 79; image of Germans on Soviet television, 35; memory of Babi Yar massacre suppressed in, 82–83
space–place distinction, 112
Spaltkopf [Splithead] (Rabinowich, 2008), 118, 119, 128–32, 133, 138, 140, 177n15; *Sterndeutung* compared with, 150
Spielberg, Steven, 95
Srebrenica, massacre of Bosnian Muslims at (1995), 71
Stalin, Joseph, 14, 82, 87
Stein, Benjamin, 2, 14, 15, 17, 96; authorial identity and, 20, 49, 102; on Judaism and Jewish identity, 43. See also *Leinwand, Die* [*The Canvas*]
Stein, Gertrude, 33
Steinschneider, Moritz, 9
stereotypes, 6, 113, 141–42
Sterndeutung [Stargazing] (Himmelfarb, 2015), 139, 147–52
Strasbourg (France), Honigmann's life in, 18, 103, 105, 114, 115; as alternative to displacement, 111; break from paternal ancestors and, 39; as diasporic place-making, 21, 102; as form of return, 106; Jewish community in Strasbourg, 35, 101; Rue Edel as temporary immigrant home, 111–16
Suche nach M. [*The Search for M.*] (Rabinovici, 1997), 21, 56, 59; interpersonal transfer of memories in, 61, 62–65; *Ohnehin* compared with, 70
Suhrkamp (publisher), 30
Sukkoth holiday, 113–15
synagogues, 6
Sznaider, Nathan, 15, 60, 61, 64

Taberner, Stuart, 159
Tagfinsternis (Rabinowich, theater play, 2014), 177n15

Task Force for International Cooperation on Holocaust Education, Remembrance and Research (ITF), 15
Tisma, Aleksandar, 29
transition, 3, 118, 121, 157; from analog to digital memory, 90; diasporic place-making and, 111; permanent, 21; transition places of migration, 123, 124, 128
Translated Jew, The (Morris), 12
translation, 9, 149
trauma, 16, 25, 67, 118, 128; dissociation and, 130; historical, 10, 15, 21, 61, 66, 70, 87; Holocaust as floating signifier and, 15; inherited, 17; memory gaps and reconstruction of, 157; memory transfers and, 62, 89; migration as traumatic rupture, 21, 119, 128; personal trauma connected to historical conflicts, 79; transmission of, 50; trauma theory, 50
travel narratives, 19
Treblinka death camp, 87, 150
"truly minor literature," 32, 33, 39, 40, 159
Tuan, Yi-Fu, 19, 112, 126
Twitchell, Corey, 180n11

Überirdische Licht, Das: Rückkehr nach New York [The supernatural light: Return to New York] (Honigmann, 2008), 107–8
Übungen jüdisch zu sein [Exercises in being Jewish] (Dischereit, 1998), 27, 29, 31; metaphors of objectification in, 36–37; on public recognition as both empowerment and debasement, 38
Ukraine, 18, 45, 81, 137, 147
United States, 5, 124, 125; emigration triangle with Germany and Israel, 120, 121, 123–24; postethnic affiliations in, 26
universality, 9
Unterhaltungsliteratur genre, 178n12
Uzbekistan, 148

Varnhagen, Rahel, 29, 32, 33, 39
Vergangenheitsbewältigung (coming to terms with the past), 65, 76
Verlorene Sohn, Der [The lost son] (Grjasnowa, 2020), 159
Vermeulen, Pieter, 16

Vertlib, Vladimir, 1–2, 17, 117–19; biography of, 119–20; on German siege of Leningrad, 79; migration from Leningrad to Vienna, 21; narrative closure undermined by, 128; refugee crisis in Europe and, 132, 134–36

Vertlib, Vladimir, works of: *Abschiebung* [Deportation] (1995), 118, 119–23, 124, 128, 138, 140; *Das besondere Gedächtnis der Rosa Masur* [The peculiar memory of Rosa Masur] (2001), 76, 117; *Letzter Wunsch* [Last wish], 1–2; *Schimons Schweigen* [Schimon's silence] (2012), 118; *Viktor hilft* [Victor helps] (2018), 118, 132, 134–36; *Zwischenstationen* [Way stations] (1999), 116, 118, 120, 123–28, 138

Vielleicht Esther [Maybe Esther] (Petrowskaja, 2014), 21, 77, 78, 81, 174n20; "archival turn" in Holocaust memory and, 88; Babi Yar chapter, 80, 81–88, 96; memory and digital media in, 88–94; poetics of similarity and, 94–97; as work of metamemory, 81

Viktor hilft [Victor helps] (Vertlib, 2018), 118, 132, 134–36

Vogel, David, 29

"Vom Verschwinden der Worte" [On the disappearance of words] (Dischereit), 31

Waldheim, Kurt, 170n8
Walser, Martin, 71
Warsaw ghetto, 87, 93, 150
Warsaw ghetto uprising, 68–69
Weiss, Peter, 4, 180n11
Weiss, Yfaat, 103, 174n6

Wenn ich einmal reich und tot bin [Someday when I'm rich and dead] (Biller, 1990), 45–46

Werfel, Franz, 180n11

White Nights (Dostoyevsky), 144

"Wie es war und wie es gewesen sein wird: Geschichtsschreibung und Literatur zur Shoah" [How it was and how it will/would have been: Historiography and literature on the Shoah] (Rabinovici), 59–60

Wilkomirski, Binjamin, 15, 43–44, 49–53, 168n11. See also *Bruchstücke* [*Fragments*]

Wissenschaft des Judentums (science of Judaism), 9, 10

witnessing, transcultural, 80, 86

Wogenstein, Sebastian, 180n11

world literature, 9

World War, Second, 14, 21, 45, 66, 81; fiftieth anniversary of end of (1995), 70; German siege of Leningrad, 79, 86, 87; Russian memory culture and, 76

xenophobia, 35, 63

Yevtushenko, Yevgeny, 82, 85, 86
Yiddish language, 6, 8, 47, 69, 94; revival of, 9; songs recorded in, 89; Yiddish literature in Poland, 167n20
Yugoslavia, civil war in (1990s), 70

Zionism, 5, 120, 154
Zunz, Leopold, 9, 10
Zwischenstationen [Way stations] (Vertlib, 1999), 116, 118, 120, 123–28, 138

KATJA GARLOFF is Professor of German and Humanities at Reed College. She is author of *Mixed Feelings: Tropes of Love in German Jewish Culture* and *Words from Abroad: Trauma and Displacement in Postwar German Jewish Writers.*

www.ingramcontent.com/pod-product-compliance
Lightning Source LLC
Chambersburg PA
CBHW030623230426
43661CB00053B/2114